UNFAIR PLAY

The Battle for Women's Sport

SHARRON DAVIES
WITH CRAIG LORD

FORUM

FORUM

First published in Great Britain by Forum, an imprint of Swift Press 2023

1 3 5 7 9 8 6 4 2

Printed and bound in Great Britain by CPI Group (UK) Ltd, Croydon, CRO 4YY

A CIP catalogue record for this book is available from the British Library

ISBN: 9781800752801
eISBN: 9781800752818

MIX
Paper | Supporting
responsible forestry
FSC
www.fsc.org
FSC® C171272

This book is dedicated to my family, who've had to put up with my crusade for justice these last few years. It's also for all the wonderful men and women who have taken on the abuse and fought alongside me for fair play, safety and the right for female athletes to have equal opportunities in sport. Sport is something I am forever grateful for. It has shaped my life.

CONTENTS

List of Illustrations   IX

Introduction   1

  1 This Is a Man's World   9

  2 Let the Doping Games Begin   29

  3 How We Were Cheated   49

  4 Moscow and the Manipulators   63

  5 Sex Matters   90

  6 Sporting Differences   103

  7 Gonads and Gotchas   114

  8 The Game Changer   129

  9 The Swimmer Who Proved the Science   158

10 The Onslaught against Women   178

11 The Gender Industry   197

12 Why Girls' Sport Matters   213

13 Green Shoots – and Swimming Turns the Tide   232

14 Truth and Reconciliation   248

Acknowledgements   275

APPENDIX 1: The Key Studies and Papers on Retained Male
    Advantage after Transition and the Meaning of Fair Play   277

APPENDIX 2: Resources   282

APPENDIX 3: Fair Play for Women's Guide to UK Equality
    Law and a Woman's Right to Single-Sex Spaces and
    Services   284

APPENDIX 4: Letter from Fair Play for Women to the IOC
    Executive Board   288

APPENDIX 5: The State of Inclusion Policies – Global
    Federations, March 2023   291

Notes   295

LIST OF ILLUSTRATIONS

1 The gender gap in Olympic sport   10

2 How long women had to wait to join men in Olympic sports   20

3 Androgenic-anabolic steroids   34

4 Mind the gap: GDR women's and men's swimming medals, Olympic Games 1976–80–88, individual events   38

5 Stasi document showing the positive tests   51

6 Petra Schneider and doping boss Manfred Ewald on the cover of GDR *Schwimm Sport* magazine, 1980   64

7 The reality of male advantage in sport   99

8 Katie Ledecky versus the boys: where the all-time great woman ranks among the best boys and men   104

9 Missy Franklin and Ryan Lochte   107

10 Shaunae Miller-Uibo and Wayde van Niekerk   109

11 GBR Olympic champions swim relay, Tokyo   111

12 The power of T: how 15-year-old boys beat the best Olympic women   112

INTRODUCTION

THERE'S a moment before an Olympic final when time stands still and the champion mindset fills the void – or not. Mental toughness plays a big part. Races can be won and lost in that gap between the whistle that calls an athlete to their blocks and the firing of the starting gun.

Friends, family, coaches, even a nation, are confident on your behalf, while you, the athlete, have self-belief built on long, hard years of work and the knowledge that you left no legal stone unturned in your preparation. At that moment your enemies are not your opponents but fear of failure, fear of blame, fear of letting down the people who've made big sacrifices for you along the way.

Knowing that the next few minutes of a race are likely to define you for the rest of your life is scary!

In fact, when I get nervous today I always look back to that moment and think, 'If I could manage that I can pretty much manage anything.' Sport has been a blessing in my life – it's made me strong, even if the strain has worn out a few bits of my body.

From a young age, my dad and coach Terry taught me to be tough, to be ready for any challenge. There were years of intense, all-consuming work before my first Olympics at 13, then four more years under huge scrutiny and expectation until I lined up in Moscow aged 17 at the Games again. This time, it meant the biggest moment of an Olympian's life: the battle for an Olympic title.

I was in the form of my life for the 400 metres medley final in
the swimming pool, but I also knew that it wouldn't be enough to
win. I might even miss out on a medal altogether because the lanes
next to me included three East German women on male steroids
and programmed to be decades ahead of their rivals.

'Take your mark…' Bang! For the next 4 minutes, 46 seconds, all
thought and energy is ploughed into being the very best you can be
when it most counts. The clock stops. It's silver ahead of two East
Germans and I've set a British record that won't be broken for more
than two decades. The 1980 Games end with me as the only female
individual medallist on the whole GB Olympic Team. That's how
hard it is to beat an unfair advantage.

Enhanced by testosterone, the winner of my race sets a standard
good enough to make most Olympic podiums and every Olympic
final for the next 41 years.

We all knew why. I'd trained every day for years knowing I was
facing that unfair advantage, knowing that I was being cheated out
of medals at every passing international competition. It was the same
for my teammates and women from countries all over the world.
And not a single person in authority raised a red flag or fought at
the top tables of Olympic power for us, for a level playing field, for
the pledges set out in the Olympic Charter.[1]

Had it not been for the German Democratic Republic (GDR)
fraud, I would have had Olympic and European titles as well
as World Championship medals to go with my Commonwealth
golds. My British teammate Ann Osgerby would also have been an
Olympic gold medallist. She would have led a totally different life
because of the opportunities that would have come her way. And
Ann was far from being the only one. So many women lost their
rightful rewards because of the GDR and because the International
Olympic Committee (IOC) failed to stop the cheating and turned
a blind eye to the truth.

We'll show you just how bad it was later in the book.

Everyone in sport knew it. Most had to look no further than the shape and musculature of the East German girls. It turned out that not a single GDR medal-winning performance among women was achieved without drugs. We didn't know precisely what those drugs were at the time, nor how they were getting away with it. When the cast-iron proof of mass systematic cheating came flooding in with the fall of the Berlin Wall in 1989, Olympic sports authorities let it go.

To this day, I feel a deep sense of despair that we don't learn from history. Having failed female athletes for half a century by refusing to take action when a whole nation doped its females with a decisive dose of male advantage, Olympic authorities have watched the transgender crisis unfold and responded in exactly the same way. They've let it go.

Yet again, it's female athletes who will pay the price. They are the only ones who will lose rewards, recognition, status, opportunities and lifelong benefits.

This time it's not artificial testosterone in doses just big enough to guarantee gold. It's the full force of male biological development that's been given a ticket to female competition, making contenders out of mediocre males' self-identifying their way out of biological reality to a new status in sport.

Having lived a lifetime of injustice, I was determined not to let it happen again. After five years of campaigning for the women's category to be ring-fenced for females, I watched unfair play reach my own sport of swimming in predictable fashion.

I was transported back four decades by the cries for help from the women who faced Lia Thomas, a 6' 4" biological male, at the American National Collegiate Athletic Association (NCAA) championships in 2022. Not only did they have to compete against an opponent fresh out of three seasons of racing as a man at the

University of Pennsylvania, but they were also threatened with exclusion and expulsion if they complained that they'd been forced to change alongside an athlete with male genitalia intact and exposed.

It was a case of sports authorities being so influenced by the politics of societal trends that they failed female athletes in monstrous style.

We've been forced to confront increased physical danger in contact sports and rising mental-health challenges because inclusion has meant invasion, injustice and ultimately exclusion from our own category. There's a denial of peer-reviewed science and wilful blindness to the loss of opportunities for women to make teams, finals and podiums or to write their achievements in CVs and on job applications. The consequences of being cheated out of such things span whole lifetimes, as we know from the fallout from the GDR years.

The threat to female sport, to women's rights, including safety on the field of play and privacy in the locker room, reaches every level, grass roots upwards. Even on primary school sports days, mixed-sex races are being encouraged, leaving young girls with nowhere to shine. What message does that send?

Females have been told that we must pretend that male development has nothing to do with meteoric rises up the rankings by biological males who on transition go from average men to champions among women. Yet again, everyone on the side of the pool or track knows the truth. Few of them have been asked by their governing bodies to speak it.

For saying such things, I've been vilified, accused of being transphobic, a bigot, even sexist (not sure how that works) and a right-wing extremist. It's got nothing to do with politics. I have always fought for everyone's right to human equality and safety to be themselves. Radical activists don't want to hear anything that they can't turn into a weapon in their cancel-culture campaigns that result in loss of livelihood and death threats – something that my family and I have faced. We're not alone.

It's a successful tactic. The insults are meant to shut you up and the lies are used to ruin reputations, inflict financial harm and drain people of their will to fight back. It's bullying, plain and simple, and we shouldn't tolerate it as some suggest we should purely on the grounds that trans people are 'an oppressed minority'. Whether they are or not, this member of a much larger, but still oppressed majority feels it's only fair to mention that the United Nations Human Rights Council (UNHRC) and related UN 2030 Agenda for Sustainable Development note that women's rights, including those on equality and access to food and education, are among the most violated on a consistent basis.[2]

In his book *Half the Sky*, Nicholas D. Kristof notes that, in the last 50 years, more girls were killed precisely because they were girls than men were killed in all the wars of the twentieth century.[3]

Numerous UN reports, including depressing projections for poverty suggesting a worsening crisis, show how a range of key problems around the world have a disproportionate impact on females, at national and international level.[4] Pay gaps across the developed world including in the UK are still a big issue.

I was one of those preparing for a forum in Cardiff in 2022, at which women just wanted to meet and discuss their concerns, when we had to inform police that trans activists were threatening to burn down the venue with all of us in it. We ought to have been shocked, but it's par for the course in the vile debate over trans rights and how they impact others.

Activists turn up to women's forums in balaclavas, hurling obscenities. Some get arrested for their attacks, yet many politicians are loath to openly defend women's rights the way they should, and the way the vast majority of the general public want them to, as polls often show us. Why is society so scared of this extremely vocal minority?

We delve into that question in the pages of this book, which include the science that explains why sport must be safe, then fair, then inclusive, in that order, not inclusive at the expense of all else.

The exclusive nature of sport is the very thing that makes it inclusive to a wide range of people across society. Where the 15-year-old is excluded from the under-tens, the younger children enjoy fair play. Where able-bodied athletes are excluded from the Paralympics and Paralympians are divided into categories, there is fair play. Where heavyweights are excluded from lightweight bouts, lightweight fighters get to enjoy sport in a safe and fair environment.

Where males are allowed into female sport, safety and fair play are crushed.

It's all such a very long way from the sport my co-author Craig and I grew up in, with our fathers as coaches. One of the myths trans activists have on repeat is that sport is based on gender not sex.

From school galas to national and international events, all the way up to the Olympic Games, for the entirety of sporting history (until very recently) sex and gender have meant the same thing: biological sex. Girls and boys or women and men. Those categories were not created to accommodate a feeling. They were created to facilitate equality.

Entry forms, starts lists and result sheets all have men's events and women's events. There has never been any other description, nor has anyone in sport I know ever assumed that the definitions of women and men have meant anything other than biological sex. The crusade to undermine this makes a mockery of sport's classifications. The option is always there to create more if need be, not ruin the present ones, but even getting respectful debate has been hard.

I realised six years ago that women's sport was about to face the same kind of systematic injustices female athletes faced during the

1970s and 1980s, during the East German doping era. My conscience would not allow me to sit back, carry on getting well-paid jobs and ignore what was unfolding. I felt compelled to spread awareness and help to stop the nightmare happening all over again.

In 2018, when tennis ace Martina Navratilova heard that trans activist Rachel McKinnon/Veronica Ivy, a biological male cyclist, had become a World Masters title winner in the women's 35–44 category, she called it insane and tweeted: 'You can't just proclaim yourself a female and be able to compete against women. There must be some standards, and having a penis and competing as a woman would not fit that standard.'[5]

It amounted to cheating, said Martina. In my opinion she was spot on. It's cheating given a green light by sports bosses breaking their own rules on safety and discrimination. But it's cheating all the same.

Martina was accused by McKinnon/Ivy of having an 'irrational fear' of something that doesn't happen. McKinnon/Ivy said: 'There's a stereotype that men are always stronger than women, so people think there is an unfair advantage.'[6]

Men being stronger than women is not a stereotype. It's a biological reality reflected in every Olympic result throughout history. In these pages, McKinnon/Ivy's ridiculous statement will be reduced to rubble, along with the other false gotchas of activists blind to the facts presented by well-qualified, world-class sports scientists and experts.

As Professor Margaret Heffernan notes in her insightful book *Willful Blindness*: 'We may think being blind makes us safer, when in fact it leaves us crippled, vulnerable, and powerless. But when we confront facts and fears, we achieve real power and unleash our capacity for change.'[7]

Women have been battling for change in sport since it all began. We've only been able to run in the marathon at the Olympics since

1984, and even though swimming got going for females in 1912, we were outnumbered by men four to one when I raced at the 1980 Games. We've fought tooth and nail to get to a better place and look what's happening now.

So let's talk human biology, peer-reviewed studies and decades of Olympic results. Let's banish the blind eye and welcome the truth.

My book is a personal quest to expose that truth and put pressure on those in authority to do the right thing, not the easy thing.

I

THIS IS A MAN'S WORLD

LET'S start where it all began. The inclusion debate needs to be understood within the wider context of sexism and misogyny in female sport throughout history. Women's claims are ignored because sport is a man's world – and few things illustrate this better than the history of the Olympic Games.

THE OLYMPICS: AN IGNOBLE HISTORY

The IOC strongly encourages, by appropriate means, the promotion of women in sport at all levels and in all structures... with a view to the strict application of the principle of equality of men and women.

– rule 2, paragraph 5 of the Olympic Charter 1996

This statement sounds good, but 'strongly encourages' is typical of Olympic guidelines, which proclaim positive sentiments all too vaguely. Sports leaders will agree to such statements but soon abandon them if they prove to be inconvenient.

When it comes to critical issues like equality and doping, which have a direct impact on the welfare and lives of athletes, the Olympic creed has more holes in it than a Swiss cheese from a dairy not far from IOC headquarters in Lausanne.

Women first joined the Olympic Games as token participants in 1900. As Image 1 shows, it was 92 years before female athletes made up more than 25 per cent of all participants at the Games. In Moscow, where I won my medal in 1980, I was outnumbered four to one. In my lifetime, there have been 19 Olympics, including the 12 I raced or worked at, and men have had the lion's share of opportunities and events to target.

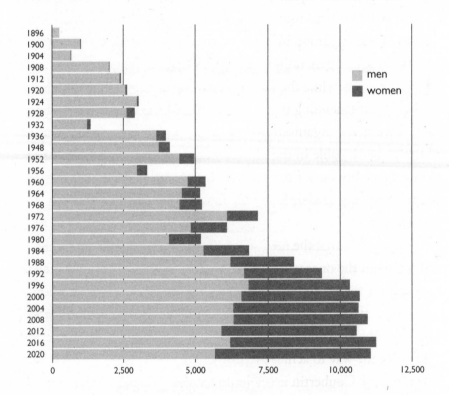

1 *The gender gap in Olympic sport.*
Source: International Olympic Committee

At the Covid-delayed Tokyo Olympics of 2021, women got closer than ever to making up half of all athletes: 48.8 per cent to 51.2 per cent.[1] This included the first three biological males to identify as women and be allowed by the IOC to compete against female athletes.

The official records don't show that those athletes were males in competition with females, just as the official books of results and records don't show that all the East German girls were on drugs at the time they won their medals. Of course, we know categorically that they were, just as we know that transwomen are biologically male.

It's against that backdrop that we're supposed to believe that 'promoting gender equality within the IOC has been an important objective of the organisation since the creation of the Women and Sport Working Group in 1995.'[2] As we'll see later, the 1990s were devastating for generations of sportswomen as a direct result of IOC decisions, while the IOC's boast that in 1996 it 'took the historic step of amending the Olympic Charter to include an explicit reference to the organisation's role in advancing women in sport' is highly questionable in the context of the inclusion model that has ripped equality out of the heart of female sport these past several years.[3] Olympic leaders know the movement has a very poor record on equality.

The truth is that the men who have run the show for over a century are not the ones who have promoted women's sport. Women's sport grew thanks to female athletes and coaches, strong mothers, members of women's rights groups and sports organisations, who had to fight long and hard every step, stride, stroke, pull, push and throw of the way to achieve equality.

Pierre de Coubertin is celebrated at every opening ceremony as the founding father of the modern Olympics. The truth is that he was the father of *men's* sport at the Games and the patriarch who effectively told women to stay out.

They could partake in the festivities in 1896 as long as they had 'chaperones' in tow – but forget the sport. That was all about a display of athletic performance reflecting men's abilities, endurance, strength, virility and courage. Women had none of that, according to Coubertin, and so their participation was pointless. He did have a job for them, though.

Coubertin, a French baron, said: 'Women have but one task, that of the role of crowning the winner with garlands. In public competitions, women's participation must be absolutely prohibited. It is indecent that spectators would be exposed to the risk of seeing the body of a woman being smashed before their eyes.'[4] He was still trotting out sexist tropes in 1919, when women dared to suggest adding track and field and other events for women at the Olympics. Coubertin scoffed at the idea and suggested it was impractical, uninteresting, unaesthetic and, he even added, 'improper'.[5]

Frenchwoman Alice Milliat was not prepared to give up in the face of these attitudes. Alice met the IOC and the International Amateur Athletic Federation (IAAF), then an organisation of men for men, in 1919. She brought a gift, a chance for the men to show their vision and allow female participation in the Olympics. They declined, and sent her back to sewing and scrubbing dishes.

So, after some hard graft, Alice founded the Fédération Sportive Féminine Internationale in October 1921.[6] After organising the Women's Olympic Games in Monte Carlo in the same year, in 1922 she set up the Women's World Games, which were held every four years until 1934.[7] Before he stepped down from the IOC presidency in 1925, the disgruntled Coubertin felt the way the wind was blowing and agreed to add fencing for women.

But men were the real show, women a token warm-up act and novelty. Concessions were made where Coubertin felt the activity was 'ladylike' enough. Golf and tennis could be played in a skirt down to the ankle, so that was allowed in 1900. Those were extremely elite sports for women to gain access to, but, by 1912, women's swimming was in. Well, sort of – at least on the surface.

The blokes made the rules and they'd been swimming at the Olympic Games since 1896. When permission was given for women to swim at the 1912 Games, the IOC restricted the number of events to just two, the 100 metres freestyle and the 4×100 metres freestyle relay. The men had six individual events in freestyle, backstroke and breaststroke and a relay twice as long.

The first women's Olympic swim champion was Australian Fanny Durack.[8] When she and fellow national swimming champion Wilhelmina 'Mina' Wylie made it known that they wanted to race at the Olympics, the New South Wales Ladies Swimming Association (NSWLASA) delivered the bad news handed down to them by the men in charge of the Australian Olympic Committee (AOC): they'd only pay for the Australian men to go to the Games, including the 21-day voyage.

Women protested and the men agreed to a compromise loaded with a gotcha. Fanny and Mina could go to the Games if they paid for themselves and the chaperones they were required to have with them. The AOC and the NSWLASA misread public opinion: Durack's exclusion was seen as a national scandal. Fundraisers were organised and the women reached their target.[9] Those women were real heroines, in my opinion. Fanny won the 100 metres to become the first Olympic women's swimming champion. Mina took silver and Britain's Jennie Fletcher took bronze.

With only two women, Australia could not enter the relay. Jennie Fletcher was joined by teammates Isabella Moore, Annie Speirs and Irene Steer, and Britain took the first women's swimming relay gold in history.[10] Years later Jennie recalled: 'We swam only after working hours and they were 12 hours a day, six days a week. We were told bathing suits were shocking and indecent and even when entering competition we were covered with a floor-length cloak until we entered the water.'[11]

It wasn't only in swimming that women defied the sexism of male event organisers. At the 1896 Olympics, pioneering heroine Stamata Revithi used the men-only marathon to prepare her answer to the sexism in her own way. Not all the blokes finished their run, but she did the day after, covering the 40-kilometre marathon course in five hours.[12]

It wasn't until Los Angeles in 1984 that women were allowed to run the marathon at the Olympics. That was 18 years after Bobbi Gibb became the first woman to run and complete the Boston Marathon.[13] She didn't do so officially, of course. The 23-year-old had to hide in a bush near the marathon start line and disguise herself in a hoodie after she was disqualified from entering the race because of her sex.

A year later, in 1967, Kathrine Switzer entered the Boston event as 'K. V. Switzer' and organisers just assumed that the name was that of a man. When the male runners spotted the woman running alongside them, Kathrine was attacked by race co-director Jock Semple, who ran her down and tried to rip the number off her sweater as he screamed, 'Get the hell out of my race!' Kathrine's American-football-playing boyfriend body-slammed Jock onto the verge at the roadside. They all ran off and Kathrine became the first woman to officially complete the race. Imagine having to have your own bodyguard just so you can run![14] Jock later made his peace with women running in the marathon.

Kathrine remembered that the all-male press were 'crabby' and 'aggressive' and made her feel 'so afraid' when they asked: 'What are you trying to prove? Are you a suffragette or are you a crusader?' When one said to her, 'You're never going to run again,' Kathrine replied: 'We'll be back and we'll be back again and again, and if our club is banned, we'll form a new club... someday you're going to read about a little old lady who's 80 years old, who dies in Central Park on the run. It's going to be me. I'm going to run for the rest of my life!' Kathrine is still going strong and is one of a vast club of female athletes who showed the way, fought their corner, refused to accept discrimination.[15]

Charlotte Epstein was another pathfinder. A courtroom stenographer, she founded the Women's Swimming Association in New York City in 1917 and became famous for promoting the health benefits of swimming as exercise. She staged suffrage swimming races and campaigned for women's rights and changes to swimsuits to allow women freedom of movement. The swimmers she coached set 51 pioneering world records.[16]

In 1923, swimming regulator the International Swimming Federation (known as FINA, the initials of its French name, the Fédération Internationale de Natation) set up a committee to consider what they called the international swimming costume for women. Charlotte got wind of it and insisted they hear from the women who'd have to wear them. It took a while, but FINA consulted her at the 1924 Olympic Games and it was agreed that the suits would have to be black or dark blue, would be cut no lower than 8 centimetres below the armpit and no lower than 8 centimetres below the neckline, and would have material that descended into the leg by at least 10 centimetres for the preservation of modesty, including a slip back and front of at least 8 centimetres.[17]

Epstein served as a manager of the US women's Olympic swimming teams in 1924 and 1928. As a Jew she boycotted the 1936 Olympics in Nazi Germany, where Coubertin was brought out of retirement to help promote the Berlin Games and sit alongside Hitler in a Swastika-filled stadium.

Coubertin and the Nazi Party were close bedfellows when it came to the role of women. In a 1933 speech, Joseph Goebbels, chief Nazi propagandist, said: 'We do not see the woman as inferior, but as having a different mission, a different value, than that of the man. Therefore we believe the German woman... should use her strength and abilities in other areas than the man.'[18]

In return for Coubertin's patriarchal promotion of what are sometimes called the 'Propaganda Games', the Nazis nominated him for the Nobel Peace Prize in 1935.[19] And the winner was… anti-Nazi campaigner Carl von Ossietzky.[20] IOC leaders still aspire to the Peace Prize. They'll probably never get it because there's something they just don't understand and possibly never will. Cosying up to Putin, Xi Jinping, the leading family in North Korea and a flotilla of sheikhs and emirs hosting and funding the Olympic Movement isn't an act of peace, nor one of understanding. For the Nobel Peace Prize, you actually have to do something noble, peaceful and courageous, like stand up to bullies and dictators and call out their corruption and human-rights abuses (in theory at least).[21]

Or, perhaps, stand up to the endemic misogyny and bullying of men in the way that Stamata, Alice and Charlotte, among many others, did. They endured the mockery of men and pressed for inclusion in the face of fierce resistance from the likes of Coubertin. Nowadays, he is celebrated as a great founding father by a generation of men who are forcing women to accept male advantage in female sport in the name of inclusion. How apt.

LETTER TO M. MACRON

At the 139th IOC session, during the controversial Beijing Winter Olympics in 2022, Guy Drut, the 1976 French Olympic hurdles champion and now IOC member, proposed that Coubertin's remains be reinterred at the Panthéon in time for the Paris 2024 Olympics.[22] Drut wrote to French president Emmanuel Macron to propose his plan. The current IOC president, Thomas Bach, thought it a wonderful proposal but he doubted the IOC could help. Bach wished Drut the best of success with his initiative.

Men are still celebrating men a hundred years on. So, early in 2023, I wrote to President Macron, too, as well as the head of the French sports ministry until 2022 Roxana Maracineanu, an Olympian and a world swimming champion for France in 1998.

I asked them to use Paris 2024 as an opportunity to celebrate the women who made it all happen for female athletes, not the misogynist who blocked them. Of course, we should not erase Coubertin from history and it's hardly surprising that the IOC and France would wish to commemorate his founding-father status at an Olympiad held in Paris. At the same time, in 2024 we should also expect, at the very least, Coubertin's regressive and sexist views to be recognised by the IOC and organisers.

Let's celebrate the women like Alice Milliat who fought for equal rights, Monsieur Macron, not the misogynist who never included women in that famous French *'liberté, égalité, fraternité'* of yours.[23]

The truth is that the spirit of that grand French national motto has only ever truly applied to men in sport.

When Qatar was making headlines over its human-rights record and not its hosting of the FIFA World Cup in 2022, Macron said that politics should be kept out of sport. By just saying that as the president of France he was of course bringing politics into sport. Perhaps diplomacy with the IOC is what he had in mind.

What he didn't mention was the scandal of France's involvement in the 2022 World Cup host bids. Perhaps the meeting before the FIFA vote that year between the French president Nicolas Sarkozy, Michel Platini and the emir of Qatar at the Élysée Palace was entirely innocent and had nothing to do with Sarkozy's desire for Qatari investment in Paris Saint-Germain.[24] What is certain is that Platini chose to vote for Qatar shortly after. Former FIFA president Sepp Blatter is on record as saying that Sarkozy had asked Platini to vote that way. Bidding has been inherently political for a long time.

We should be asking serious questions about whether countries with some of the world's worst human-rights records, including with regards to women's rights, should be hosting major sporting competitions. This is particularly the case when it comes to football.

It's striking that 2022 World Cup host Qatar was close to the bottom of the World Economic Forum's 'Global Gender Gap Report' that year.[25] This tracks gaps between women and men in employment, education, health and politics. Rights groups say that the Qatari legal system and its male guardianship law hinder women's advancement and are highly discriminatory.[26] There is a discussion to be had about whether sport should get involved in any debate about the practicality or advisability of imposing Western moral values on Islamic countries.

That issue cropped up during the World Cup in 2022, but with narrow focus: there was constant coverage of protests in support of the LGBTQ+ community but we heard very little about the lack of equality for women, which affects a much larger number of people.[27] It often appears that the rights of males, including gay men and transwomen, come right at the top of the political agenda in sport. Women are an afterthought or not even thought of at all.

Sports leaders who claim to be staunch supporters of gender equality and have been telling female athletes to be reasonable, stop complaining and be more welcoming to a new wave of biological males self-identifying as transwomen are the same men who voted to have Qatar, a country with no elite female athletes, host its showcase events.

It's no use Macron or anyone else saying we should keep politics out of sport. Sport is up to its neck in politics, power, business and the money that it generates.

Think back to the pre-World Cup press conference in Qatar. FIFA boss Gianni Infantino tried to brush aside all the human-rights concerns about football's controversial choice of Qatar as host when he said:

Today I feel Qatari. Today I feel Arabic. Today I feel African. Today I feel gay. Today I feel disabled. Today I feel like a migrant worker. Of course I am not Qatari, I am not an Arab, I am not African, I am not gay, I am not disabled. But I feel like it, because I know what it means to be discriminated against. To be bullied, as a foreigner in a foreign country. As a child I was bullied – because I had red hair and freckles.[28]

Spot the missing 'I am'. Infantino didn't mention feeling like a woman. At least not until a journalist pointed out he'd missed half the world, to which the Italian official answered: 'I feel like a woman too!'[29]

He hasn't a clue what it feels like to be a woman. This is all about the business of men.

SWIMMING TO EQUALITY?

From the start of the modern Games, women have had to fight tooth and nail with every passing Olympics to get closer to true equality. It's been a long haul. In 1900, there were just two women-only events. Men had 95. Parity has been hard fought for. Even where a sport includes both men and women, women have often been deemed incapable of covering the same distance, enduring the longer match, taking on the same number of events. We're still not there when it comes to tennis or the decathlon.

Women started swimming at the Olympic Games in 1912, but it was 2021, in Tokyo, before the women swam the same events as the men. Some of the gender gaps in Image 2 are breathtaking.

Women swimmers did quite well. They only had to wait 16 years to compete at the Olympics. For athletes and gymnasts, it was 32 years, speed skating 36 years, equestrianism 52 years. Women couldn't be trusted with a gun for 72 years; rowers waited 76 years, cyclists 88 years, women water polo players 100 years. But the prize for the record wait is wrestling, a sport that has been part of the Olympics from the beginning in 1896: 108 years.

SPORT	MEN	WOMEN
Swimming	1896	1912
Athletics	1896	1928
Gymnastics	1896	1928
Equestrian	1900	1952
Shooting	1896	1968
Basketball	1936	1976
Rowing	1900	1976
Cycling	1896	1984
Football	1900	1996
Water Polo	1900	2000
Weightlifting	1896	2000
Wrestling	1896	2004
Boxing	1904	2012

2 *How long women had to wait to join men in Olympic sports*

The governance gender gap has been even worse. It's hard to believe, but when I raced at my second Olympics in 1980 there had still not been a single woman member of the IOC. The first one was elected in 1981: one woman and 14 men. Today, there are more women but still five times more men than women at senior executive level and twice as many men in the boardroom overall.[30]

At executive level, there are five senior positions, only one of which is occupied by a woman, Nicole Hoevertsz, from the Dutch island of Aruba in the Caribbean, who finished eighteenth out of the 18 duet teams in synchronised swimming at the 1984 Olympic Games with teammate Esther Croes for the Netherlands Antilles.

In simple online searches for news and features from around the world, I cannot find any references to a single one of those women speaking in support of female athletes in the trans debate. Nor do I see any support for inquiry, truth and reconciliation over the East German doping decades.

In total, there are 102 full members of the IOC, 43 honorary members and one 'honour member' (Henry Kissinger). Of the 146 members in total, just 38 are women. The list includes two kings, six princes and three princesses. Of the 38 women, 16 are from countries where women are distinctly treated as second-class citizens and suffer life-shaping discrimination of the kind illegal in many parts of the world, including the UK, according to the country profiles of organisations such as Amnesty and Human Rights Watch.[31]

And we're not even talking about the standard, ever-present struggle highlighted by the World Bank on International Women's Day in 2022.[32] It noted that about 2.4 billion women of working age are not afforded equal economic opportunity and that 178 countries maintain legal barriers that prevent women's full economic participation. More than a dozen female IOC members hail from countries that human-rights groups cite as places of deep discrimination towards women. The human-rights violations perpetuated by these countries include beatings, stoning and differences in the age at which men and women can marry, with girls as young as 12 being forced into arranged marriages with men decades older than them.

There are more than 50 countries in the world, including IOC member nations, where rape within marriage is still legal. No surprise, then, to find that women are not encouraged or even allowed to participate in elite sport in many of those countries that are represented in decision-making roles at the IOC.

The governance structure and gender gap in my own sport, swimming, provides insight into many Olympic sports. In 2020, the 'Third Review of International Federation Governance', published by the Association of Summer Olympic International Federations (ASOIF), put FINA at the bottom of the league, along with weight-lifting and judo, over matters of discrimination and transparency.[33]

A glance at the gender gap in swimming governance highlights one of the key findings of the governance survey. Founded in 1908,

FINA was 113 years old before it included a single woman on its top team, now known as the executive. It took until 2000 to add a single woman to its board.

Reform is now reshaping the sport, and, in December 2022, FINA was renamed World Aquatics and a heartening decision was taken to set a minimum quota for women on the board (or bureau) that works out at just shy of 40 per cent.[34]

There's more work to be done. By the end of 2022, there was a commitment to reduce some of the 400-plus voluntary governance roles on 27 committees at FINA, which are 80 per cent male and at least half of which are occupied by political appointees. On the cusp of reform, 11 of the 27 groups had no women representatives even though their work involves particular focus on issues that affect women.

Between 1998 and 2021, there has been a tenfold increase in delegates from the Middle East and countries that have very few male elite aquatic athletes and almost no female athletes of any standard. This means that men from countries where women's rights are restricted have risen to key positions of authority in FINA.

It is true that there are women involved in sports governance, and there is no doubt that there are some good women in governance positions today. But when I look through the ranks of those who are there, I can't help thinking that they represent what men in sports governance may well consider to be the *right kind* of women: those who will cause them no problems, will do good work to a certain level but will never raise a red flag on a whole range of big issues because to do so would probably mean that they would lose their positions.

Frankly, it's been very disappointing to see how many strong women go into governance and then prove totally ineffective. I understand that these people have sometimes fought to get to those places. There must be something in them that motivated them in a good way. But it's frustrating to see fine athletes who must have had a fighter instinct to win races as sportswomen just roll over and become part of the machine, keeping their heads down, staying on message, avoiding issues if they aren't convenient to the leadership.

Those women who do get into positions of authority in FINA have faced a rampantly misogynistic culture. Craig once interviewed Julio Maglione, the Uruguayan president of FINA, in the lobby of a five-star hotel. Just as the interview was about to start, the FINA boss spotted an old friend and shouted out, 'Eh! Hijo de puta!' – meaning 'son of a whore' – as women and children wandered past. He engaged in a short but foul-mouthed exchange that the two individuals had dragged straight out of the locker rooms of their youth.

At the time, Maglione was staying in the suite, had a chauffeur and limousine at his beck and call, an 'executive volunteer' credit card and enormous, often pre-paid privileges that extended to first- and business-class travel, all meals, and a daily allowance of over $500 even though he had no expenses. They were all covered. It's not my definition of a volunteer.

Where Maglione might have been considered one of the boys for his foul language, a woman would be deemed a disgrace if she spoke that way. Where a man might be called aggressive, a woman is a bitch or, that favourite, a 'difficult woman'. If a girl is said to have slept around she's a slut, whereas a man doing that is just a lad. We're in the 2020s and that negative terminology used for women is part of the culture that keeps us in our places, and men in the driving seat.

Some of that old culture left with the departure of Cornel Mărculescu after 34 years as FINA director, and the reform process under way is already reaping fine dividends, as we'll see in Chapter 14.

The old guard are well past their sell-by date. For far too many years, they've been telling sportswomen what to wear – and like it. We've had volleyball players being told they're not showing enough bottom and that the shorts men wear just wouldn't be aesthetic enough.[35] There are countless other examples, many infuriating. I know young gymnasts who were asking to be able to do their routines in more comfortable, athletic kit, like shorts, not leotards, and being told they couldn't. Then transgender competitors arrived on the scene and all of a sudden they were allowed to wear shorts.

AN ILLUSION OF PROGRESS?

Sport is a tough place: females already have less prize money, less access, less media coverage and less profile in general. Now we're also supposed to compete at a disadvantage, against known males who have gone through male puberty. The consequences include loss of places on teams, loss of chances to make finals, loss of chances to win medals and gain access to all the related opportunities that follow.

Despite this, the success of the Lionesses and Emma Raducanu, and the fact that the media like to boast of having a women's sports correspondent on their team these days, has given the impression that we're talking about a new golden era for women's sport.

But just from my own experience I know that isn't true. It actually means more coverage for women's football, rugby and cricket or any Brit who wins a big pro title. But this isn't the case in many other sports. When it comes to female swimming, the new coverage has displaced much of the old. In many sports, historically there was no need for a women's correspondent: sport-specific specialist correspondents like Craig have been writing about women in sport for decades, and in my racing days we had three international matches a year, all televised. We had big companies like Esso and Green Shield sponsoring youth and senior swimming. Now, apart from track and field, Olympic sports are lucky if they make TV once a year, and often that's on a red button.

If you take a straw poll on the high street, and ask people to name five female Olympians, they'd probably end up naming mainly retired ones, or a couple of track stars who appear on yoghurt adverts. They'd struggle to name the current top British female swimmers, even the ones who won relay gold medals in Tokyo. And that's because we get less coverage between Olympics now than we did in my racing days.

The 'Gender in Televised Sports' report, issued by the Center for Feminist Research at the University of Southern California, was published in 2010 and covered the 20-year period from 1989 to 2009, citing a survey of early-evening and late-night TV sports news across a range of broadcast media. By 2009, men received 96.3 per cent of all airtime, women 1.6 per cent and neutral topics – whatever they are – 2.1 per cent. Another study ten years on found that the picture was practically unchanged and that 80 per cent of the televised sports news and highlights shows included zero stories on women's sports. Not one. The findings were written up in a paper subtitled 'The Long Eclipse of Women's Televised Sports, 1989–2019'.[36] The research is excellent, the findings truly depressing.

While women are no longer portrayed in demeaning ways as sexual objects or as the brunt of commentators' sarcastic 'humour', editors pay less attention to women in general. It is not only women who are overlooked. Seventy-two per cent of airtime goes to men in just three sports: basketball, American football and baseball – all traditional magnets for advertising revenue and generators of the biggest audiences that accounted for the bulk of coverage even out of their season. The popularity of individual sports has to be taken into account, but there's more than a little 'chicken and egg' about it: if people don't ever get an opportunity to see certain sports and women in them, it's obvious that there won't be an audience to grow. The rise in popularity of women's football has surely made that point.

That said, governing bodies could do so much more to grow the viewing figures for women's events, like putting major games on after the men's matches at venues such as Twickenham and allowing full stadiums to stay and watch. Invest to grow. Stadium numbers are increasing. Mainstream TV stations are airing big finals with big build-ups, especially in team sports. And the women are delivering. We can see the skill and fitness of the women's game. Men are also chatting about the tactics and talent in women's games. That's a very recent trend. It's heading very slowly in the right direction but men in boardrooms could still do so much more.

Olympic sports federations have a constitutional obligation to 'grow' and promote their sports, but the difference between the periods of popularity during a Games every four years and what happens in between is often stark. Why? Where are they going wrong and what might be done about it? In the digital age, when organisations seem to think they have it covered by appealing directly to 'the fans', where is the engagement with the mainstream media that provides a fundamental part of coverage in big pro sports? You can't grow a sport if you only ever talk to those who already love you.

Tributes to Dickie Davies, the frontman on ITV's *World of Sport*, who passed away in February 2023 aged 94, included a clip from his 1981 review of the year in which he tells viewers: 'Whatever the sport we cover – and that's right across the spectrum – there are those moments that occur that enliven, humanise and soften the serious business of competition. They so often spark off sporting chat in the pubs and living rooms and they provide us with warm and amusing memories.'[37]

'Right across the spectrum' is the key phrase. It's not happening in the UK today because emphasis is so heavily on the top handful of sports that take up all the oxygen in the media room. Craig tells me that things are different in Germany, where TV sports shows and even news bulletins still cover a wide range of sports and celebrate any German athlete who excels in any sport, regardless of whether the audience is the size of football fandom or that of handball fandom. Success makes the news and feeds into follow-up profiles written by print media and television documentaries.

If those news stories and profiles get no airtime or column inches in print, then success is something we only celebrate for those engaged in the most popular of activities. If we set sport aside and turn briefly to music, we find that, in the United States in 2018, pop, hip-hop and rock accounted for 56 per cent of all album sales, while classical accounted for 1 per cent. Does that mean we can't find public and commercial broadcasts and constant newspaper reviews of classical music? No.

Of course, unequal treatment by sex and sport is not confined to media coverage. Men's teams travel with dieticians and personal chefs, while the women muck in at the hotel buffet or tournament canteen. In 2019, the Lionesses flew from London to Nice for the World Cup on a British Airways flight and then made headlines when they took an EasyJet flight to a friendly in Portugal months after the England men's under-21 squad had flown to their European tournament on a private jet, the class of travel the England men's team has become accustomed to.[38] In 2020 the Lionesses flew to the United States for the SheBelieves Cup in premium economy and returned business class.[39] While the return journey was a step up from the economy class that most Olympic athletes travel in, the Football Association's decision on the women's flights came less than two years before the England team lifted the European trophy and attracted the biggest TV viewing figures for a home tournament in history, highlighting the ugly gap between women and men in the Beautiful Game.[40]

Similar things happen far and wide. Sedona Prince, the Oregon Ducks basketball star, highlighted the same issue in the United States in a video revealing the difference between the NCAA women's and men's weight-training rooms.[41] Women got the IKEA flat-pack version in a tiny room while the men got a state-of-the-art palace of pumping to work in.

However, we do need to retain a note of realism. We pay male footballers millions of pounds: their female equivalents get less in a year than a male Premiership footballer gets in a week. Some say that this situation should be equalised, but the hard truth is that the market for that is just not there. I do understand supply and demand. Sometimes women prefer to go shopping, or to watch *Strictly*, *Coronation Street* or *The Kardashians* rather than sport. Fact: there are a lot more male spectators on a Saturday afternoon than there are female spectators.

It also needs to be said that if women want to have equal prize money, then women need to run as far and play as many sets. We shouldn't have a heptathlon on the track in the Olympics for women. We should have decathlons for men and women. If men can do ten events over two days, so can women. None of those events in the decathlon is anything that's not done by women as an individual sport today. If it's about the ultimate athlete, then the ultimate athlete does ten events, not seven. Let's have real parity.

There are grounds for optimism. We all saw the outpouring of love for the Lionesses and that has to be a positive development. The problem is that the bosses still think of them as economy-class ticket holders and it's yet to be seen how long the drive to promote the women's game will last. I know they have had sessions in the UK Parliament to discuss how to harness all this enthusiasm. I hope it lasts longer than last time!

Whether it's big professional or Olympic sport, there is often only a small window of opportunity for women to grab attention, while men's sport gets huge coverage every single day.

2

LET THE DOPING GAMES BEGIN

SPORTING CRIME OF THE CENTURY

Let's face it, female athletes have been abused, denied, discriminated against, ignored, robbed, sacrificed and starved of justice by men manipulating women and breaking fair-play rules for as long as anyone can remember. To those of us still haunted by the ghosts of East German doping in the 1970s and 1980s, that era serves as a particularly cruel reminder of past wrongs.

Two groups of men bear responsibility for that dark chapter in Olympic sport.

First, we have the all-male leadership of the Communist GDR, hungry for success in sport to promote its political ideology at all costs. And then there are the Olympic bosses who not only failed to protect athletes through adequate policing of the scam unfolding on their watch but actually placed some of the leaders of the East German doping programme on the committees tasked with catching cheats and keeping sports clean. The aim of those GDR leaders was to guarantee that a nation of 17 million people punched well above its weight in sports based on speed, strength and endurance.

To do that, the leaders and those following their orders doped generations of athletes with anabolic steroids. Cheating with banned substances proved immensely successful for the politicians and perpetrators, but catastrophic for female athletes on both sides of the Cold War in sport.

What might be called the 'sporting crime of the twentieth century' was highly misogynistic. Success relied overwhelmingly on administering testosterone to teenage girls to give them some of the male advantages that naturally come from the steroid. As we'll see in Chapter 5, the best boys can beat the best ever females in a range of sports by the age of 15.

I was just 11 when I raced at my first junior international for Great Britain, and 13 in 1976 at the first of my three Olympic Games. At the same tender age, some East German girls in sports such as swimming, rowing, track and field, cycling, weightlifting and gymnastics were on a schedule of testosterone pills and injections and on their way to becoming Olympic, world and European champions, some as young as 15.

GDR athletes were weaponised in the biggest clinical trial on athletes in history, females the key target. Estimates suggest that up to 15,000 athletes, known as 'ambassadors in tracksuits', had been doped between the late 1960s and the fall of the Berlin Wall on 9 November 1989.

The girls were very strong and very fast, and had male physical characteristics as they lined up against us. In some of the sports that relied heavily on explosive force and strength, like shot-put, javelin and hammer-throw, GDR women were the size and shape of men as a result of the huge doses of testosterone they were given.

Brigitte Berendonk, who competed in track and field for West Germany and later became an author and lifelong, award-winning campaigner for clean sport, and her husband Professor Werner Franke, an oncologist who was also honoured by the German state for his anti-doping work, were two of the leading voices for truth and justice on GDR doping. They helped save hundreds of official state-secret documents from the shredders as East German security police tried to get rid of the evidence the moment it became clear that the days of the GDR were over.

In a 1997 paper presented to the Doping in Sport Symposium in Leipzig, they summed up what they had unearthed in 1990, and what Berendonk had published in her book *Doping: von der Forschung zum Betrug* (Doping: from research to fraud) in 1992, as follows:

> Several thousand athletes were treated with androgens every year, including minors of each sex. Special emphasis was placed on administering androgens to women and adolescent girls because this practice proved to be particularly effective for sports performance. Damaging side effects were recorded, some of which required surgical or medical intervention.[1]

Olympic shot-put champion Heidi Krieger was among those given doses of testosterone in her youth so extreme that medical intervention was required. By 18, Krieger had developed many masculine traits. East German records noted by Prof Werner Franke and Brigitte Berendonk show that she was administered with 2,600 milligrams of male steroids in 1986 alone. That's nearly 1,000 milligrams more than Ben Johnson took when cheating ahead of being banned during the Seoul 1988 Olympics.

In 1997, at the age of 31, Krieger underwent sex-reassignment surgery and changed name to Andreas. A year later, Andreas would testify against the doctors and coaches, who were convicted of bodily harm. Krieger has since married former East German swimmer Ute Krause, who was also a victim of systematic doping in the GDR. Andreas told Heidi's story and his story of transition in a moving documentary for the US Anti-Doping Agency (USADA) in 2015.[2]

The architects of cheating put national glory above human safety. Some of the banned substances used were even tested on teenagers who had been hand-picked at six years of age, measured for expected

growth and development, allocated to a sport they and their parents were told they were suited to, and placed in special schools. It
appeared to be an honour, but what no one told the families was
that coaches and doctors awaited the youngsters with a toxic tonic
of banned substances.

Among those given drugs were many who never made it to international competition. During the doping trials in 2000, some of the
athletes described themselves as guinea pigs in the GDR experiment
to find the champions whose names we got to know. I'd never heard
of Jutta Gottschalk and Martina Gottschalt (we learned from the
doping trials that the latter was an age-group backstroke champion
at 13, around the time she was put on a doping regime), but their
evidence in the trials was among the most moving. Jutta's daughter was
born blind while Martina's son was born with a club foot. *Der Spiegel*
reported from the trial that Dr Lothar Kipke, the senior swimming
doctor in charge of doping, had told his bosses that in pregnancy
embryos could be damaged by the anabolic steroids. He wrote: 'During
pregnancy, transplacental virilization of the female fetus.'[3]

In an interview with *Die Zeit* in 2018, Katja Hofmann, then
44 and a former GDR discus thrower, revealed a horrifying list of
symptoms that her doctor had told her would contribute to prema-
ture death as a result of the steroids she was given in youth. The 21
debilitating and life-threatening conditions included an enlarged
heart, thrombosis and pulmonary embolism, liver damage, obesity,
arthritis in the spine, hips, shoulder, ankle and thumb joint, hypo-
thyroidism, underdeveloped ovaries and uterus, pain-medication
intolerance, and insulin resistance.[4]

She also suffered burnout, chronic fatigue and depression, had an
eating disorder and still experienced signs of virilisation, including
facial hair growth, male-pattern pubic-hair growth and elevated
testosterone levels – decades on. Basically, they ruined her life. She
told *Die Zeit*:

In my sports club in Berlin, I would be given packets of powder. I was 13 or 14 years old the first time. The word Dynvital was on the label. I had no choice but to swallow it. My coach told me they were vitamins. She made sure that I always took it and acted as though she was doing me a favour. I trusted her, but she deceived me. I also know that she was only at the very end of the chain of command. I loved my sport... 'We are better than the West,' we were always told. It was also constantly said in East German sports that: 'Individuals don't matter.' We were guinea pigs.[5]

The East German medal factory was a regime of experimentation, cruelty and intimidation unparalleled in sporting history. The children were even told not to discuss details of their training with parents. Mum and Dad would simply not understand the world of sport, so best not worry them with any mention of the infamous little blue pills of Oral Turinabol. This was the brand name of the most common GDR steroid, which was used in a range of testosterone-based and other banned substances at the heart of the state secret. Here's a glimpse of just a part of the toxic nature of the 'supporting means' [*unterstützende Mittel*] fed to East German athletes, some as young as 11, reported by Franke and Berendonk in the 1990s. The sole purpose of these substances was to enhance performance and all are still part of the cocktail cabinets of cheats who risk their own health in sport to this day.

Athletes, particularly in sports such as swimming, where doping regimes started with children aged as young as 11 and 12, were told to take the 'vitamins and minerals' handed to them at the end of training sessions to help them grow strong and recover faster from the hard work they were doing.

The masterminds of the doping programme knew in the early years of experimentation that the list of side effects of the chemicals used was long and truly disturbing. Had parents been presented with

3 Androgenic-anabolic steroids

ORAL

Oral Turinabol (tablets)
Steroid substance 646 [Mestanolone]
Steroid substance XII
Steroid substance 482
Steroid substance 648
Dianabol [Methandienone, methandrostenolone]

INJECTABLE

Testosteron-Ampullen [Testosterone propionate]
Testosteron-Depot-Ampullen [Testosterone enanthate]
Testo-Tropin-Ampullen
Turinabol-Ampullen [Nandrolone phenylpropionate, Durabolin]
Turinabol-Depot-Ampullen [Nandrolone decanoate, Deca-Durabolin]

NASAL SPRAY

Testosterone esters
Androstenedione

STIMULANTS

Amphetamine
Methamphetamine (Pervitin)

POLYPEPTIDE HORMONES

Human growth hormone [Somatotropin][6]

Source: W. Franke and B Berendonk (see first note for Chapter 2)

that information and been given a choice, they would surely have withdrawn their children from the programme.

In sports such as athletics, swimming and rowing, men had an advantage over women of between 10 and 14 per cent at the time, but the architects of GDR fraud didn't need anything like as much to guarantee gold in women's sport. Their research told them that just a touch of masculinity would do the job.

The more testosterone a girl gets, the bigger and stronger she will be, and the harder she will be able to train. Guess what happens when you repeat all of that many times over for years and continue to train when your rivals cannot because they need to rest in order to allow the body to recover naturally. These girls had an artificial winning edge. That's what the rest of us faced. It was unsporting and unfair, and, of course, it broke the rules, but the rule-makers failed to hold inquiries into dubious results after questionable dominance at every passing international competition.

Actually, it was worse than that, because that second group of men responsible, Olympic bosses, put some of the GDR doping masterminds on the IOC's medical, scientific and anti-doping committees tasked with staying one step ahead of cheats. In fact, those GDR officials were there to make sure they stayed *three* steps ahead of the anti-doping police to avoid detection.

The science and biology that underpinned East Germany's fraud has several parallels with the transgender debate.

It comes down to the fundamental difference between the men's world champion and the women's world champion in any given event. As we shall learn in Chapter 5, the levels of testosterone males get from the womb and throughout life sets them apart from women.

East German scientists had already drawn the same conclusions in the late 1960s and in subsequent studies. They had established all those decades ago that 'androgenic initiation has permanent effects in girls and women', as Franke and Berendonk noted in their presentation to the Doping in Sports Symposium in Leipzig in 1997. With hindsight and the use of statistics showing the rate of decline in performances of shot-putters in the years that followed the collapse of the GDR, the authors concluded that after a sustained period of steroid use 'a higher performance level is reached that does not return to pretreatment values after the drug is withdrawn. In this respect, many of today's top athletes still profit from their previous androgenisation'.[7]

The conclusions reached half a century ago can very comfortably be applied to men who identify as women and gain access to female sport today. Indeed, it's even worse, as biological males have far more testosterone-driven advantages over women than any GDR female in sport ever had.

THE BIGGEST HEIST IN SPORTS HISTORY

The GDR crime began with men sitting around a table in the 1960s agreeing that if they could make a woman more like a man then the chances of her beating other women in speed and strength sports was extremely high.

The biggest heist in the history of world sport was a clandestine operation, an official state secret ordered by the ruling politburo, the GDR government's all-male cabinet. Only one woman ever made it to the position of government minister in the GDR, Margot Honecker, and she was the wife of the head of state and leader of the ruling Socialist Unity Party of Germany, Erich Honecker.[8] 'State Plan 14.25' was the official name of the cheating programme from 1974 onwards.[9] It remains the most successful medal factory in Olympic history in terms of the might of one nation relative to its population. Here's a brief overview of key statistics:

- The GDR competed at 11 Olympic Games, five summer (the Soviet-led boycott of 1984 kept them away from Los Angeles) and six winter, between 1968 and 1988.
- They had 1,714 athletes in total, and claimed 192 gold and 519 medals in all, compared to the 250 gold and 591 medals won by the United States, which had 2,832 athletes drawn from a population more than ten times greater than the GDR's during those years.
- At the five summer Games, the GDR won 126 gold and 409 medals from 1,394 athletes drawn from a population of 17 million. In comparison, Great Britain claimed 27 gold and 153

medals from 2,037 athletes drawn from a population of between 55 and 57 million.

- Three-quarters of the GDR's medals came from five sports: athletics, swimming, rowing, canoeing and gymnastics, with cycling, boxing and weightlifting also making significant contributions.

- Across all of the Olympics between 1968 and 1988, women won more than 70 per cent of medals for East Germany and more than three-quarters of all gold medals in athletics and swimming. Since women had almost as many chances to win medals in those two sports as men (though even then there was a disparity), these are the two sports that allow the most accurate comparison between the performance of male and female GDR athletes.

- The GDR was hugely dominant in female Olympic swimming across all events between 1976 and 1988, discounting the 1984 Games, which they boycotted. GDR women claimed more than 80 per cent of all gold medals, as well as 60 per cent of all world titles, in five global championships between 1973 and 1986, and a staggering 92 per cent of all European titles and 90 per cent of all medals at the continent's championships between 1973 and 1989.

That level of dominance in women's swimming by one nation over the course of almost two decades was and remains unprecedented. GDR men came nowhere remotely close to the success rate of their female teammates. We know they were also given illegal drugs, but they made nowhere near the same impact.

By the time we arrived in Montreal for the 1976 Olympics, we were all aware of the East German powerhouse. In swimming, the GDR women's team had claimed 21 gold medals, more than 70 per cent of all available, at the first two World Swimming Championships in 1973 and 1975. GDR men claimed three gold medals at those championships, courtesy of one swimmer, Roland Matthes, one of the most outstanding swimmers in history.

4 *Mind the gap: GDR women's and men's swimming medals, Olympic Games 1976–80–88, individual events*

WOMEN			MEN		
GOLD	**SILVER**	**BRONZE**	**GOLD**	**SILVER**	**BRONZE**
27	18	15	2	3	3
MONTREAL 1976					
Ender (3)	Priemer	Gabriel			Matthes
Thümer (2)	Treiber (2)				
Richter (2)	Pollack				
Anke	Tauber				
Pollack					
Tauber					
MOSCOW 1980					
Krause (2)	Diers (2)	Diers	Woithe	Pytell	Pytell
Reinisch (2)	Metschuck	Schmidt (2)			
Schneider	Schneider	Dähne			
Diers	Kleber	Riedel			
Geweniger	Polit	Treiber			
Metschuck	Pollack	Knacke			
Geißler	Schönrock				
SEOUL 1988					
Otto (4)	Friedrich	Meissner	Dassler	Baltrusch	Dassler
Friedrich	Strauß	Stellmach		Kühl	
Hörner	Zimmermann	Möhring			
Nord	Weigang (2)	Sirch (2)			
Hunger		Hörner			
		Hunger			

Roland was coached by Marlies Grohe, the only GDR swimming coach to have refused to take part in the doping of swimmers and remain in the job, as one of the senior scientists on the doping programme told Craig in a 2006 interview.[10]

In rowing, GDR women had lifted five of the six world titles up for grabs in 1975, while in track and field, the first sport in which young girls were used as guinea pigs in the GDR's pharmaceutical experiment, East Germany had already dominated athletics events at the 1972 Olympics, with six golds and 13 medals, a haul which took them to the top of the medals table.

The Montreal Olympics of 1976 introduced the muscled might of East German women to the bigger Olympic audience in a wide range of sports. One of the iconic pictures of the Games was of swimmer Kornelia Ender holding the rails with both hands as she climbed the steps out of the pool after winning one of her four golds with eight Olympic podiums. That image summed up how I saw the East Germans. They were big, heavy, muscular – built like the men on our team. We hadn't seen anything like it before.

Many years later, after the Berlin Wall fell in late 1989, Craig was the first Western journalist to interview Ender, for *The Times*. By then a physiotherapist with her own children, one of them with her first husband Matthes, she recalled the little blue pills of Oral Turinabol. 'There were also injections to help us to recover and recuperate so the athletes could get back to hard training session after session without breaking down or being in need of a day off,' she said.[11]

The rest of us had to build rest and recovery into our programmes while GDR doctors propped their athletes up with artificial strength. More work, more power, greater fitness all added up to bigger artificial advantage over those who played fair and had to follow a natural rhythm of recuperation from heavy training. It wasn't that we were putting less effort in, but our bodies just didn't have the ability to repair themselves in the same way after intense periods of training. And as females we just couldn't build the muscle bulk.

THE LEARNING CURVE OF MY FIRST OLYMPICS AT 13

At 13, I wasn't a contender for medals. Montreal was about having fun, gaining experience, seeing how much I could improve. It was a massive learning curve in my career. The sheer scale of everything was new and fascinating. To help everyone find their way around, organisers had painted coloured lines on the floors. The blue line led to the changing rooms, where I was one of many women who thought they'd walked into the men's side by mistake.

It turned out we were in the right place. The deep voices on the other side of the lockers belonged to the East German women. If that was strange, what really struck us about them was their physical presence and how sad they often appeared.

Swimming is a hard sport, and you have to be dedicated, disciplined and determined to get through tough times, but it felt like the East Germans were more like machines, programmed to win. Once racing was done I was used to having some fun on swimming trips. We'd be bouncing off the walls and ceilings, playing jokes on each other, getting up to all sorts of innocent mischief. For the East Germans, it was almost like it was just a job, and they would be herded around like soldiers, not being allowed to mix.

People still talk about what was suspected back in the 1970s and 1980s but we actually knew. I knew – we all knew – what was staring us in the face: they were cheating and it had to be drugs. We just didn't know the details or how they were managing to escape detection.

We couldn't ask the girls themselves because there was no social contact. The coaches and team officials kept a close watch on the athletes, and journalists were fed propaganda and lies. When East

German coach Rolf Gläser was asked in Montreal to explain why the teenage girls on his team had deep voices, he remarked tersely: 'They didn't come to sing, they came to swim.'[12]

Between 11 and my selection for the Olympic Games as the youngest member of the Great Britain team at 13, I was busy getting experience on the European race circuit. Terry, my dad and coach, took me to competitions all over Europe, where the Continent's best juniors cut their competitive teeth. It's where we got to know our opposition, learn and form friendships.

Neither I nor anyone else outside the GDR knew it at the time, but my first summer of senior international selection coincided with the official adoption of 'State Plan 14.25'.[13]

I was up to scratch on flares and *Top of the Pops* but not so much on politics, though at 13 and on my way to my first Olympic Games in 1976 I was already learning. I remember seeing teams from Africa packing up and leaving the Games as their nations joined a boycott of 29 countries from their continent.[14] They were protesting against the IOC's refusal to ban New Zealand after its rugby union team had toured apartheid South Africa earlier that year.

Boycotts would affect two of the three Olympics I competed at, in 1976 and 1980. In 1976, the Cold War came to the Games. I was aware of the GDR girls and the attention they were getting, but at 13 my lasting memories were things like being madly in love with David Wilkie, Britain's breaststroke gold medallist; the fun we had at the opening and closing ceremonies; the extreme discomfort of the heat wave that affected our training camp at Crystal Palace that summer; and feeling absolutely shattered from not getting much sleep.

I shared a room with my 15-year-old teammate, Kim Wilkinson. She's still a good friend of mine and we laugh about the ways we tried to cool down: by putting our sheets in cold water, wringing them out and seeing if that might help us sleep. It didn't.

By 1976, I'd got to know a lot of the girls I would race at major championships in the coming years. But not the East Germans. We rarely saw them. We'd never heard of many of them. Girls would appear on the GDR team after making spectacular improvements in the six months before any championships. They'd make the medals and, within just one or two years, they were gone.

The story of Petra Thümer is a case in point. We first heard about her when she was 15. She won the European junior 800 metres freestyle title in 8:59.31 (8 minutes, 59.31 seconds), and took the silver in the 400 metres freestyle in 4:27.08, behind a teammate. Thümer entered 1976 well off the pace she would need to have a chance of winning a medal at the Olympic Games seven months later. Over 400 metres, she was in no sense a contender. Her best time was 13 seconds slower than American Shirley Babashoff's world record and outside the fastest 50 times in the world.

Just six months later, at trials a month before the Olympics, she set a world record of 8:40.68 in the 800 metres freestyle and finished second to compatriot Barbara Krause in the 400 metres freestyle, both women inside Babashoff's world record of 4:14.76.

Krause's new world record of 4:11.69 was amazing back then, but she did not make it to Montreal. At the Games, East German officials told the media that she was ill. Years later, however, state documents would show that she had returned a positive test for an anabolic steroid because doctors had miscalculated the dose of the banned substances they had given her, and they could not risk Krause testing positive in competition.[15]

For the GDR, she was dispensable. After all, they had another lined up for gold. Thümer took the 400 metres and 800 metres Olympic titles in the astonishing times of 4:09.89 and 8:37.14, respectively. Her curve of progress was, like those of many other East German swimmers in that era, off the chart. That era remains a distinct blip on the curve of women's progress in the pool down the years.

Thümer would go on to break the world records in those two events once more to take the 1977 European titles. And then she was gone, at 16. We never saw her in international waters again, but we would, eventually, find out why.

My dad had understood what I faced long before I did. Dad studied all sorts of magazines from around the world, checking out rivals, monitoring progress, showing me the names, results and times of the swimmers I was likely to race. In the years after Montreal and before the Moscow Olympics, he would take me to America, Canada and Australia to train with some of the leading coaches in the world.

I was constantly learning – and so was Dad, busy soaking up cutting-edge coaching knowledge before returning home to call on friends and contacts in business and the navy, and anyone else who could help him build contraptions like pulley machines that a swimmer could use to replicate swimming movement on dry land (this was what the Americans were doing). He left no stone unturned. He was one of the first coaches in the UK to incorporate dry-land training. It was intense and all consuming.

When I broke both bones in both forearms at 11, he wrapped a plastic bag around the casts, taped them up and told me, 'There's no reason why you can't do kick.' So that's what I did, my broken arms resting on a float, my legs working hard. The following year, I tore all the ligaments in my right knee at school sports day, so he tied my legs together and I swam arms-only for months. No injury was allowed to stand in the way of training. Needless to say, I wasn't allowed to do school sports any more!

All of that effort made it all the more frustrating to hear, down the years, sometimes from our own federation and media in Britain, that we weren't working hard enough, weren't as clever as the East Germans, who were doing things that we weren't capable of. That explained why they were champions and we had failed to beat them or, if we raised questions, why we were called sore losers.

WHY SHIRLEY BABASHOFF WAS A HERO

When Shirley Babashoff questioned the GDR results in Montreal, she made headlines around the world. Her home media in the United States dubbed her 'Surly Shirley', 'shrill' and 'angry'.

When I think of the hateful labelling by trans activists of those standing up for hard-fought-for women's rights, it reminds me of Shirley and her teammates Wendy Boglioli, Jill Sterkel and Kim Peyton, who against the odds took the one gold for American women in the pool in 1976 when they defeated the GDR in the 4×100 metres freestyle relay. Arguably, it remains the greatest team victory by any American relay in swimming history and was the subject of the 2016 film *The Last Gold*.[16]

As things turned out, Shirley wasn't surly at all. She had every reason to raise a red flag. She would have been one of the golden greats of our sport, probably with several gold medals in Montreal, but she went home with one relay gold and several silvers and bronzes and was written up as a 'sore loser', alongside anyone else who dared question the GDR 'success story'.

In 1976, it was not the GDR conquerors that I looked up to but Shirley. She was a hero to me, one of the greats of swimming. She went home as the most medalled American woman in Olympic swimming history, with a total of eight podiums from 1972 and 1976 combined, her tally matching the biggest career total ever, held at the time by Australian legend Dawn Fraser.

Dawn has spent most of her life as an official 'National Living Treasure' down under, reaping the rewards of that status.[17] It was a very different story for Shirley. She coached swimming after her retirement, but to make ends meet when her son was born, she took a job as a postwoman for the United States Postal Service in Orange County, California. And that is how she spent much of the rest of her working life, never having been able to capitalise on her real status and achievements as an athlete, for want of an Olympic gold in a solo race.

All the gold medals in Shirley's solo events in 1976 – the 100, 200, 400 and 800 metres – went to East Germans Ender and Thümer. Shirley had little to do with swimming for many years, but in 2016 told her story in *Making Waves*, her fine autobiography, written with Chris Epting.[18]

I had no connection to the East Germans. I had no explanation for what they were doing. No official was asking any questions, so there were no answers when it came to why they were so muscled and spoke with such deep voices, why some of them had excessive body hair and serious acne that stretched well beyond facial pimples to scarring of the skin across the shoulders and down the back.

I don't know if the GDR girls even knew that we were angry that they were beating us, but, as I said before, they rarely seemed pleased, sometimes even embarrassed, so maybe they did.

We had the feeling that it wasn't that they didn't want to mix with us – they just weren't allowed to. They weren't allowed to change with us or go on the same buses. I would often bring gifts of make-up or tights for a Russian friend I had made, because during the Cold War they struggled to get luxury items, and I remember once smuggling some to one of the GDR girls in the green room before a relay race.

Even though they were beating us, we felt sorry for them. We understood it wasn't as if they had any choice in the matter. We also felt it was important to tell the truth about what didn't seem right, but we were told to keep quiet. Coaches like my dad got left off teams because they did speak out and bosses felt uncomfortable.

And there's another parallel with the transgender debate. It wasn't that you had no empathy with the East German girls – it was just that it all felt so very unfair to all of us who were following the rules and playing fair. It felt as though the truth was being quashed by those in charge.

All the better for the rogues of the GDR, who relied on Olympic bosses to look the other way. Years later, in 1990, after the first details of the doping programme were revealed on the eve of German reunification, the head of the doping programme, Manfred Höppner, would tell the German magazine *Stern* that the GDR knew that there were no effective doping controls back in the 1970s.[19]

He also knew that the IOC-accredited laboratory at Kreischa in Saxony was part of the dark secret. Instead of trying to catch cheats, they tested in order to detect and hide positive results, and therefore to make sure that anyone who might get caught, like Krause and Thümer, did not travel outside the country.

Those who did show up had already got away with it. They were officially 'clean'. The drugs had already built the winning machine. Fair play was dead and Olympic bosses have never even held an inquiry into any of it. Kreischa remains an anti-doping facility to this day.

East Germany's rise was meteoric. From nine golds and 25 medals in all sports in 1968, the GDR took 20 golds and 66 medals in 1972. In 1976, the GDR forced the United States into third on the overall medals table. Its 40 golds and 90 medals in Montreal were second only to the score of its political master, the Soviet Union.

SINKING THE BIG LIE OUT OF SIGHT

A hero's welcome awaited the East Germans back home. They were met by heads of government at the airport. There were national honours, prize money for their medals, perks that extended to flats and cars – all this despite the fact such things were forbidden under amateur rules at the time.

The prestige derived from these athletic feats had to be protected at all costs.

The conditions under which the GDR competed were even different to those of their Soviet opponents. I remember watching people like Olga Korbut breezing through the food hall in the athletes' village in Montreal, but I never saw the East Germans. I didn't know at the time, but since then we've learned that they stayed on boats on the St Lawrence River. We would later learn that every team had athletes, coaches and officials hired by state police to spy on teammates and report any suspicions or signs of defection or disloyalty to the regime.

The big lie had to be protected. In 2009, news agency The Canadian Press explained just how dark the deceit was even during the Games in Montreal. It reported:

> After injecting athletes with performance-boosting drugs at the Montreal Olympics, East German officials dumped the leftover serum and syringes in the St. Lawrence River, newly uncovered documents indicate.
>
> A chance discovery in the Berlin archives of the notorious Stasi, the East German secret police, led University of Waterloo history professor Gary Bruce to a 95-page file on the spy service's operations at the Montreal Games.
>
> A Stasi officer's final report on the Games contains a none-too-subtle reference to the drug program under the subheading, 'Destruction of the Rest of the Special Medicine.'
>
> About 10 suitcases of medical packaging, needles, tubular instruments, etc. were sunk in the St. Lawrence River.[20]

Bruce explained:

> The documents make it clear that Stasi chief Erich Mielke saw the Games as a means to improve East Germany's standing in

the world by ensuring all went well on the athletic field and that nothing went wrong away from it. He put the fabled Markus Wolf, head of the Stasi's foreign espionage wing, in charge of Operation Finale, a tightly controlled effort to monitor East German athletes in the years leading up to the '76 Olympics as well as during the 16-day sporting festival... Officers from the Stasi and other East Bloc security services met at KGB head-quarters in Moscow before the Games to coordinate efforts.[21]

To the GDR, sport was about business, power and politics. For me, the Montreal Games were all about soaking up the incredible experience. Four years later, at 17, I would be a contender and the significance of GDR cheating would sting me and my teammates not just on the day, but for decades after.

My Olympic-debut focus was the 200 metres backstroke. I entered as the third fastest on the British team and left the competition as the fastest Brit, midfield among all the world's best swimmers. A key definition of satisfaction in performance sport is seeing the rewards for all your hard work.

The East Germans worked hard, too, some of them enduring regimes that were beyond what many of us could manage without breaking down, sustaining serious injury or burning out. The big question, one that ran through our heads at every passing competition, was: how were they getting away with it?

The truth started to flow not long after the fall of the Berlin Wall in 1989 – but not everyone wanted to hear it.

3

HOW WE WERE CHEATED

WHEN *Stern*, one of the world's leading magazines, published state-secret documents proving that a six-time Olympic gold medallist and three of her East German teammates tested positive for illegal anabolic steroids, Olympic bosses shrugged and looked the other way.[1]

It was November 1990, the month of German reunification, and there in black and white was the truth we'd all been waiting for, alongside what amounted to a signed confession from the head of the East German doping programme, Manfred Höppner.

The headline proclaimed 'How the GDR made winners!' Right next to it was a shot of the explosive document showing that swimmer Kristin Otto, who, just two years earlier, at the Seoul Olympics, had achieved an all-time, all-sports record haul of six golds at a single Games, had tested positive for a male anabolic steroid.

The timing of these revelations meant that there was absolutely no chance of the IOC or anyone else claiming that a statute of limitations stood in the way of any inquiry or the start of the much-needed truth-and-reconciliation process. The healing of generations of female athletes, on their side and ours, depended on it.

But Olympic leaders took no action, even though Höppner confirmed key details of the secret state doping programme, which *Stern* poured out over eight pages of painful revelations. Höppner was the top doctor in the fraud and one of the three most senior figures at the helm of the GDR's official state-secret and dream-smashing fraud.

The other two were Erich Honecker, leader of the GDR between 1971 and 1989, and his sidekick Manfred Ewald, minister of sport from 1961 to 1988, a man who would often be at major international sports events or there to greet the returning doped heroes at the airport with a handshake. The president of the National Olympic Committee (NOC) of the GDR from 1973 to 1990, Ewald, like Höppner, was convicted in the German doping trials of 1998–2000 for his role in the state-sponsored swindle.[2]

Extraordinarily, both Honecker and Ewald remain on the list of those honoured by the IOC to this day.[3] Olympic bosses appear to have no understanding of just how toxic their names are to generations of athletes from the GDR era. Their failure to take action after *Stern*'s explosive revelations was perverse and infuriating in 1990 and remains so.

In the middle of the *Stern* spread was an interview with Höppner that suggested that his defence of the doping programme could be summed up by the title of Édith Piaf's great classic 'Non, je ne regrette rien'. 'I could sing along with that,' Höppner replied. A decade later a Berlin court would convict him of bodily harm against minors who'd been pumped with harmful substances purely in pursuit of sporting glory for a Communist state that had, by then, been disbanded.

Still Olympic bosses did nothing.

The damning document showing Otto's positive test was typed up on the headed paper of the GDR's Central Institute of Sports Medicine Services, complete with the address of the IOC-accredited laboratory at Kreischa in Saxony. It was signed on 9 August 1989 by one of the leading doctors working in the GDR doping programme, Claus Clausnitzer, the director at the Kreischa facility.

He listed the bad news about Otto alongside adverse findings for three of her national teammates. Fellow Olympic champions Heike Friedrich and Daniela Hunger and GDR swim-team newcomer and future European and Olympic champion Dagmar Hase all had a 'positive X' reading next to their names (see Image 5). If those results had been reported to the IOC, as they should have been by the Kreischa laboratory, all four swimmers would have been suspended in 1989 and the GDR game would have been up.

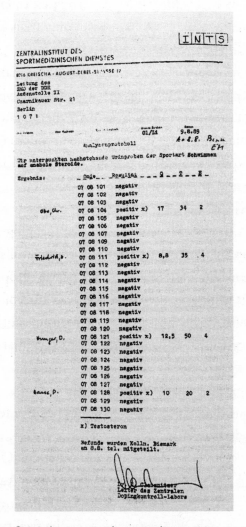

5 *Stasi document showing the positive tests*

But the Olympic laboratory hid the 7 August tests and used the information to instruct doctors to clean the girls up before they raced to titles and medals at the European Championships just a week after failing drug tests.

Dr Clausnitzer was used to the process. As we'll see in Chapter 7, he'd led a 1982 study showing how doctors had learned to turn a positive testosterone test into a safe negative within three days.[4] Otto and co. were duly cleaned up and sent to Bonn for the Continental showcase, where they added five solo titles to a total of 14 out of 16 gold medals for the GDR. That was part of a pattern over the seven European championships between 1974 and 1989 at which East Germany's women claimed a staggering 92 per cent of all gold medals and 90 per cent of all medals available to them.

Those 1989 positives and the last competition at which we saw East German swimmers racing in GDR colours coincided with my swimming comeback, which occurred at the very tail end of two decades of steroid-fuelled dominance for East German women in a range of Olympic sports.

Just over a year later, Höppner was peddling his version of events to *Stern*. He spilled the beans with some of the most incriminating evidence of mass cheating ever seen. It's truly galling to think that the head of GDR doping could confess in the way he did in 1990, with no regrets, to a world-renowned magazine that everybody respects, but that no one, neither the IOC, nor international federations, nor anyone else in any position of authority in sport, was prepared to sound the alarm. Höppner and his accomplices should have been slapped with immediate temporary suspensions pending a full inquiry. Instead there was silence from those with the power to act.

It's difficult not to reflect on the parallels with what happened at the Sochi 2014 Winter Olympics, where urine and blood samples were switched through holes concealed by fake power sockets in the walls from the official anti-doping laboratory to a hidden one operated by scientists and their state-security minders in Russia.

The award-winning documentary *Icarus* captures the darkness of it all.[5] It was like an updated version of the GDR's way of avoiding positive tests. The outcome was the same – systematic cheating – but still the IOC passed the buck to international federations and others to sort the mess out.

Höppner was not only in charge of the doping programme in the GDR. He was a member of the IOC's Medical Commission, dispensing advice on good health and clean sport, and spying on the anti-doping testing programme so that he could go home and tweak procedures to make sure that no GDR athlete was ever caught.

Fewer than a handful of GDR cheats were ever caught by international testers, but Kreischa had a fat record of the vast number of positive tests for banned substances over a 20-year period. Höppner and co. made sure it never came to light when the fraud was a state secret. So did Dr Lothar Kipke, who served on the medical commission of FINA, the international federation in my sport, swimming. He was vocal about clean sport abroad but back home was reported by Höppner for the brutality with which he rammed steroid syringes into the backsides of teenage girls. Kipke was convicted of the crime of bodily harm to minors and sentenced to a suspended prison sentence of 15 months in January 2000 by the Berlin Regional Court. The then 72-year-old had confessed to having been involved in 58 cases of administering anabolic steroids to underage swimmers between 1975 and 1985 to enhance their performance but without medical indication.[6]

The spymasters had spies in every camp, including the medical committees, the organising committees – even the IOC, where the boss was only too happy to seek the advice of people who would turn out to be doping masterminds.

Höppner told *Stern* in 1990 that IOC president Juan Antonio Samaranch had asked him and his colleagues to determine where medical support for athletes ended and doping began. Samaranch might as well have asked the world's biggest diamond thief if he wouldn't mind helping pick out new security systems for the Guggenheim.

Testing was required only in competition in those days to avoid athletes cheating on the day. It wouldn't have done to have had officials snooping around inside East German training centres, or showing up unannounced at the Kreischa laboratory when athletes were having the steroids flushed out of them at the adjacent clinic.

In 1990, Höppner even had the nerve to suggest that GDR athletes were far better off than many others because they had constant medical attention. It was tantamount to saying that we'd all be better off in the care of criminals. In one extract from state-security documents, Höppner acknowledges that a strong increase in sex drive is a side effect of the steroids given to teenage girls, who were told not to tell their parents about the pills and injections. He then advocates secret abortions at a state clinic:

> Should a pregnancy occur while anabolic steroids are being taken then it is recommended in all cases that an abortion is carried out. Children born to athletes who had taken steroids are to be delivered in a Stasi clinic so that a decision could be taken as to what to do in the event of complications.[7]

There was a serious risk of disabilities in children developed in the wombs of women on a toxic diet of anabolic steroids, he noted. He also lamented that a well-trained athlete would be lost and no longer available to the GDR's medals factory.

As noted in Chapter 2, all of these files and facts are with us because of the work of two-time Olympic discus thrower for

Germany and campaigner for clean sport Brigitte Berendonk and her partner and leading oncologist Professor Werner Franke. They helped recover and compile official state research documents on the GDR doping programme with the help of good colleagues who kept the record safe at the Military Medical Academy in Bad Saarow.

Stasi volumes detailed the names of athletes, coaches, doctors, spies, banned substances, dosages and much more. No wonder *Stern* asked Höppner whether the future of sport was to be all about which athletes had the best doctors.

Since *Stern*'s revelations and Brigitte Brendonk's book *Doping: von der Forschung zum Betrug* (Doping: from research to fraud) confirmed all we needed to know about East German cheating, successive IOC leaderships have been in denial. They even failed to act after the doping trials in Berlin from 1998 to 2000 handed down a series of criminal convictions to doctors, scientists, coaches and politicians.

They should all have gone to jail for years, but the numbers involved were overwhelming for the special division of the German criminal police, the Central Investigations Office for Government and Reunification Crimes (ZERV), that was put in charge of investigating doping crimes.[8] Of the 1,000 athletes invited to testify at the trials, only 300 ended up doing so, in part because a time limit of October 2000 was set and all cases not tried by then escaped being called. It's the kind of judicial process that leaves victims, survivors and observers frustrated.

The sentences were token measures, with suspended jail terms of a few months to two years backed by fairly paltry fines, and most of it concentrating on bodily harm to minors rather than any of the other forms of crime that might have been considered. By the time the trials finished, the IOC had shifted its justification for taking no action away from the need to ask for more information to the claim that it could no longer act because of the statute of limitations. How convenient!

THE COSTS AND CONSEQUENCES OF CHEATING

I went home from my first European Championships in 1977 with bronze medals in the 400 metres medley and the sprint freestyle relay with my British teammates. I also finished fourth in the 200 metres medley. I was still only 14, and, had it not been for GDR doping, I would have been the youngest European 400 metres medley champion in history. I would also have claimed silver medals in the 200 metres medley final and another in the medley relay. Sue Jenner would have won the 200 metres butterfly instead of the bronze, and the silver medal instead of coming fourth in the 100 metres; there would have been a bronze for Cheryl Brazendale in the 400 metres freestyle, and for Maggie Kelly in the 100 metres breaststroke – and we would have had a bronze medal in my medley relay.

So, it was three bronze medals instead of the two gold, three silver and three bronze it should have been. We, along with women from swimming nations all over Europe, spent our careers battling that curse, and despite libraries stacked with the evidence of cheating, not a single result, record or outcome has been the subject of any official inquiry by Olympic bosses, with international and domestic federations frozen to the spot until the IOC tells them when and how they can move.

Years later, after the Berlin Wall had fallen, all our fears were confirmed. Ahead of me in the 400 metres medley in Jönköping, Sweden, back in 1977 were Olympic champion Ulrike Tauber and her GDR teammate Sabine Kahl. Tauber became the youngest champion ever in 1974, on her way to the Olympic gold in Montreal. She was coached at the sports club SC Karl-Marx-Stadt in Saxony with other winners at the championships in 1977: Petra Thümer, Birgit Treiber, and Berliners Barbara Krause and Andrea Pollack.

In 1994, all of them would be named by Franke and Berendonk as having tested positive for anabolic steroids.[9] Still the IOC failed to act.

We didn't know the precise details back in the 1970s – we just knew something was very wrong, and that's why Terry, my dad, told me that our 1978 focus would be on the Commonwealth Games in Edmonton, Alberta. It was our chance to show what we were truly capable of out of the shadow of GDR doping. And that's what I did, by winning both the 200 and 400 metres medley titles for England ahead of the Canadian athletes who had claimed Olympic silver and bronze behind the GDR'S Tauber in 1976: Cheryl Gibson and Becky Smith.

I was very proud of my progress: I'd come from sixteenth at the Olympics two years before all the way up to beating the two Canadians who would have been Olympic gold and silver medallists at a home Games in Montreal had it not been for GDR doping.

There was a sense of relief to be free of the feeling you were being cheated out of what should have been. I remember being ecstatic when celebrating relay medals with my roommate, Heidi Turk.

Heidi was also one of those who would've won more medals in Sweden. Instead, she often missed out through her career, like so many. We had been friends since we met as children at school competitions. Sadly, in 2012, shortly after her fiftieth birthday, Heidi died of breast cancer. Her husband set up the charity Heidi's Heroes, which I am a proud ambassador for, to raise money to teach children from areas of deprivation to swim, a life-saving skill.[10] I still miss her. She's just one of those who didn't get what they deserved and now never will.

I finally got to leave a race thinking the fight had been fair and that I'd got the medals I deserved, the reward my dad had pushed so hard for. Part of any story of success in sport is acknowledgement for the huge sacrifices a family makes so that a daughter, son or sibling can become a world-class challenger. When the athlete is then robbed of their rightful reward, they all feel a deep sense of loss. It's one of the hidden sides of the GDR fraud: the impact on the mental health of athletes, coaches and parents down the decades cannot be overstated.

My family made massive sacrifices. There was no funding or National Lottery in those days. We used to go on holiday to Cornwall when I was very young, but from the time I started to show promise in the pool at ten we didn't have a family holiday. I remember overhearing my parents talking about going without: no new washing machine, no meals out, no new school uniforms for my younger twin brothers. We all got bikes when my grandma sadly passed away, but even they were second-hand. Don't get me wrong – we didn't go without food, love or a roof over our heads, but money was always tight.

Dad had been invalided out of the navy when he lost sight in one eye and Mum helped in his various projects at a time when he was coaching me four to six hours a day on top of doing a job. Their spare finances were used to support me to do my sport and that meant that they didn't have enough money to come and watch me when I raced.

My parents scraped enough together to get Dad to Moscow for the 1980 Olympics, but both Mum and Dad missed both Commonwealth Games, the European Championships, the World Championships and even the 1992 Olympics, when I made my comeback. They watched me making podiums on the telly back home, sometimes in the middle of the night, the clock ticking towards their next shift, since they were parents with jobs to get to.

For all those reasons, the decision to focus on the Commonwealth Games was obvious. Just two weeks after Edmonton, we were in West Berlin for the 1978 World Championships. Except for the curiosity of a trip through Checkpoint Charlie, this was a sort of non-event for me, because I'd achieved what I wanted that summer in Canada, but, to everyone's surprise, the GDR dominance we expected didn't happen.

ATHLETE REVELATIONS

Christiane Knacke, with a pioneering swim that made her the first to race inside the one-minute mark in the 100 metres butterfly, and double Olympic champion Petra Thümer, with three golds over 200, 400 and 800 metres in Sweden, were among those expected to mop up in West Berlin. But something strange happened on their way to Checkpoint Charlie and they never showed up. Journalists at the championships in Berlin were told that the two swimmers were out of action because one had caught a bad cold and the other had slipped in the shower.

When Knacke was allowed to leave the GDR in 1988 after marrying an Austrian, she approached the media in her new country and told the truth. The reason that she had not shown up in Berlin for the 1978 World Championships was that she and Thümer had tested positive for anabolic steroids.[11]

They were pulled out of the queue awaiting transfer from East to West Berlin with teammates, driven three hours south in a van to Kreischa, put on static bikes for hours on end and told to keep drinking water. 'They were trying to clean us up, but it didn't work in time,' she told my co-author Craig in 2006 at a GDR athletes' reunion.

While Knacke would make it to the Moscow Olympic Games two years later, Thümer's senior career was over. Two golds on her Olympic debut at 15, three European freestyle titles at 16, a positive test for doping – and gone almost as fast as she'd arrived. Swimmers of that calibre didn't just arrive at 15 to leave the scene at 17 without a reason. No explanation was ever given. Speculation was rife because, the year before, in 1979, we finally got the first statement from a leading East German swimmer that banned substances were being used by the GDR: Renate Vogel suggested that testosterone was the GDR fuel of choice.

In 1973, Renate, a breaststroke specialist and 1972 Olympic silver medallist in the GDR medley relay, took three gold medals at the first World Swimming Championships. When she finished second to a West German in the 100 metres breaststroke at the European Championships in 1974, she was treated like a failure.

She complained to her coach and others that her voice had deepened, but when she asked to come off the drugs and quit her sport she was told that she could not, and that she could not leave the programme.

So Renate hatched a plan to flee. She travelled on holiday to Hungary, still within the Soviet bloc, and with the help of friends on the other side of the Berlin Wall was given a West German passport, a false identity and a ticket from Budapest to Munich. It was a high-risk plan for a citizen of a country whose leadership had given shoot-to-kill orders at the borders for anyone caught attempting to escape the GDR.

In Munich, Renate told her story about the GDR talent scouting and the process of selecting children for sports schools – and about the secret, systematic doping programme.

During an interview with the Austrian public broadcasting network ORF in Vienna, she had to be given bodyguards after receiving threats from East Germany's ruling Communist Party.[12] Renate said the steroids she had been fed were injected and mixed into her food at sports school from the age of 14. Nothing was done when this information was made public. The IOC know it all to be true, and these days Renate's 1979 revelations are even included on her profile on the official Olympics website, even though the organisation has never done anything to reinforce its rules, neither historical nor prevailing.[13]

A decade later, after being allowed to leave the GDR to live in Vienna with her new husband, Christiane Knacke echoed Renate's story when she told Austrian media that she had been given steroid pills by coach Ralf Gläser from the age of 13.[14] In the year leading up to her historic swim in 1977 she had put on 15 kilos of muscle.

And listen to this. When the GDR border came down in 1989's peaceful revolution, Renate and Christiane travelled to Lausanne, Switzerland, and booked an audience with Olympic don Juan Antonio Samaranch. The swimmers explained how the systematic doping had worked, pushed their medals across the table and asked that they be given to their rightful owners.[15]

Samaranch, a Spaniard whose career in sports administration blossomed when he was a member of the Franco dictatorship, pushed the medals back, saying: 'Keep them, you were not the only ones.'

The signal had been sent: a line would be drawn under a dark chapter of Olympic history and no shame would be acknowledged. There would be no further discussion. There has been no inquiry or any action in all the years since, despite several petitions calling for justice to be done and enough evidence to chuck them all in jail and throw away the key.

Four months after Knacke made headlines around the world with her doping revelations, the days of the GDR were done and the Stasi were desperately trying to shred evidence of their crimes.

Thankfully, there was just too much of it, and many good people kept it and passed it on to those such as Berendonk, Franke and Giselher Spitzer, a leading sports and social science researcher, who compiled comprehensive histories of the crimes and their impact.[16] The work of all three would earn them prizes, while Spitzer was part of the project team that put together a vast volume of incriminating evidence.

German Thomas Bach must have noticed all of it. He became an IOC member in 1992, when Berendonk's book was making headlines around the world. By 1995, all the evidence that could ever be needed to prove the existence and details of the biggest pharmacological experiment in sports history, one that had unfolded on the watch of Olympic leaders, was available to investigators, and judge Peter Faust, who would preside over the doping trials in which Petra Schneider, the East German who had beaten me to gold in Moscow 1980, testified against those who doped her.

The IOC has never called anyone to account.

We had no idea just how dark and deep the GDR's doping system was as we approached the Moscow Olympic Games in 1980, but we did know that every medal had an East German name on it. It would be my job to muscle in on that as best I could.

4

MOSCOW AND THE MANIPULATORS

WOULD have loved to start this chapter with a celebration of Olympic gold, but I can't. 'Sportsperson 137', beefed up on steroids from a state-doping programme, got to the wall ahead of me at a grey, totalitarian Games in Moscow in 1980.

Finishing second in what many rate as the toughest of all Olympic swimming races, the 400 metres individual medley, is something to be proud of. It's also a curse when you're denied gold by cheating.

My signature event requires supreme fitness and skills in all four swimming strokes built over years of six-hour training days, six days a week, without respite. There's no time to rest even when you break both your arms or when glandular fever strikes.

'Sportsperson 137' was Petra Schneider, and in 1980 she was racing at least five Olympic Games ahead of her time. Her winning time in Moscow, 4:36, would have won the title at any Olympics from 1984 to 1996. It would have placed her on the podium at all Games until 2008. Petra would still have made the Olympic final just shy of the podium in Tokyo in 2021. She remains the German record holder as this book goes to print in 2023.

Her 1982 world record of 4:36.10, 0.19 of a second inside her pioneering time in Moscow two years earlier, is by far the oldest national record of any among the top swimming nations of the world.

6 *Petra Schneider on the cover of GDR* Schwimm Sport *magazine in 1980, with doping boss Manfred Ewald, handing a prize to Jorg Woithe, the GDR's only male Olympic champion in the pool in Moscow that year (top left), and Vladimir Salnikov, the Soviet hero of a home Games, during a GDR vs URS friendly (bottom left, third from right)*

It worked out like that because the German Swimming Federation (DSV) chose politics over athlete welfare. It could have acknowledged the *Stern* revelations of 1990 and pressed for an inquiry. It could have started with a clean slate, but it decided to adopt all the GDR's records as the new standards of a reunified country, knowing that they were achieved with doping. And even when Petra asked the DSV to strike her record from the books in 2005, the DSV took no action.[1]

The drugs do work. They also do harm. They were life-changing for Petra and all the women she beat in unfair circumstances. What the DSV failed to see was what trans activists refuse to see today: if you make girls compete against opponents who bring male advantage to the race, eventually they'll give up and find something else to do. It's the role of governors and guardians to deliver a clean, safe and healthy experience for athletes and set that culture for its community on all levels.

Petra was a pawn in a corrupt Communist state's game of East vs West chest-beating, a display of strength that relied on what a German court would judge to be criminal abuse of minors.

As we noted in Chapter 3, East Germany placed its spies on international committees, and they were the men in charge of the IOC-accredited laboratory. Their loyalty was to a dictatorship that made cheating an official state policy. Anyone who revealed the truth could be charged with treason.

East German heads of doping were welcomed and even honoured in the tight Olympic network run by Spaniard Juan Antonio Samaranch – a former minister in Franco's dictatorship – who was president of the movement at the time when the head honchos of East German doping, Erich Honecker, head of state, and Manfred Ewald, sports minister and head of the GDR's NOC, were awarded the Olympic Order.

Samaranch was appointed Spanish ambassador to the Soviet Union and Mongolia in 1977 when democracy was restored in Spain. The post helped him to gain the support of the Soviet bloc countries in the election to the presidency of the IOC, held in Moscow in 1980.[2] In my opinion, he ran the biggest multi-sports show on earth with no regard for women's right to fair treatment until his term ended in 2001.

He took the presidency in the Russian capital just before my mission in Moscow began on the first day of swimming at the Olympics on 26 July 1980. It had been a challenging time just getting to the

Games. There were far fewer competitions back then, and in 1979 there had been no major internationals for us. It was hard work all the way and I got a bout of glandular fever. My dad's answer was to work through it and that meant a really hard winter for me going into the Olympic year. He thought that I just couldn't afford time out given the East Germans I'd be facing.

I wasn't even sure if I'd make it to Moscow, because at the end of a crap year we got news that the West might boycott the Games over the presence of the Soviet military in Afghanistan. Deadlines came and went, fruitless negotiations were held and we athletes were talked over, discussed, told we would be boycotting if it couldn't be sorted out. US president Jimmy Carter even proposed moving the Olympics to Greece on a permanent basis to strip politics out of their hosting, but the IOC rejected the idea and pressed ahead with Moscow.[3]

President Carter barred American athletes from the 1980 Games, but his idea of having a permanent Olympic base may well be worth revisiting bearing in mind the present cost of the Games, the bidding scandals and some of the bad choices sports organisations keep making when they take their showcase events to places with appalling human-rights records.

They don't ask athletes about such things today, just as they didn't ask athletes what they thought about the boycott back in 1980: we were told by the UK government to set aside all the hard work, ambition and dreams, and, as it turned out, the Olympic boycott had absolutely no impact on the events that gave rise to it. The only people affected were athletes.[4] It was frustrating. We spent six months getting up at the crack of dawn for the first session of the day without knowing whether any of it would be worth it. Politicians were telling us that we had to give up on our dreams while they continued to trade and travel back and forth.

We came under a lot of pressure not to attend the Games, but with the help of Britain's NOC, known as the British Olympic Association

(BOA), a lot of us made it to Moscow along with many from other countries, including some of our toughest rivals from Australia.

I'd never been to the capital of the Soviet Union before. I found it harsh and depressingly grey. Our team of about 150 people was tiny compared to the 550 who competed for Britain at the London 2012 Olympics. In 1980, most of our sponsors pulled out after pressure from Margaret Thatcher and we weren't allowed to fly the flag.[5] Not being allowed to parade under the Union Jack has always been a source of sadness for me as a proud Brit. There was no anthem when British athletes won. We accepted our medals and then watched the Olympic flag inch up the pole as a symbol of our neutrality in a world taking sides.

We knew that would be the case when we first came to Moscow. Swimming starts on day one at the Games, so swimmers are always some of the first to arrive in the athletes' village. One of the strangest things about Moscow was the lack of children. Those who were due to be part of ceremonies were hidden away, and many other children under the age of 16 were bussed out of Moscow, some with their families, to youth camps for the duration of the Games.[6] There certainly seemed to be no children in playgrounds. It was a little eerie. The Games lacked colour – there were no advertising hoardings, no graffiti or rubbish anywhere. There was very little sign of normal life in this big cosmopolitan city, but we did see the odd farmer driving a tractor down the middle of the high street. It was all a bit surreal.

Even the training facilities were not what we were used to. The tiles in some of the pools were popping off and we were cutting our feet when we did tumble turns because the cement hadn't been smoothed off. Health and safety didn't seem to be that important in Russia.

On the plus side, they put on circuses, ballets and operas as entertainment for athletes in the village. It was all very beautifully done, even though it wasn't necessarily what a 17-year-old was after. Mostly, we were bored and looking for distraction.

We found it in the canteen. The food wasn't great. Olympic food halls are incredible places these days, offering cuisine from all over the world 24/7. It was quite different back then. We were told that ordinary Russians had lost all their meat rations because they'd been sent to us at the Games. There wasn't much that I wanted to eat, but we did put the rock-hard bread rolls to good use. We'd jump on the athlete bus that went around the circuit of the Olympic Village, and if we could get a smile out of one of the guards, in full winter regalia with Kalashnikovs over their shoulders, one of us would jump off and put a GB Olympic pin in his pocket. If he didn't smile we'd throw the rolls at him.

A food fight broke out in the food hall between teams one evening. It's not something I've heard of happening at another Games and not something I'm terribly proud of, but we were young, it was fun and it brings back fond memories for those who were there.

On another occasion, we were on our way back from a training session when we met the GB men's rowing squad. All eight were over 6' 4", except the cox, now Colin Moynihan, fourth Baron Moynihan. We were waiting in line at a humour-free security checkpoint, and the rowers said, 'Watch this!' They'd made a tinfoil gun and taped it to the inside of Colin's kitbag. I'll let you guess what happened next.

These were rare moments of light relief in Moscow. Montreal had been a fun-filled roller coaster and a learning experience by comparison. This time, I was a contender and there was much more pressure to perform. I was really glad my race was on the first day so I didn't have long to wait for what I'd worked so hard for.

RACING AGAINST THE ODDS

I knew I'd made good progress since winning two Commonwealth medley titles for England in 1978. I'd set the Commonwealth 400 metres record in an invitational duel against Sweden in Blackpool earlier in 1980. I was on form.

My 4:46 still left me seven seconds behind Petra's eye-watering world record, but it meant that I arrived in Moscow seeded no. 3. That put me centre stage, in lane four of the first of three heats. It's a tricky place to be in swimming. The fastest eight times from all heats make the final. If you're in the first heat, you try to win in a way that conserves energy for the final but isn't too slow: there were 16 women still to race after our heat and my time set the target for all of them.

I felt good, and I won the heat comfortably in 4:52.38, ahead of Russian Olga Klevakina, one of my old sparring partners and friends from the European race circuit. We both made it through, alongside three East Germans, including Petra, the clear favourite and world-record holder, and Ulrike Tauber, the defending Olympic champion from 1976 and by then Petra's part-time coach in Karl-Marx-Stadt.

Moscow was the last Olympics that allowed three swimmers per nation in swimming, and the GDR filled every slot in women's events with a potential medallist. By the time the racing was done, East German women had amassed an unprecedented 26 out of the 35 medals that it was possible for any country to win in one sex category. Their haul included 11 of the 13 golds, world records in both relays and four individual events, including mine, and six podium sweeps that locked the rest of the world out of the medals in more than half of all solo finals.

Like many others, I'd gone to Moscow knowing the GDR would dominate women's swimming and that I couldn't match Petra's speed. Australia's Michelle Ford was the only Western woman to win gold in the pool, in the 800 metres freestyle.

In Moscow, I wasn't facing men but our East German opponents had had enough male strength pumped into them to guarantee an edge at any distance, swimming any stroke. The more explosive the event, the bigger the advantage. Like me, Petra was 17 when she entered the medley final knowing that gold was in the bag. She'd been programmed to win on testosterone pills and injections since she was 14.

Years later, on the eve of testifying against her abusers in the German doping trials in January 1998, Petra told German media: 'I was given three or four 5-milligram tablets [Oral Turinabol] every day in a cycle of two or three weeks. Later, in preparation for big competitions, they made it seven weeks, but I always stopped taking them long before a race. They did it all very scientifically.'[7]

I was the only Western swimmer in the final in Moscow, alongside the three East Germans, two from Poland, a Russian and a Bulgarian. The worldwide swimming community tuned in to the race that day knowing something was very wrong. Petra was swimming at a pace we didn't see in women's medley racing for decades.

She dominated from the start, setting a blistering world record of 4:36.29. The only stroke she was not the fastest in was freestyle. I got that one! The swiftest concluding two lengths on freestyle in a race with three East Germans affirmed the heavy workloads I'd endured. I not only beat two of the GDR girls but my fast finish lifted me from third to second place, the bronze going to Poland's Agnieszka Czopek.

Media reports described the difference between Petra and me as that between a nuclear torpedo and a dolphin. Years later, Werner Franke, who helped save evidence of GDR cheating from state-police shredders, told Craig: 'Davies was not racing another human swimmer that day; she was fighting a different species, a young girl manipulated by men who altered her physiology and psyched her to win. She was an experiment. It worked for them, not so well for her in life.'[8]

Franke passed away in November 2022, but the work he did to expose the truth and help athletes bring their abusers to court earned him the German Order of Merit in 2004 and is a lasting reminder of the IOC's inaction and shame.[9]

In 1983, Petra was beaten by a teammate at the European Championships. Illness had set in – and it would last a lifetime. One virus followed another. In 1984, as the GDR boycotted the Los Angeles Olympics, Petra suffered a serious inflammation of the heart, a known side effect of steroid abuse.

She'd retired by then, but her swimming days were not done. GDR scientists, aware of the damage to health they'd caused, insisted on an intensive detraining programme that lasted up to two years. It was a case of clean them up, wash them out and wash our hands of it. Petra's coach told her she was probably getting sick because of her lack of dedication. It was only when she was able to read her secret police file that she fully understood what had happened to her.[10] You can't remove the horrendous side effects of testosterone by swimming it out.

DOPING TRIALS AND THE STASI ARCHIVE

Investigators brought documents to a series of German doping trials that unfolded in Berlin between 1998 and 2000. The evidence included instructions to coaches of teenagers, such as: 'The swimmers must never see the packets or the prescriptions'; 'You must put the pills in their hands and make sure they take them'; and 'No one can be sure what the side effects will be in ten to 20 years' time.' My heart bleeds again for these young girls, whose health mattered so little to those in charge of them.

On the trail of the crime with a film team for the Channel 4 documentary series *Joe Public* in 1998, I got a glimpse of what life was like for athletes and their families in the GDR.[11] They were constantly spied on. I visited the Stasi archives with the crew and my three-month-old daughter Grace.[12] We could choose from files selected for public viewing to show how neighbours were instructed to spy on each other. Some of it was trivial, some of it life-threatening for those criticising the state or plotting to escape.

There were dozens of rooms full of shredded documents slowly being pieced back together and rows of glass bottles on shelves. Every time someone was called in for questioning by the state police, a sweat swab was placed on a small yellow duster and popped into a sealed jar to make it easier for sniffer dogs to track them down if ever the state felt the need.

In sport, every travelling squad included at least one spy hired to report back on their teammates. We were shown videos of experiments on young athletes at clandestine clinics in which electric shocks were sent through biceps and quadriceps in a crude attempt to stimulate muscle growth. Biopsies were routinely taken without anaesthetics to check the effects of drugs.

In swimming, there were flumes, or tanks with strong-flowing water, like wave machines. GDR swimmers would later describe how frightened they were when white-coated scientists pulled a contraption that looked like a gas mask over their heads and told them to jump in and swim against the current. A tube fed oxygen into the mask but the supply would be switched off to deprive the swimmer of air until they got close to the point of collapse. It was all about testing limits and understanding which drugs could boost natural human capacity, performance and recovery.

Parents were often unaware of these sport versions of torture chambers. The strain was heartbreaking for the likes of Petra, literally. As Franke put it: 'A viral infection of the heart is the most frequent sequel to steroid abuse. Which can of course lead to heart failure. Petra's doctors would have known this. To have given 20 milligrams a day to a young, growing woman was nothing less than criminal.'[13]

Shot-putter Birgit Boese said that the damage the steroids had done to her and many others meant that simple things such as going for a swim, or to the theatre, to the cinema or on a day out at the shops were major strains.[14] She was fed a diet of steroids and other banned substances from the age of 11. Just like Petra, she would later suffer from an irregular heartbeat. Birgit also had to take pills for high blood pressure, diabetes, nerve damage and kidney problems. Much of the damage done to the female athletes was irreversible. All they could do was treat and manage their conditions. Nature did not design female bodies to be pumped full of male hormones.

Birgit was among the 170 ex-GDR athletes awarded €9,250 each in compensation in 2006 from the German Olympic Sports Confederation (DOSB) and the drug company, Jenapharm, that developed and produced the steroid Oral Turinabol.[15] The out-of-court settlement was the first of three compensation processes that have paid victims more than €25 million so far. The work of the organisation Doping-Opfer-Hilfe (whose name means 'help for doping victims'), founded in 1999, prompted the German government to award €10.5 million to GDR athletes in 2016.[16] Compensation for the GDR's doping victims became a well-oiled machine: within half a year, 240 of the 400 athletes eligible for payments from that particular pot had had their applications approved.[17]

There has never been any such organisation campaigning for justice, truth and reconciliation for generations of women on the other side of the crime.

Down the decades, I've campaigned for justice for those denied, those who have suffered breakdowns and mental-health problems as a result of feeling robbed, seeing their parents and coaches pass away without ever having had their efforts recognised. Craig, half of whose family are from East Germany, has campaigned on this issue as a journalist, too. It's always felt like we've been running continually into a brick wall. Back in the day, it often felt like it was just me and my dad against the world. For speaking out he was never selected as a British team coach even when he had several swimmers on teams.

And bear in mind that he was also the only coach in the UK to have an individual female medallist on the British team in Moscow.

It's not all been gloom and doom, however. I've also had a lot of lovely people and organisations introduce me as an 'Olympic champion', and when the BBC put together a documentary about all of Britain's living Olympic champions ahead of London 2012, they included me. That was really touching. Mostly, it's been a battle against men who do nothing and never invite strong women to be part of the discussion and the decision-making process.

I finished my final in Moscow in 1980 thinking, 'It's over, I'm done.' Sadly, I didn't get to swim my second-strongest event, the 200 metres medley. In 1976 and 1980, the IOC had sought to trim the size of the Games by cutting some events. For no apparent reason, swimming leaders chose the 200 metres medley, which had been on the programme before 1976 and has been a part of the Olympics ever since 1984. My team also finished fourth in the freestyle relay, another medal missed because of doping, but I had the main medal I'd come for to reward Dad for all his passion and sacrifice down the years. A weight had been lifted from my well-trained shoulders. I felt free from massive expectation. I hadn't let anyone down and the tough road had made me strong, but there are still moments when the injustice of it all creeps up and kicks me in the teeth.

I could never have imagined all those years ago in 1980 that we would still be fighting more than 40 years on because the guardians of sport have blanked out all recognition of the achievements of generations of female athletes denied by doping.

There are still so many struggling with a lack of recognition from those dark days.

Once we had finished racing we were sent off home. By going home early, we didn't get an opportunity to support many of our teammates in other sports. I'd been lucky to have my big race on the first day. With some time on my hands, I went to see Daley Thompson and Seb Coe, good friends of mine. Seb had been beaten in the better of his two races by Steve Ovett. It was the one Seb was expected to win. He was the world-record holder, but Steve held him off and it was a Britain 1–2 but a painful result for Seb.

I went with Daley to see if we could cheer him up. He was refusing to get out of bed, looking miserable lying there, so we yanked the curtains open, pulled him out of bed by his feet and told him to stop being a pain in the arse and get on with it. Seb went on to win the 1,500 metres, which Steve had been tipped to win, both of them having shared the world record. They both got gold, just the opposite way round to what everyone predicted. That's Olympic sport for you.

It can be a lonely place when the powers that be don't lift a finger even when a crime is proven. They're in it for the wrong reasons and won't step an inch beyond any line that might threaten their positions in a grace-and-favour system vulnerable to corruption, as we'll see in Chapter 8.

Athletes are often caught in the middle. It certainly felt that way in 1980 when we got home from Moscow. There were no street parties for us because we'd competed despite Margaret Thatcher's vehement opposition to it. There were no honours or visits to the palace. I had to wait until after my second retirement for my MBE, following my Olympics comeback in Barcelona in 1992. Seb didn't have to wait that long. He was made MBE in 1982, the year I was banned from making a comeback because I'd broken amateur rules. I'd accepted a £40 fee for being on a TV game show, while Seb had benefited financially from his athletics career because athletics had set up individual trust funds for its stars. It made no sense to me. Even after all that time I was still the British record holder (in fact, I held the national 400 metres medley standard for 24 years until 2004). I'd also held the Commonwealth record for nearly ten years during a career in which I raced at three Olympic Games in three different decades between the ages of 13 and 30.

Our lack of recognition at home on our return just added to the misery generations of female athletes endured for decades because of the drug-fuelled GDR era. My teammates Ann Osgerby, beaten into fourth by three East Germans in the 100 metres butterfly, Helen Jameson, Maggie Kelly and June Croft – who, as a foursome, formed the women's 4×100 metres medley relay team – would also have been Olympic champions in Moscow.

LIFE AFTER STOLEN GOLD

My competitive swimming career stretched from before I was eight to when I was 31, with a break between 18 and 27 forced on me by Olympic amateur rules even though I never made a penny from swimming.

I had a choice: go to the United States on a university scholarship after Moscow or go on the dole, as social security was referred to in those days. I went to America for a term on a university road trip after doing entrance exams at Berkeley, Stanford, the University of Southern California and UCLA. I was offered places and chose Berkeley, but to maintain my scholarship I needed to swim for the university straight away. I had not had a break from training longer than two weeks for over ten years. I was very jaded and needed time out and a chance to learn to love my sport again. I was just 18. There was no support or advice. My parents had just split up and there was no spare cash.

I knew full well that a fortune in family terms had already been spent on me and my sport. There was no National Lottery back then, and even sponsorship was not allowed. I was training 18 to 22 hours a week, more with land work and physio. I couldn't hold down a full-time job and train, and there were no sports universities in the UK like there are today.

So I came home because I thought my mum needed me and I wanted a break, just to be normal for a while, to be a teenager, without every single minute of my day decided for me.

I was offered the chance to present a kids' TV show, and moved into a flat with my friend and Olympic gymnast Suzanne Dando. Sue, Kathy Taylor, Liz Hobbs and I were all part of a stable of female sports talent that found itself in what we now know to have been the dark world of Max Clifford, the promoter who ended up in jail for indecent assault on four teenagers.[18] It was crazy in many ways, a serious baptism of fire. I arrived in London in a rental car with my suitcases and no money. The first night I was there my car was broken into and everything I owned was stolen, including all my Olympic kit.

They say what doesn't kill you makes you stronger!

So I took charge of my life. I didn't have much choice. But there was always a sense of unfinished business with swimming. Many were not able to find the strength to deal with the past as it unfolded, and none of us really shook off the sense of loss at not having our achievements recognised for what they truly were. Years later I made a comeback at a time when it was almost unheard of to have a swimmer a few years shy of 30 make a third Olympics after nine prime years out of the sport. I've now been to 12, with TV work, and every single one was unique and special.

While working for New Zealand radio at the 1988 Olympics, I shared a flat with the wonderful Olympic pentathlon champion Mary Peters. She said to me: 'Sharron, do not go through life wishing you had or saying what if.' So I got back in the water. It was crazily hard and I started working my way back to race fitness for the 1992 Games in Barcelona.

Within a year of getting back into full training in the pool, I was very proud to make the British team for the European Championships in the summer of 1989. I even made the 200 metres medley final in Bonn in a race won by East German Daniela Hunger. Remember her? She was one of several Olympic champions who'd tested positive for steroids just a week before we raced (see Chapter 3).

The East German doping factory was still in full flow, but that summer we didn't know that we were just a few months away from the fall of the Berlin Wall and the revelations that we believed would mean that we'd finally be recognised for our real achievements.

The year after, it was like being back in 1978 and feeling the relief of not having to face East Germans when I raced to two relay medals with England teammates at the 1990 Commonwealth Games – though this time we knew we'd never have to face competitors from the GDR again. There was great optimism that our true achievements would be acknowledged at last and that swimming was entering a new era. We would finally be free of systematic cheating.

Little did we know that China would take off where the GDR ended and that the IOC would do nothing to prevent all of that cheating still being a part of its official record of honours and history.

THE SEARCH FOR JUSTICE

After retiring from swimming for a second time I was determined to seek justice. By the time the German doping trials began in 1998, huge amounts of evidence, witness statements and confessions from coaches and doctors had been compiled by a special police task force in reunified Germany ahead of doping trials.

Something similar was clearly needed worldwide. In swimming alone, 1998 was a bumper year for drug scandals. It started with Petra telling a German magazine that she now knew the full truth of what had happened to her and would testify against her coaches and doctors, alongside around 300 other athletes.[19]

At the same time, the IOC was coming under pressure from my campaign for justice alongside fellow British Olympians, as well as Australian, American and Dutch athletes. It was all getting very embarrassing for Samaranch. So he announced that he and the IOC he led would discuss the latest revelations about GDR doping at a meeting in Nagano, Japan. Of course, Samaranch had already made up his mind, and the book of results and records would not be touched. His line was the IOC's official stance: despite the fact that GDR medals were tainted by confirmation of systematic doping, the history of Olympic results and what unfolded would not be rewritten.[20]

By then, the GDR Mark II Express was well on its way down the tracks. China had spent the last few years of the GDR era and the 1990s up to its neck in illegal drugs. A few days from the start of the 1998 World Swimming Championships in Perth, Australia, Yuan Yuan, a 15-year-old female swimmer, was caught in transit at Sydney Airport with 13 vials of human growth hormone in her kitbag.[21] It was enough to supply the whole team for the duration of the championships. Of course, the teenager had not put the drugs there. She was an unwitting mule. The sport's reputation was on the line, swimming left fighting for its life, as leading niche magazine *SwimNews* put it.[22]

By the time the decade ended, China had more than 90 positive doping tests on its score sheet. The vast bulk of the cases involved teenage girls fed a diet of steroids, human growth hormone and diuretics to help them pee the evidence away. Very GDR.

Yuan was suspended for four years and was never seen again, while her coach Zhou Zhewen was banned for 15 years. No doctors, sports scientists or bureaucrats were called to account. Four other swimmers were banned, along with their coaches. When global swimming regulator FINA launched an inquiry, it did so noting that it had no jurisdiction to undertake police work in China, so its solution was to hand the whole investigation over to... the Chinese![23]

Around the time Yuan and co. were being questioned by police in Australia, anti-doping testers Al and Kay Guy arrived at the home in Ireland of Michelle Smith, the controversial triple Olympic champion of 1996.[24] The urine sample they collected would be declared 'spoiled' by whiskey in concentrations so high that had the Irishwoman ingested that much, said experts, she would not have survived. My co-author Craig broke the news of the anti-doping case that would cause her downfall.[25] FINA imposed a four-year suspension for manipulation of a sample.[26] Smith appealed to the Court of Arbitration for Sport (CAS) but the decision to suspend her was upheld.

One of the highlights of the appeal hearing attended by Craig was when Smith's lawyer anticipated what he thought the FINA lawyer was about to say and was overheard saying: 'You said you wouldn't mention the Andro.' FINA submitted evidence from Jordi Segura, head of the IOC-accredited laboratory in Barcelona, that the swimmer had androstenedione, a testosterone precursor, in her system.[27] The Guys had requested the sample in January 1998, a month after the IOC had added androstenedione to its list of banned substances ahead of some professional sports organisations, as the case of American baseball player Mark McGwire highlighted in 1998.[28]

However, FINA opted to pursue a charge of manipulation. The sample was reported to have been spoiled by alcohol – and it landed Smith a suspension that she never came back from.[29]

I had trained with Smith a few years earlier in Canada, with one of the best coaches in the world, Deryk Snelling. Oddly, he couldn't draw out the supremacy that appeared as if by magic at the Atlanta Olympics in 1996. By then, Smith was training alone, under the guidance of her partner Erik de Bruin, a field athlete who had already served a drugs ban in his career.[30] She had raced for Ireland for many years and I knew when working for the BBC at the poolside that there was a lot of speculation in the run-up to the Atlanta Games that her performance was not fuelled by training alone. We weren't allowed to say anything on air, of course, but I understood all too well the frustration of those athletes who left Atlanta convinced they had been cheated out of their medals in much the same way I felt I had been when I left Moscow back in 1980. Smith kept her three gold medals and the silver she claimed in 1996.

I keep my medals in a Union Jack box alongside a GDR swimsuit from the 1976 Olympics. To me, that suit has always been like another bloody medal! The GDR girls weren't allowed to give their suits away and I honestly can't remember who gave it to me, but it's in the box to remind me of the only thing that beat me at the Olympic Games: cheating.

Our fight to have that recognised by the IOC goes on, but no one's holding their breath. Olympic bosses never had my back nor the backs of generations of women they know were cheated out of rightful rewards and the lifelong opportunities that flow from Olympic success.

On the podium in Moscow there was satisfaction and joy. I was really pleased to have set a Commonwealth and British record under pressure when it counted most. My national standard stood for a very long time and would have been good enough to win medals at the next Olympics and Commonwealth Games. I was Britain's only female medallist in individual events at the 1980 Olympics, something I'm very proud of, but it's extraordinary when you think that women on the British team – known after 1999 as 'Team GB' – won so many medals in Sydney, Athens, Beijing, London, Rio and Tokyo.

There is so much to be happy about, but the truth is there was a silent tear that reflected a stolen gold, a moment diminished by the horrid truth that comes back to haunt me every time I look at the race video or the footage of the medal ceremony, any time anyone introduces me at an event as 'silver lady' Sharron Davies, or when my BBC colleagues tell the nation how amazing the GDR's Kristin Otto was or that Becky Adlington's fabulous victory (which it definitely was) in the 400 metres freestyle at the Beijing Olympic Games in 2008 was the first Olympic swimming gold for a British woman since 1960.

Mostly, there's been no recognition, and there's never been an asterisk on any of the thousands of competition results in several sports dominated by East Germany's steroid-fuelled army of female athletes. The IOC made that official policy in 1998 when it rejected the petitions from Britain, driven by me, and the United States on behalf of its own women swimmers.

There were many headlines about us wanting to have the GDR girls stripped of their medals. That was never the case. Neither petition, from the United States or Britain, asked for that. We simply wanted appropriate medal recognition. It was the IOC's chance to reach for reconciliation in the form of duplicate medals and an asterisk in the record book, showing the rightful winners. It was an opportunity to be introduced as an Olympic champion, for many others to be recognised as medallists, and for us to be able to explain what happened in an official account.

In rejecting the petitions in the 1990s, the IOC stated that it wanted to discourage any such appeals in the future. 'The executive board considers that unfortunately there are too many variables involved to attempt to rewrite Olympic history,' said François Carrard, the IOC's former director general, who passed away in 2022.[31]

Instead, the executive board recommended that any athletes who used prohibited substances or methods and wished to demonstrate sportsmanship donate their Olympic medals to the Olympic Museum in Lausanne – 'to serve as a memento to this period in Olympic history', Carrard said. He went on: 'The IOC expresses its regret that Olympic athletes who followed the rules in good faith may have been victimized by those who did not.'[32]

And that is the only nod the IOC has made to the entire criminal catastrophe that impacted the lives of so many women on both sides of the Cold War.

The lack of a proper apology from the men who were supposed to be the caretakers of Olympic sport hurts. I will never understand what 'too many variables' means. We had personal confessions, evidence in black and white on legitimate documents stating who had cheated, with what and when. The rules had been broken. Where were the variables? What sort of deterrence was it to any nation thinking of doing it again?

The official paperwork I saw when we made the *Joe Public* documentary for Channel 4 said that the introduction of steroids to young girls would produce on average a 9 per cent benefit. If you take that advantage away from Petra Schneider she would have been 16 seconds behind me and out of the final.

It wasn't only the IOC and international federations that let dark bygones be bygones. At the end of the 1980s, Petra was not allowed by GDR authorities to accept an invitation to attend her induction ceremony at the International Swimming Hall of Fame (ISHOF) in Fort Lauderdale. All the East German winners can be found in that official repository of swimming history. Many who should be there are not, even though the Americans who own and run ISHOF know the truth.

In 2022, ISHOF finally started to recognise the achievements of Americans who did not get to race in Moscow because of the boycott. Many of us athletes always thought it perverse that the Land of the Free chose to take away its athletes' passports so they couldn't compete at the 1980 Games. In Britain, we were also aware that trade continued to flow with the Soviet Union even though we were supposed to stay away from the Olympics. I was always so grateful that the BOA, which was not funded by the UK government, stood up to Mrs Thatcher and the tokenism of depriving young athletes of their once-in-a-lifetime dream.

One of the biggest campaigners for athlete welfare, clean sport and a robust anti-doping system in world sport, Michele Verroken, founder and head of the website Sporting Integrity (see Appendix 2), tells us that Craig Reedie, then head of the BOA, read the room when a meeting of sports leaders in 1997 backed a proposal to call on the IOC to recognise the claims of athletes beaten by rivals whose performances were enhanced by doping. He offered to take on the issue but Michele noted that not only was there no further action on this, but her efforts to get the truth told were not appreciated.

Michele made sure Werner Franke was given a public platform in Britain to present the Stasi and scientific documents that proved the systematic doping. The man who helped save critical information from state shredders in the dying days of the GDR, Franke had published some of his work in German but a lot of it had not yet filtered through in English.

Michele not only made sure that he was able to present his work at the annual UK Sports Council National Drugs and Sport Seminar in September 1997, but arranged for Franke's paper, written with Brigitte Berendonk, to be printed in the journal *Clinical Chemistry*, the first published evidence of the Stasi doping regimes in the English language.[33]

It was the year before the doping trials began – and the world was able to tune in aware that the crime was real thanks to the exposure Franke's work received. You'd think the guardians of sport in Britain might have given Michele a prize or a bonus. Sadly, she received strong personal criticism from Reedie for her efforts.

I also had cause to feel deeply disappointed with Reedie. He never came back to me with any details of how he was fighting for us, any discussions he'd had with Olympic leaders. He later became an IOC member and head of the World Anti-Doping Agency (WADA). The ghosts of the past survived his era, but I'm grateful for all the efforts made down the decades by people like Michele.

Meanwhile, in 2022, Craig Beardsley, an American world butterfly champion and record holder, was the first of those denied by boycott to enter ISHOF without ever having raced at the Olympic Games. We who did race there and were beaten by cheats have never been recognised.

ISHOF notes on Petra Schneider's profile page: 'Doping Disclaimer: In a German court of law, after this swimmer was inducted into the International Swimming Hall of Fame, team officials confessed to administering performance enhancing drugs to this swimmer, who therefore obtained an illegal and unfair advantage over other athletes.'[34]

Why are we still celebrating wins we know were fuelled by drugs? Tragically, the same profile also includes this:

From this great swimmer, a note on how she does it time after time: 'For me swimming is the most beautiful of all sports. Although I have been training for very many years and have taken part in a great number of competitions, I always find something new in this sport. And this I'm sure is greatly to the credit of my coach, Eberhard Mothes, who takes my training sessions at the sport club in Karl-Marx-Stradt and never fails to come up with something interesting or challenging in the course of the work. I am the kind of person who likes being expected to achieve as much as I possibly can.'

These words are not Petra's. They were handed to her by the Stasi for her to sign and include in her reply to ISHOF explaining why she wouldn't be attending.[35]

In 1998, when I visited Petra to film the documentary for Channel 4, she said: 'I was forgotten by my country. The Swimming Hall of Fame in Florida invited me to attend my induction but I was instructed by the authorities in East Germany to say I could not attend for family reasons.'

She clearly came to despise the coach who handed her the pills before training on many mornings – he claimed that they would 'help me to recover and recuperate from hard training and allow me to do more work but not be so tired', Petra told Craig in a 2005 interview.[36] Mothes, who died in 2018, aged 78, warned her that she should not tell her parents, but that if she did not take the tablets she would never reach the top.[37]

Not long after she gave testimony at the doping trials, Petra returned home to find the word 'traitor' painted across her front door. Petra was a pawn in a political ideology that drove a state to drug its children. Today, we have a different form of ideology doing damage to women all over again.

On 18 November 1991, Mothes was among 25 East German swim coaches who signed a statement confessing that they had doped their swimmers under instruction from the state.[38] Stasi files also include a note referring to double Olympic and triple European freestyle champion Petra Thümer's last-minute withdrawal from the 1978 World Championships. The excuse given to the media in Berlin was that she had a cold, as we've mentioned. In fact, she had tested positive for anabolic steroids in a sample analysed at the IOC-accredited laboratory in Kreischa. The Stasi note quotes Mothes as saying: 'You should explain that throughout the country we have worked with specific medicines… on grounds that such things are required in performance sport.'[39]

The spy filing the note signs off with his code name 'IMS [informant] Ullrich', aka Dr Ullrich Tolkmitt, the doctor assigned to the squad in Karl-Marx-Stadt that produced a string of Olympic and world champions and record holders – all women.

Given the overwhelming evidence, it always felt to me as though the IOC manipulated their process to protect themselves from prosecution. Samaranch, as *Stern* reported in 1990, invited the head of the GDR doping programme to draw the line at which medical support ends and doping starts. The point of a legal supplement is to aid recovery from heavy physical work, but some substances that can also be used for the same purpose, such as testosterone, are banned because they enhance performance but also put the long-term health of the athlete at risk. Samaranch was also the man who sparked outrage in 1998 when he said he wanted the banned-substance list reduced.[40]

The same excuses from sports leaders epitomised the China crisis of the 1990s. A month after a squad of teenage girls dominated the 1994 World Swimming Championships in Rome, seven Chinese national-team swimmers were caught red-handed in one go getting off a plane to the Asian Games in Hiroshima. They had taken banned substances on the flight but were surprised by a team of out-of-competition anti-doping testers in the arrivals lounge. All their samples were positive for banned drugs. Soon after, Samaranch gave China a clean bill of health when he said: 'I do not think the Chinese are using drugs. And they are certainly no worse than many other nations in this regard.'[41]

In 1998, Kevan Gosper, an IOC executive board member for Australia, said that revisiting the truth about the GDR 'would be a bottomless pit'.[42] The IOC could have deferred a decision, pending the end of the doping trials in Germany, but Samaranch had made up his mind eight years before when he rejected the request of GDR swimmers offering to have their medals handed over to those who deserved them.

Their decision had nothing to do with the best interests of athletes, the welfare of women or the integrity of sport. It was all about them saving face and covering their tracks because they knew their rules had been broken and that they had looked the other way. Ever since the fall of the Berlin Wall it's been hard to find a man prepared to fully atone for his role in harming athletes.

It took a woman to do that. Dr Dorit Rösler, aged 50 at the time she was fined in the doping trials in 1998, was the only doctor and scientist in all the trials to break down in court and express deep sorrow for the victims with her apology.[43] For many years afterwards, she ran a clinic in Berlin free of charge for doping victims suffering health problems believed to have developed as a result of the steroids they were given in their youth. In contrast, Samaranch's stance is one that current IOC bosses have stuck to.

The Lords of the Rings, a book about corruption in the ranks of the IOC by award-winning investigative journalist Andrew Jennings, considered what the IOC meant when it referred to the 'Olympic Family'. He pointed to Samaranch's role in Franco's government and likened the *omertà* operated by the Mafia to that at work in the IOC. Jennings viewed the Olympic Family through the prism of a totalitarian regime.[44]

Not my kind of family at all. My family is the one where my dad Terry, along with my daughter Grace, arranged a special surprise for me for Christmas after London hosting the Olympics brought home just how big an injustice it all was. They hatched a plan and popped a mysterious present under the tree. When I opened the box, there was my silver medal from Moscow. Only it had been professionally plated in gold, to reflect how they perceived my achievement in Moscow. That's what family means.

It also means a swimming family that recognise your right to rewards denied by East German doping. In 2022, the British Swimming Coaches Association (BSCA) issued special 'Historic Achievement Awards' in response to an article in *The Times* in which I spoke with my co-author Craig Lord about the first official backing in swimming for a truth-and-reconciliation process.[45]

The BSCA made an official statement in which they said that, regardless of what the IOC had to say on the matter, it was 'an historical fact' that the East German team was doped with banned substances and as such it would recognise all those who coached Olympic swimmers who'd been 'deprived of their medals or medals of an appropriate colour'.[46]

It was a special moment. There at the top of the list was my dad. He had waited 42 years for that recognition from peers and at 86 was delighted to see his name next to mine and other swimmers he'd coached. Coaches Keith Bewley and Mike Higgs didn't live to see the day but would have been delighted with the recognition of their work with the Olympians of 1980.

Dr Mike Peyrebrune, a former international swimmer and sports scientist who works with the British team, put the list together for our Moscow 1980 team:

- Sharron Davies (400 metres medley) / Terry Davies (gold)
- Ann Osgerby (100 metres fly) / Keith Bewley (gold) posthumously
- June Croft (200 metres freestyle) / Keith Bewley (bronze) posthumously
- Margie Kelly (100 metres breast) / Dave Haller (bronze)
- Ann Osgerby (200 metres fly) / Keith Bewley (bronze) posthumously
- Peter Morris (200 metres fly) / Paul Stait (bronze)

4×100 metres medley relay

- Helen Jameson / Terry Davies (gold)
- Margie Kelly / Dave Haller (gold)
- Ann Osgerby / Keith Bewley (gold) posthumously
- June Croft / Keith Bewley (gold) posthumously

4×100 metres freestyle relay

- Sharron Davies / Terry Davies (bronze)
- Kaye Lovett / Terry Denison (bronze)
- Jackie Wilmott / Mike Higgs (bronze) posthumously
- June Croft / Keith Bewley (bronze) posthumously[47]

5

SEX MATTERS

THE FACTS OF LIFE

So why are there such stark differences in athletic and sporting performance between men and women? To understand this, we need to go to the science.

Human sex is dimorphic. There are only two biological forms of the species, female and male. It's been like that for more than two million years – since sex chromosomes developed as a key part of the evolution of our species. And it's been about 320 million years since the dawn of X and Y, when sex determination in DNA was triggered in life on earth, according to oodles of research.[1]

A chromosome is a structure found in the nucleus of every single cell, carrying the unique code, or DNA, of each and every one of us. Humans have 46 chromosomes; 22 pairs are called autosomes and look the same. The twenty-third chromosome pairing is special. It determines sex.[2] Females have one pair of identical X chromosomes – XX – and males have one X and one Y chromosome – XY.

A minority of humans have a trisomy, a chromosomal condition characterised by an additional chromosome.[3] A person with a trisomy has 47 chromosomes instead of 46. Down syndrome, Edwards syndrome and Patau syndrome are the most common forms of trisomy.

There is also a 47th chromosome variant. Jacobs syndrome, also known as '47,XYY' syndrome, is a rare genetic condition that occurs in about one in a thousand male children. There is also a sex-chromosome condition in females in which either the whole or part of the X chromosome is missing: Turner syndrome, or '45,X', which is the most common sex chromosome abnormality in females.[4] It affects one in between 2,000 and 2,500 live female births. We say 'live' because about 99 per cent of gestations affected by X-chromosome monosomy do not survive to birth – and the 45,X genotype is found in at least 10 per cent of all spontaneous, naturally occurring miscarriages.

Take careful note of the male and female references in those potted explanations. As with all other atypical sex chromosome trisomies, XYY does not mean that sex is indeterminate.

Everyone born with Jacobs syndrome is male, just as everyone born with Turner syndrome is female. In all cases human biology delivers a male or a female. Female gametes are ova or eggs, which develop into another human when fertilised and nestled in the womb, which only females have. Male gametes are sperm, the most prolific little swimmers in the race of life.

The first sperm that gets to the egg has a shot at developing into the next little female or male. No human, including those with any disorder of sex development (DSD) or who are – to use an old-fashioned and much-maligned term – 'intersex' has ever produced both eggs and sperm. It's impossible.

There is no such thing as a human hermaphrodite – and, as we're about to see, the word 'intersex' was thrown in the bin of history by scientists in 2005.

Let's hope sports bosses are paying attention to the facts. There's not much evidence so far to suggest they have been. They've been busy listening to trans activists telling them that sports categories are based on feelings, not biology, and that the reason Britain's male Adam Peaty is 12 per cent faster over 100 metres breaststroke in the pool than the female US Olympic champion and world-record holder Lilly King comes down to this: Lilly's a bit lazy.

We'll start where that kind of nonsense belongs, in the grave. DNA testing is so good these days that archaeologists can dig up an ancient Egyptian here, a Roman over there and a Viking somewhere else and determine whether they've found a male or a female. The latest technique tests the enamel on teeth, because even the 4,000-year-old gnashers of a mummy speak the truth.[5]

You can't dig up and test a feeling. Nor can you reverse the vast bulk of the strength, size, shape, aggression and other factors that testosterone (also referred to as 'T' in this chapter) builds in males at ten to 20 times the level females have access to. And in sport that matters.

Scores of scientific and medical references confirm what Dr David Gerrard, a former swimming international from New Zealand and a leading sports doctor, told the eighth International Working Group (IWG) World Conference on Women and Sport in New Zealand in November 2022:

> The words sex and gender are not interchangeable, and those who conflate these terms dismiss incontrovertible genetic fact. Unlike sex, which is biological and fixed, our gender is a psychosocial construct which may change at will during life (like a name). And post-pubertal sex differences especially in physique, speed and strength reveal an undisputed male advantage. Therefore respecting equity and fairness, female and male elite competition must remain separate. And in collision or combat sports, concerns for safety reinforce this argument.

As Dr Gerrard told his audience:

> The endogenous (natural) hormone testosterone is an anabolic, androgenic messenger, essential to healthy female and

male development. It is liberated in a biological cascade we call puberty. Athletes experiencing male puberty are permanent beneficiaries of most of these endowments, and despite testosterone suppression, transwomen retain their physique, and most of their power and strength with clear implications for safety in collision sports.[6]

THE POWER OF T

Testosterone is a steroid and an androgen, a word derived from the Greek *andro*, for 'man' or 'male', and *gen*, which comes from the Greek for 'to be born, become'. Outside its naturally occurring levels, testosterone has been a banned substance in sport for half a century.

Dr Carole Hooven notes in her must-read 2021 book *Testosterone: The Story of the Hormone that Dominates and Divides Us* that 'all the evidence points to the same conclusion: a male level of T, in puberty and adulthood… is the master key for superior performance in most sports'.[7]

In a 2020 peer-reviewed research paper, University of Manchester developmental biologist Dr Emma Hilton, the creator of the website Sex Matters (see Appendix 2), whose Twitter name is @fondofbeetles, and Dr Tommy Lundberg, an exercise physiologist at the Karolinska Institute in Sweden, concluded: 'The biological advantage, most notably in terms of muscle mass and strength, conferred by male puberty and thus enjoyed by most transgender women is only minimally reduced when T is suppressed as per current sporting guidelines for transgender athletes.'[8]

In other words, when it comes to the vast bulk of male development locked into a male body early in life, there is no mitigation anywhere close to the point at which male inclusion in female sport could be considered fair in any shape or form. Gender identity is irrelevant in that context and should have no part to play in the equation of safety, fair play and equality already enshrined in sports.

Even when muscle mass dropped by 5 per cent after a year's hormone-reduction therapy, the loss of muscle strength in transwomen was negligible, according to Hilton and Lundberg. The biological males were still much stronger than any of the women they were demanding to compete against just because they felt like it.

Statistically, male athletes are on average 40 per cent heavier, 15 per cent faster, 30 per cent more powerful and 25 to 50 per cent stronger than their female counterparts irrespective of hormonal intervention. Let's look at some of the facts and figures set out in presentations such as that delivered by Hilton at the Woman's Place UK conference held in association with Fair Play for Women (see Appendix 2) in July 2019, and in many of the peer-reviewed studies listed in Appendix 1:[9]

- Women are on average about 9 per cent shorter than men.
- Men are 40 to 50 per cent muscle by weight and women are about 30 to 35 per cent muscle by weight.
- Men, on average, have larger heart and lung capacity and higher metabolic rates.
- The strongest 10 per cent of females can only beat the bottom 10 per cent of men in a hand-grip contest.
- Women's ligaments are thinner and softer than men's, which is why women in combat training sustain far more injuries.
- Men's longer arms give a greater reach and can generate more speed on a cricket ball.
- Men's bigger handspans allow them to palm basketballs more easily.
- Men's longer legs and narrower pelvises lead to better running gaits.
- Males need fewer strides to cross a distance and the strides they take are more efficient.
- Females have a significantly higher Q-angle and hip-joint internal-rotation angle, as well as a significantly lower arch height index than males. This means that women are much more susceptible to lower-limb and foot/ankle injuries.

- Males have around 40 per cent more muscle mass, even when height is taken into account, and 40 per cent less body fat.
- The muscle men have is denser, with more and larger fibres. Higher numbers of muscle stem cells make new muscle fibres, donate nuclei to strengthen existing muscle fibres and help healing.
- Men have higher proportions of fast-twitch fibres (responsible for explosive movement).
- Men have stiffer connective tissue – ligaments and tendons are tighter springs – which means greater storage of potential energy and even more explosive power, so male muscles can move way more quickly and with far greater force than female muscles.
- Men have larger hearts, lungs and haemoglobin pools – which can feed them more oxygen.

That's the tip of the iceberg – and it's nothing new. As Emma Hilton put it, the physical differences between males and females were already apparent when our ancestors emerged from the trees.

We can, and do, measure such things precisely in modern sport these days. Males can run faster, jump longer, throw further and lift more than females. Males outperform females on average by 10–13 per cent in running, 9–12 per cent in swimming and around 30 per cent when throwing various objects.

A male of equal weight to a female but not taller will punch 160 per cent harder. That differential would be lethal in contact sports, particularly fighting sports, if males were allowed to compete with females.

Those huge performance gaps are set aside by researchers out to prove that having males in female sport can be fair. They want to replace the 'fair play' of the rule book with what they call 'meaningful competition', another way of saying that some women are faster, stronger, taller and more talented than others so it's reasonable to

allow a transwoman reducing testosterone to compete among females
as one more example of a point along a spectrum of strengths. For
me, 'meaningful' means that they just want to bypass the 'fair-play'
principle that recognises the need for sex-based categorisation.

Dr Jon Pike, senior lecturer in Philosophy and the Ethics and
Metaphysics of Sport at the Open University, shot that notion
down in flames in a February 2023 paper titled 'Why "meaningful
competition" is not fair competition' (see Appendix 1). He concludes:

> There is, then, no obvious argument to suggest that global sports
> authorities – and female athletes – should accept Meaningful
> Competition as a replacement for fair competition, or to adopt it
> as part of an ameliorative project. To do so would mean accepting
> that male advantage is permissible in female sport, and this con-
> tradicts the standard justification of female sport; the provision
> of fair equality of opportunity for sport success, which, in turn,
> requires the exclusion of male advantage. It is possible to argue,
> coherently, for the abolition of female sport. It is not possible to
> argue coherently for female sport, but also for the permissibility,
> within that, of male advantage. Such advantage is not fair in
> female sport.[10]

The term 'meaningful' is often used by some of the key figures who
have helped shape IOC policy that discriminates against female
athletes, as we'll discuss in Chapter 8. Pike says the response 'ought
to be that competition is only meaningful when it is fair. So-called
Meaningful Competition is a snare and a delusion.'[11]

I could not agree more. Biological sex has long been the starting
point of fairness in sport and it's why we find men and women
divided at the gateway to a sports world in which segregation is the
best way to achieve a model of inclusion that upholds the principle
of sport for all.

WHY WE HAVE CATEGORIES IN SPORT

Sport is full of categories – for instance, athletes are divided by sex, age, weight and ability status, and sports played by schools, colleges, universities or the military exist in their own separate spaces – all in the name of fair play. The model spreads opportunity and achievement across society, so that each community is able to support, celebrate and share in the striving and the success. Event organisers are at the heart of those communities and do so much good: the Invictus Games, the Paralympics, the FISU World University Games (formerly the Universiade) and the Gay Games are all fine examples.

Identifying as a woman, however, should not be the checkbox required to drag male advantages into female sport.

One of the most vocal of trans activists is Rachel McKinnon, who now goes by the name Veronica Ivy. Born a boy called Rhys McKinnon, McKinnon/Ivy transitioned at 29. Never an elite athlete as a young man, McKinnon/Ivy summed up the radical ideology in a Twitter exchange about what trans activists call TERFs – trans-exclusionary radical feminists. 'I… want them to die in a grease fire,' tweeted McKinnon/Ivy[12] – a person who 'advises various national and international organisations, including the International Olympic Committee'[13] on gender issues when Olympic medal-winning female athletes have not had their voices heard.

McKinnon/Ivy suggests women are just being self-defeatist for thinking themselves not as capable as Usain Bolt of running 100 metres down a track in 9.58 seconds, 10 per cent faster than the swiftest woman ever. Or as capable of swimming like 17-year-old David Popovici, who swam the 100 metres freestyle in a world record of 46.86 seconds, 12 per cent faster than the fastest woman ever.

Women have no chance of matching those speeds without the levels of testosterone that make men of boys and boost performance in males from womb to tomb. Yet McKinnon/Ivy says:

We've seen the gap in performance sport between elite men and women is closing in every sport. As the men are improving and new records are being set the women's records are being set faster. The gap is closing. It's misleading to take the current gap and say that will always be the case.[14]

In fact, the gap is not closing. Not even close. After Title IX became American law in 1972 and banned sex discrimination at schools and colleges that receive federal funding, women's performance did increase relative to men's, but only for a decade. Since 1980, it hasn't budged.[15]

That decade of women gaining a touch on the pace of men coincided with systematic and clandestine use of steroids between 1972 and 1980, the year a doped East German beat me to Olympic gold in Moscow.

Between 1972 and 1980, when I was working my way up from a top junior in Britain to Commonwealth titles and Olympic and European medals, we women were put on a treadmill to try to keep up with East Germans on steroids. The drugs were significant in the gap between the best men and women being cut from 17 to 13 per cent in running and 13 to 11 per cent in swimming. That average gap in my sport has stayed at around 11 per cent ever since. As Image 7, taken from the 2019 paper by Hilton and Lundberg (see Appendix 1), shows, male advantage over females in sport is highly significant.

The point was not lost on Larry Krasnoff, the department chair at the College of Charleston, South Carolina, where McKinnon/Ivy once worked. In a long note reproduced in full by Dr Linda Blade, former Canadian track-and-field athlete and now kinesiologist and coach, and journalist Barbara Kay in their insightful book *Unsporting: How Trans Activism and Science Denial Are Destroying Sport* (2020), Krasnoff pointed to a blip in McKinnon/Ivy's trans mission.[16]

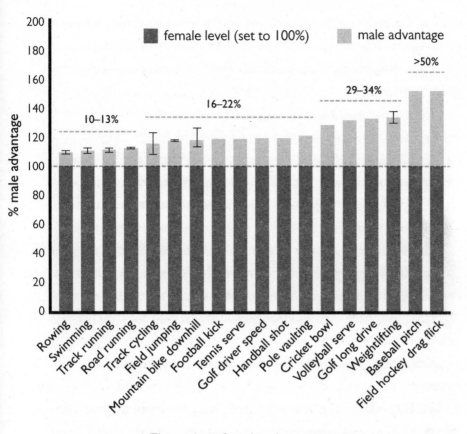

7 *The reality of male advantage in sport*

I represents range of advantage in sports with multiple disciplines

Source: Hilton and Lundberg (see Appendix 1), reproduced with permission of the authors

As part of his 2019 review of his staff's performance, he wrote to McKinnon/Ivy pointing out that the standard distinction between men and women in sport was for many based on physiological differences in the biology of the only two sexes. He followed up by asking the following: 'You challenge this argument in many ways but you also have thus far evaded what might seem like the theoretically most important question, what is the normative basis for the distinction between men's and women's sports?'

None of McKinnon/Ivy's arguments in the trans-inclusion debate, he added, 'challenge your opponents' conviction that biology is the dividing line between men and women in sport'. Krasnoff concluded: 'Maybe you don't have to have an answer of your own to this question but then you need a compelling answer to the question of why you don't have to answer it.'

In other words, he was suggesting that McKinnon/Ivy needed to explain why sport should be split along biological lines at all if a person's biological sex did not determine categorisation in sport. Why not just have one big melting pot, in which it wouldn't matter how McKinnon/Ivy identified because men and women would all be physically equal?

There's been no answer to that from the trans cyclist at the time of writing. I suspect that's because even McKinnon/Ivy knows that removing sex categorisation from sport would mean that only the biggest, toughest, fittest, strongest males would ever qualify for competitions in a large number of sports, let alone make finals or podiums, win prizes and enjoy the financial benefits that come with success.

Professional sport is a job these days. Discrimination in the workplace is illegal and allowing male advantage into female sport affects the opportunities and earning power of females.

A growing number of experts in a variety of fields and approaching the problem from different angles, like Krasnoff, appear to think so too. Biologists, doctors, kinesiologists, academics, lawyers, and many others have come out very strongly in support of the science and simple truth: sex is dimorphic.

Not a single cell in the human body is capable of changing sex, no magic can alter our chromosomes. Sex is a biological reality, not a feeling.

Children must not be lied to. Biological sex is not a spectrum that includes male and female and many sex varieties in between. It's just female and male. The spectrum trans activists talk about is not about the science and reality of sex, but about feelings, and how a human may identify for a variety of reasons, including the influence of stereotypes of what it is to be feminine or masculine. Bound up in that are false and damaging representations of what it is to be a woman.

Lines have been deliberately blurred. I'd support anyone to be as unique and original as they want, wear what they want, clothes or make-up, in total safety with as many rights as the next person – but not more. Biology doesn't say that sex is wearing high heels, red lipstick and a pair of fishnet tights. That's society and sexuality. Human personality is complex but basic biology is not.

The biological divide is critical in sport and is one reason why the UK Equality Act 2010 (see Appendix 2) and similar laws elsewhere in the world, including Title IX in the United States, afford single-sex rights. That provides the answer to Krasnoff's question to McKinnon/Ivy. The UK Act notes sport as one of six areas where females have a right to single-sex protection in a way that specifically excludes transwomen.

The Act specifically says that it is lawful to exclude people born male from women-only competitions. Section 195(3) of the Act defines the expression 'gender-affected activity'.[17] If the physical strength, stamina or physique of average persons of one sex would put them at a disadvantage compared to average persons of the other, it's a gender-affected activity. The exclusion extends to people born male even if they self-identify as transwomen and/or have changed their legal sex status. Reasons cited for such exclusions include fair play and safety.

Sport must be split along biological lines because anything else would be grossly unfair to females. There's one overwhelming reason why that's the case.

T divides, says Hooven, who notes that the primary evolutionary function of testosterone is to coordinate a male's body and behaviour in the service of reproduction.

To achieve its goal, it leaves no stone unturned: even the brain gets masculinised, not just the body. T influences the development of neural circuitry that then gets activated later in puberty. It changes everything, not just at puberty but for the whole of male life. Hooven notes that T touches the body and the brain first in the womb as the child grows, then again shortly after birth, before another explosion of changes occurs in puberty. T shapes behaviour and our social environment – it triggers a chain of events.

The power of testosterone is precisely why the entrance to sport has two gates: men and women, male and female, the definitions of which are not societal but biological.

6

SPORTING DIFFERENCES

Let's take a detailed look at how the biological divide translates into real performance differences in sport.

A good example is to compare the results of the women's swimming finals at the Covid-delayed Tokyo Olympic Games in 2021 with the same year's finals from the European Junior Swimming Championships for boys (up to 18). In 14 races with eight swimmers – that's 112 chances – just one woman makes one lane in one final, and she finishes last. That's against teenage boys, not fully grown men.

That one outstanding woman among all the world's outstanding women swimmers is Katie Ledecky, a living legend of her sport with seven Olympic and 19 world titles to her name – a female Michael Phelps of her time, a once-in-a-generation pioneer who has set a punishing pace for her opponents in distance freestyle events.

In a race with boys, let alone men like former teammate Phelps, winner of an other-worldly 23 Olympic golds, Katie would not make a junior US team. Forget medals and even finals, because Katie would never make a US Olympic team or even a national junior squad if she had to race junior boys. Her Olympic victory over 800 metres freestyle in Tokyo would have placed her fourteenth in the heats of the European junior boys championship 800 metres freestyle in the same year, while her world record from 2016 – one of the most outstanding swimming standards in history – would have placed her sixth among junior boys. Impressive. At world level, she would not make the boys final.

8 *Katie Ledecky versus the boys: where the all-time great woman ranks among the best boys and men*

	8:12.57 Tokyo 2020 Olympic Gold	8:04.57 World Record, Rio 2016 Olympic Gold
Best Junior Boys, Aged 15–18 2022	17th	12th
All-time Senior men best performers	Outside top 1,200	Outside top 650
All-time Senior men best performances	Outside top 15,000	Outside top 12,000

Performers = the best time of any single swimmer
Performances = all performances of each swimmer

Sources: Swimming Rankings Database (Thierry, Lord, Weidlich, private resource) and World Aquatics

Photo: Katie Ledecky, courtesy of Patrick B. Kraemer, www.magicpbk.com

At her very best, Katie is swimming at the pace of the best men around the time of my first Olympic Games in 1976. Against the best of boys at the past two World Junior Championships, her 800 metres world record would not make the top eight. When it comes to comparing the all-time performance rankings of men and women across all swimming events, you have to go many thousands deep on the men's lists before you get to the women's world record.[1]

Such stark realities explode the trans-activist myth that the overlap of male and female performers' capabilities is so closely aligned that the female who wins the women's competition could beat the male who comes last in the men's final. This is clearly a fantasy. When men are allowed to enter women's sport, they will win, fill finals and take away team places even if they were very average when they competed as men.

This is amply proven by the results of many hundreds of competitions around the world and the media coverage of it all, much of it reached by a simple online search. Take the website the Sports Room, among many news outlets listing the growing numbers of transwomen excelling in female sport. In a June 2021 feature, it noted 30 cases of transwomen achieving a status in sport well beyond the level they reached when competing with men.[2]

The cases include the following.

- 2012: Laurel Hubbard, a 35-year-old New Zealand weightlifter, transitions and thereafter qualifies for 11 international women's tournaments, including the Olympics in 2021. As a man, Hubbard did not make international selection.
- 2014: Chelsea Wolfe transitions and, in the same year, takes up BMX cycling after having competed as a boy in previous years. Wolfe switched to BMX freestyle after that became an Olympic event in 2017, and in 2021 went to Tokyo as an alternate on the US women's Olympic Bicycle Motocross (BMX) freestyle team. Wolfe did not compete but became the first transgender Olympian on Team USA.

- 2015: The Australian handball player Calum Mouncey transitions, taking the name Hannah Mouncey. Previously Mouncey made 22 appearances for the Australian men's handball team, scoring 0 goals. After transitioning Hannah was allowed to play for the Australian women's handball team, scoring 23 goals in 2018.
- 2017: The Jamaican-American athlete CeCé Telfer, previously ranked three hundred and ninetieth among male NCAA Division II athletes in the 400 metres hurdles category, transitions and, in 2019, becomes national NCAA Division II women's champion with an eye on Olympic selection.
- 2017–18: Rodrigo Abreu, a volleyball player in Brazil's men's Superliga A and B divisions, becomes Tiffany Abreu on the way to breaking Brazil's women's Superliga's single-game scoring record against a team that contained three Olympic gold medallists. The first transwoman to play in the Superliga, Abreu is estimated to be a dollar millionaire.
- 2018: US athlete Terry Miller identifies as female and, in 2019, wins the girls' 55-metre dash at the Connecticut Open Indoor Track Championships, breaking the girls' state indoor record. Second place goes to Andraya Yearwood, who is also a transwoman.
- 2020–1: The US swimmer Will Thomas transitions to become Lia Thomas. In autumn 2021, Thomas races among females for the first time and then in March 2022 becomes the first transgender NCAA Division 1 swimming champion in history, ahead of three Team USA female Olympic silver medallists.[3] As a man Thomas was not even close to that status in sport – as we will see later in this chapter.

These are just a few examples of very average male athletes transitioning and stealing races and titles that were designed for females to win. There are many more. And the list is growing every single week, especially in Masters events designed to reward retired female athletes or those who discovered competitive sport later in life. And we're talking about a female community that already has far fewer opportunities than men in sport.

WHY FEMALE AND MALE MUST BE EQUAL BUT SEPARATE

Let's illustrate the sex-based performance gap further by making some specific cross-sex comparisons.

Image 9, a slide from a presentation given by former US swimmer Nancy Hogshead-Makar in May 2022, shows the difference between swimmer Missy Franklin and her American teammate Ryan Lochte.[4] It's a snapshot of why women and men should compete 'equal but separate', says Nancy.

- Missy Franklin and Ryan Lochte
- They are both multiple Olympic and world champions in swimming.
- Both had first class training, coaching, and support.
- Both are 6'2" with reported 6'4" wingspans.
- Both held the world record in the 200 meter backstroke.
- But Ryan's best time of 1:52.96 is a half lap ahead of Missy's at 2:04.06.
- Missy's world record time would tie for 50th in the U.S. men's Olympic Trials.
- #SexMatters

Women's Sports Policy Working Group

9 *Missy Franklin and Ryan Lochte*

Both athletes are 6' 2" and were Olympic champions in the 200 metres backstroke. They have lots of other excellence-related things in common and are outstanding examples of achievement in their respective sex-based categories. The one thing, on many levels, that makes a massive difference to their time on the clock is obvious: biological sex.

The gap between their best 200 metres times is 11.1 per cent: 2:04.06, a world record for Missy between 2012 and 2019, and 1:52.96, the 2011 best of Ryan, who remains the fastest ever in a textile suit, unaided by materials banned in 2010 because they boosted performances to a different degree in different swimmers and introduced unfairness.

There were well over 1,500 men capable of swimming faster than Missy at the time of her London 2012 Olympic victory. At those Games, she would not have beaten a single swimmer in the men's 200 metres competition. Missy was a phenomenal female athlete during a career that ended after the Rio 2016 Olympics, the best women's 200 metres backstroke swimmer and a supreme champion using the biology available to her.

In London, the time it took to make the semi-finals for men, 1:58, is highly unlikely to be matched by women in my lifetime. Missy's then-world-record time is about the pace of the best men back in the early 1980s – and the pace of progress is slowing down.

The same picture can be found if we compare athletes Shaunae Miller-Uibo and Wayde van Niekerk, in this second slide from Nancy Hogshead-Makar's presentation (Image 10).

Whichever angle you take when looking at any chart of male advantage over females in sports like swimming and athletics, there's no escaping the obvious. And remember that, as we saw on the chart from Chapter 5, swimming, with an 11 per cent average speed advantage of men over women, is at the lower end of the big performance gap between the sexes across a wide range of sports.

- Shaunae Miller -Uibo and Wayde Van Niekerk
- Both are reigning Olympic Champions in the 400 meters.
- Wayde is the current men's world record holder and Shaunae is the fastest female in history never to have been associated with doping.
- Both have had access to first class training, coaching, and support.
- Both are about the same height (6'1"/185 cm and 6'0"/183 cm) and weight (152 and 154 pounds).
- Wayde's best time – 43.03 – is over 5 seconds faster than Shaunae's– 48.37.
- #SexMatters

Women's Sports Policy Working Group

10 *Shaunae Miller-Uibo and Wayde van Niekerk*

Here's what that gulf means: more than 10,000 male performances over 800 metres freestyle are faster than Katie Ledecky's stunning world record of 8:04.79, and more than 10,000 male swims are faster than Missy Franklin's pioneering 200 metres backstroke effort in 2012.[5]

A comparison between Michael Phelps and Katie brings the picture into particularly sharp relief.

In all those 23 Olympic gold-winning efforts, Michael had a 0.2 per cent advantage over his competitors. Now add 11 per cent to Michael's best in his signature event, the 200 metres butterfly, and we get a time on the clock that is four seconds slower than the winner of seven golds at the 1972 Olympics, Mark Spitz. He remains faster in 2023 than any woman who has ever swum. Meanwhile, Michael, the most versatile swimmer in history, with world records in five individual events, had only one of those global standards left just six years after he retired in 2016.

To suggest, as trans activists do, that there's overlap between the best men and women in sport and that women are catching up is untruthful. Michael still holds two senior national records but his great standards are going and will be gone long before the next 40–50 years are up. That's how far you have to go back in time to find men's records in swimming at around the level of the best women's standards today.

Katie, meanwhile, is 2 per cent better than her nearest competitor over 800 metres freestyle. That's not unknown, but is an amazing advantage within a sex category. It reflects Katie's status as one of those rare pioneering athletes who set standards that may last well beyond their era. Both Michael and Katie have been Olympic champions over 200 metres freestyle. Michael won the men's crown in 2008 by an impressive 1.8 per cent, while Katie won the women's 2016 title by 0.3 per cent. The gap between their winning times is 10.5 per cent.

Sex-based categories are essential. In the Summer Olympics alone there are more than 70 categories within men's and women's events that are ring-fenced specifically on the basis of physical size and strength. There are also mixed events these days in which men and women who train together also get to compete alongside, but not against, each other. A prime example of this is from my own sport. In swimming, we now have mixed relays in which each team has two men and two women.

In the 4×100 metres freestyle, the men race each other first on the opening two legs before the women, 60–80 pounds lighter than their male teammates, go in, because if women were to race men, they would be washed away at the first turn by the bow wave created by huge male sprinters pushing off the wall like orcas chasing a seal supper. The order of line-ups is sex-based, but usually because each team wants to have the best chance of winning. You get a mild glimpse of that in the 4×100 metres mixed medley, which is now an Olympic event, the first title having been won by Britain in a world record at the Tokyo Games in 2021.[6]

I was there to interview the new champions Kathleen Dawson, Adam Peaty, James Guy and Anna Hopkin on the poolside as they celebrated gold. I took a snap of the joyful foursome (Image 11). It's a poster for sex-based categories in sport.

11 *GBR Olympic champions swim relay, Tokyo, taken by Sharron*

None of those athletes gets to select their Olympic category on the basis of a feeling. Their physical nature allocates them to a category ring-fenced to uphold rules on fair play. There is no rule in sport that prioritises a gendered feeling and demotes sex to a minor matter, which is why some sports are now working on an open classification that delivers for all concerned.

For the same reason, it's not embarrassing for the Arsenal women's football team, on their way to an international cup win, to have played a friendly against their club's under-15 boys' team and lost 5–0.[7] Those boys had less experience on the pitch than the women they were playing but their experience of testosterone is what got them past the defence and into the net five times.

The same picture can be found just about everywhere you look in sport. Jake Teater runs the excellent website Boys vs Women, which is stacked with fascinating interactive graphics.[8] The site is swimming in statistics that show how waves of boys of 14 to 18 years of age can beat the best Olympic women in the world in various sports.

12 *The power of T: how 15-year-old boys beat the best Olympic women*

Position	Track and Field 100 metres	Track and Field 200 metres	Swimming: 50 metres freestyle LC	Swimming: 100 metres Freestyle LC
1st	10.44	20.71	22.30	50.09
2nd	10.45	20.78	22.95	50.28
3rd	10.46	20.94	23.02	50.96
4th	10.48	20.95	23.19	51.04
5th	10.51	21.07	23.31	51.06
6th	10.53	21.10	23.36	51.26
7th	10.60	21.34	23.66	51.28
8th	10.63	21.37	23.68	51.34
9th	10.71	21.78	24.07	52.70
10th	10.83	21.88	24.09	52.70
11th	10.86	22.15	24.11	52.99
12th	10.86	22.21	24.13	53.04
13th	10.90	22.31	24.15	53.08
14th	10.92	22.34	24.19	53.24
15th	10.94	22.65	24.42	53.30
16th	11.80	22.69	24.69	53.36

■ High School Boys – NBNO Finalists / SJNC Finalists

■ 2016 Olympic women's finalists

Track and field: 2016 High School Boys NBNO Finalists vs 2016 Olympic Women's Finalists; Swimming: 2016 High School Boys SJNC Finalists vs 2016 Olympic Women's Finalists. None of the women's finals performances met the qualifying time to enter the boys' competition.

Reproduced with permission from Boys vs Women.

In a battle of American high school boys vs female Olympians, taking athletics times run at the National Scholastic Championships and the Olympic Games, it's a hands-down victory to the males: 28 gold, 27 silver and 26 bronze to one gold, two silver and three bronze for the plucky best-of-class women, aka the most outstanding Olympic track-and-field women in the world.

A comparison of the records of high school boys (aged 14–15) in the United States alone to women's world records shows that, in running, the marathon is the only event in which a female pioneer is faster than an American 14- or 15-year-old boy. The performance gap extends to every level of sport and is why there are no female players in any of the major men's professional leagues (see Image 12).

The proof of stark sex-based difference in sport is to be found almost everywhere you look. According to a Duke Law study, a specific example of this performance gap includes Olympic, world and US champion Tori Bowie. Her 100 metres personal best of 10:78 was topped more than 15,000 times by men and high school boys in 2017 alone.[9]

The same holds true for Allyson Felix, the most decorated track athlete in Olympic history, with seven gold, three silver and a bronze. Felix's 400 metres best, 49:26, is hugely impressive, but more than 15,000 men and high school boys got past it in 2017.

T really does divide us. On that score, sports bosses have been getting it wrong all along.

7

GONADS AND GOTCHAS

Y OU don't need to be a genius to make sense of the science, but it helps to have the logic explained by an expert in exercise physiology. Dr Ross Tucker says testosterone (T) measures should never be used as a ticket to female sport for men identifying as women. They're a red herring.[1] Tucker, the chief scientist at World Rugby, the first international regulator to bar transwomen from female competition on grounds of safety, says that sports bosses have been looking at the issue from the wrong angle.[2]

Trans-inclusion policy in women's sport has been based on the theory that a transwoman can spend a period reducing testosterone levels during transition and keep the level below a set limit, and that this alone will make competition fair.

It does no such thing. It just leads to the kind of meaningless narrative found in coverage on trans athletes. Here's an example from Wikipedia on the huge former men's Australian handball player:

[Hannah] Mouncey's testosterone levels were well below the required levels of 10 nmol/L by July 2016. Mouncey hoped to play in women's competition in October 2016, and to be selected in Australia women's national handball team. Her request to play for the ACT representative team in October 2016 was refused by the Australian Handball Federation, citing insurance concerns

because she was still three weeks short of the IOC guideline of
12 months of hormone therapy.[3]

Once androgenisation has occurred during puberty, most of the male
development that follows is irreversible. Women's sport exists to
exclude males for all the reasons we've understood for years. Yet still
the IOC and many sports federations following Olympic 'guidance'
insist that if you reduce the impact of nature a little with chemical
and medical intervention, a man can be a woman and female athletes
should welcome the newcomer into their races and spaces.

The whole idea is farcical and the IOC knows very well why.

Any snapshot of T levels, which can tell anti-doping agencies
if there's cheating on the day, does not test the actual problem, as
Tucker points out. Testosterone has already done the work long
before the race or the moment an athlete is tested: from the womb,
through every year of life and male development.

The East Germans were able to get the added testosterone out of
their systems in time for drug tests at all major Games and championships in just days. They learned that trick half a century ago,
and it's a method of avoiding detection used to this day by cheats
in various ways, including microdosing, the art of taking enough of
a banned drug but flying under the radar.[4]

In 1982, before a new method of testing for testosterone was
introduced, East German scientists had a solution, after running a
study on 241 male and female athletes.[5] If they made the measures
in the method of their cheating more precise, by injecting 25 milligrams of testosterone into athletes, it took just three days for the
ratio to fall back to less than 6 nanomoles, the limit beyond which
an athlete is positive.

That knowledge led to the East Germans writing a new proto-
col to get round doping controls. No athlete would be injected less
than four days before a competition. They perfected the scam in the

following years and worked out how many hours it would take for an athlete to return to legal levels of testosterone. How useful that must have been when international anti-doping controllers were kept waiting for hours at Checkpoint Charlie for their visa to be approved when supposedly unannounced out-of-competition tests began in the 1980s.

Fast-forward to 2020, and Dr Emma Hilton and Dr Tommy Lundberg note that with the right cocktail of pharmaceuticals, it is possible to reduce a man's testosterone to castration level (zero) within 12 hours where there's a medical need to do so, such as in cancer patients.[6] Cheats in sport have long shown their willingness to take what's been designed to help people with life-threatening conditions and use it to defraud rivals.

The chances of East German-style manipulation, and cheating similar to behaviour that we've seen from around the world, most particularly in China and Russia over decades of doping scandals, are alive and kicking. It would be easy for an athlete self-identifying in the gender opposite their birth sex to achieve compliance for any scheduled test requiring 10 nanomoles per litre of testosterone or less without having to reduce normal male levels of testosterone throughout the training year, says Hilton.

In theory, any athlete identifying as a woman and behaving in that way would, effectively, be training and competing in conditions no different from those of a male athlete.

That's precisely what happened during my career as an Olympic swimmer: rules were set, cheats found a loophole and guardians looked the other way. The knowledge and experience of all that harm are something trans activists turn a blind eye to when they trot out whatever 'gotcha' they can think of. You'll hear their ill-informed sympathisers say that Usain Bolt has higher testosterone levels than teenage girls but some of the very best might run 800 metres faster than him so that must mean that T can't be that important for performance. This shows a deep, and in some cases wilful, mis-understanding of physiology and its application in sport.[7]

As Tucker notes, a single test of T levels invites disingenuous and dishonest claims about just how important testosterone is to male and female differences in sport. Arbitrary testosterone levels that biological males must show they have not exceeded at a given moment of their choosing are irrelevant and open to manipulation. At present we don't even have robust ways to test and monitor such things.

In many cases, we're told we should not raise the possibility that a trans athlete might intend to cheat, while certification and 'proof' of testosterone levels are only required from a doctor who knows the athlete and may even work in the sports system and get paid by the athlete and his or her club or programme.

Contrast that with the experience of the vast majority of other female athletes, who are subject to a very different level of scrutiny. Anti-doping tests are there because we assume and know that humans cheat. Testing is not carried out by a friendly doctor but by independent testers who arrive unannounced to do spot checks. The who, when and how are often unknown to the athlete.

It's not hard to see that those two versions of scrutiny are not the same in terms of their intensity, even though all athletes are supposed to be subject to the same rules and competition environment.

So, in the case of transwomen and testosterone, who decides who gets tested? And if checking testosterone levels set specifically for trans athletes is to be part of the random out-of-season inde-pendent testing females have to submit to, what would happen if a trans athlete was over the legal T level? What happens to trans athletes who register 7 nanomoles when it's supposed to be less than 5 nanomoles? Would they also be banned for four years?

Apparently not, because the IOC seems to think the woman might be cheating and the penalty is at the high end of the suspension scale, but the transwoman is assumed to have just made a silly mistake, and so Olympic bosses have made it a one-year penalty for them. It's one rule for us, another for biological males taking on female athletes.

So much science and logic has been buried down the many rabbit holes trans activists spend time digging to confuse as many people as they can. For every scientific argument, there's been a 'gotcha'. We're not going to burrow down all those holes, but here are just a couple of examples of trans-lobby gotchas.

NON-BINARY

For me, non-binary is a nonentity. Whatever anyone wishes to identify as, there are still only two sexes. Non-binary status is not protected in British law. I don't personally believe in the whole non-binary thing. If people don't want to conform with their bio-logical sex, or, more specifically, with a stereotype of what a man or a woman is perceived to be by society, absolutely fine. If Sam wants to wear a dress, fine by me. Sam can wear and present however Sam likes. I'm cool with that. But Sam will always be biologically male and can never be both sexes or 'neither'. How 'they' expresses himself is totally unique and perfectly acceptable in a progressive society. People were already doing that in the 1980s without saying they'd changed sex!

A light was shone on the misuse of language and the hypocrisy of it all in 2022 when Jacob Caswell picked up a $5,000 prize for fin-ishing the New York City Marathon as the first 'non-binary' runner home.[8] Overall, he was 172nd. His time of 2 hours, 45 minutes and 12 seconds is that of an average club runner.

New York Road Runners coughed up the non-binary prize. Five non-binary runners received a total of $15,000. All of them were male, which caught the eye of the parent of another non-binary athlete who called on the marathon organisers to split the non-binary category into non-binary male and non-binary female winners. So, non-binary would be binary after all!

It wasn't hard to spot what organisers had created: more opportunities for men to win more prizes, as British marathon ace Mara Yamauchi pointed out in an article for the website LetsRun in November 2022.[9] The whole trend leaves women unequal on various levels. The system evolving in American marathons means that men can be men, and that biologically male trans competitors and transmen can pick and choose whichever competition category suits them best, including the women's category and/or 'non-binary'. And it's OK for a transwoman to refuse to stay in the category that represents their male biology, because if they did they'd be average athletes and not the elite stars they aspire to be in women's sport.

The winner of the non-binary category in the London Marathon on 23 April was Irishman Sam Murphy, in 2 hours, 24 minutes and 14 seconds. Mara noted on Twitter that the winner of the New York City Marathon's non-binary race was also a man. She noted that he'd 'won $5000 for 2:45:12, slower than 146 men and 25 women, most of whom won nothing. More easy NB money.'[10]

In summary, there are plenty of options open – so long as you're not a non-trans biological female.

DISORDERS OF SEX DEVELOPMENT (DSDS)[11]

DSD is the next gotcha. They say some variations prove that sex is not binary and human hermaphrodites do exist. Horribly, they've used South African runner Caster Semenya as the champion of their cause.

That's worse than being wrong. The word 'intersex' was replaced because it implied a person could be between sexes when that's not true. It gets used all the time by trans activists and media to suggest that a human can be whichever sex they like and even both at the same time. It's a lie and really insulting to the people with DSDs. I've spoken to many of those affected, people who try very hard to put the trans lobby right but who just get knocked back.

Researchers who helped at the birth of the term 'DSD' during an international consensus conference in Chicago in 2005 wrote a paper explaining why terms like 'hermaphrodite', 'pseudohermaphrodite' and 'intersex' were inaccurate.[12]

Fifty renowned international experts were asked to review inter-sex disorders and find a better and more respectful way of describing the five types of sexual anatomy first labelled in the nineteenth century.[13] They wanted the new descriptions to be understandable to patients and families while being psychologically sensitive. They decided that words such as 'hermaphrodite' and 'intersex' should be abandoned. The term 'disorder of sex development' was born to define atypical congenital conditions.

Basically, they wanted to reflect the truth in accurate but sensitive language and get rid of mythology. But lobbyists still use controversial terms to create confusion.

The Caster Semenya case has been used by some to bolster such claims because the South African runner was often described as 'intersex' during years of controversy and challenge at the International Amateur Athletic Federation (IAAF; later World Athletics) and the Court of Arbitration for Sport (CAS).

Caster has a DSD of 46 XY 5-ARD, or 5-alpha-reductase deficiency (internal testes, sometimes referred to as ovotesticular disorder).[14] In general, 46 XY is a condition in which a person has one X chromosome and one Y chromosome in each cell, the normal pattern found in males, but also has genitalia that may not be clearly visible at birth. Caster's condition means that male levels of testosterone from the Y chromosome have helped build an adult human with male traits.

The controversy surrounding Caster came to a head in 2019 when the South African Olympic 800 metres track champion from Rio gave CAS no choice but to issue a ruling that meant Caster could not defend the crown at the Tokyo Games.[15]

The IAAF ruling said that Caster had to reduce testosterone to 5 nanomoles. Caster didn't want to, so challenged the ruling – and lost. Caster was barred from competing in a range of women's events after CAS noted that 46 XY 5-ARD athletes have 'circulating testosterone at the level of the male 46 XY population and not at the level of the female 46 XX population. This gives 46 XY 5-ARD athletes a significant sporting advantage over 46 XX female athletes.'[16]

Media coverage of the CAS decision included a ton of references to intersex people making up 1.7 per cent of humanity. The BBC cited a UN document when it reported: 'According to a 2016 report by the UN, between 0.05 and 1.7 percent of children are born with intersex conditions. For the upper level that's roughly the same as being born with red hair.'[17]

That's misleading and biased. The 1.7 per cent figure comes from biologist Anne Fausto-Sterling's book *Sexing the Body: Gender Politics and the Construction of Sexuality*, published in 2000, and is still anchored to the five types of sexual anatomy superseded by the new DSD definition that emerged in 2006.[18]

Fausto-Sterling used a very broad definition of 'intersex', one that has been challenged by a host of other experts, including Dr Leonard Sax, an American psychologist and a practising family physician best known as the author of three books for parents: *Why Gender Matters* (2005), *Boys Adrift* (2007) and *Girls on the Edge* (2010).[19]

Sax notes that even if one chooses to use the term 'intersex' and confine it to its traditional meaning – that is, those who have XY chromosomes with predominantly female anatomy, XX chromosomes with predominantly male anatomy, or ambiguous or mixed genitalia – then the rate of intersex births works out at just 0.018 per cent.[20]

All of which makes the outcome of the 2016 Olympic women's 800 metres final on the track in Rio all the more crazy: even though births like Caster's are extremely rare, all the medals in that 800 metres final went to African athletes reported to have the same DSD: Caster, Francine Niyonsaba and Margaret Wambui.

If that doesn't shine a light on the role testosterone played in that women's final, I don't know what will. The first biological female home with XX chromosomes got no medal. It would be wrong to think of the rogues coercing and making cheats of their own athletes in the GDR in the same way we think of the DSD athletes who made the 2016 podium, but it is fair to note that however male advantage finds its way into female competition, female athletes pay a high price, and when I see it, I'm reminded of the horrible, sinking feeling I had watching British teammates like Ann in the six East German podium sweeps at the 1980 Olympics. In the 100 metres butterfly final, Ann was the first home without male advantage, without being fuelled by banned levels of testosterone – which left her fourth.

Ross Tucker represented Athletics South Africa and Caster at CAS in their challenge to IAAF rules in athletics. He believed one of the IAAF's studies used against Caster was flawed. Even so, when asked how big an advantage the presence of the Y chromosome in women's sport is, he described it as the 'the single greatest genetic advantage a person can have'.[21]

Trans activists like to talk about the lack of science and the need for more research. By all means do research, but let's not have more live experiments in female sport like we did over more than two decades in the East German doping era. The women's sports category should not be used as a laboratory that male sport will never have to endure.

There are huge aspects of Caster's case that absolutely require us to show empathy and understanding. But that should not prevent us from asking for truth so that decisions can be based on facts. In the 2019 CAS case, Caster described the DSD condition that lends the runner the advantages of being biologically male as a genetic gift. Many media outlets reported that Caster had unusual levels of testosterone for a female, but the truth is that those levels of testosterone were very normal for a 46 XY human.

CAS knew it and insisted she reduce T to 5 nanomoles, but Caster didn't want to. That uncomfortable truth was ignored by a lot of media. Some reports were deliberately misleading, in my opinion. Caster has a Y chromosome. It's incredibly unfortunate that it wasn't spotted and the consequences understood when Caster was younger.

We should all empathise, but, at the same time, Caster has good reason to want to remain in female sport and race in signature events. Caster has been on a conveyor belt of funding, fame, notoriety, sponsorship, endorsements, honours and elevated status. It's not easy to step down from all that.

But nor is it easy to be invisible, never to be recognised for the reward that was rightfully yours in female sport because you were robbed of it by the male biological advantage of her testosterone levels being so high that CAS referred to in its rulings on Semenya. It's not easy to be a survivor of the system. Just as it was in my racing days, females, again, are now being asked to accept unfair play.

Can you remember the names of the first three biological female athletes home in that Olympic 800 metres track final in Rio? Here they are: Melissa Bishop, fourth in a Canadian record, Poland's Joanna Jóźwik, fifth in a personal best, and, sixth, Britain's Lynsey Sharp, who spoke out and was wickedly vilified for being a bad loser. Try to appreciate after a decade or more of intense training and sacrifices what fourth, fifth or sixth place in an Olympic final means in terms of lost fame, funding, sponsorship, honours and status. And how much more frustrating it is to know that you were beaten to a medal by rivals possessing male biological advantages. Those girls live with that every day.

SEX TESTING

Trans activists don't seem to care and the IOC has their backs. Olympic bosses are not even trying to be neutral any more. In part that's because their record of handling such matters is not pretty, each change in policy on sex tests and then trans inclusion seemingly correcting but also compounding previous errors.

Here's a reminder of the history of sex testing, or biological verification, in Olympic women's sport:

- 1948 to 1966: Women are required to arrive at major competitions with a medical certificate from their home country verifying their sex.
- 1966 to 1967: Women are required to parade naked before a panel of gynaecologists before competitions so that sex can be confirmed depending on the appearance of genitalia.
- 1968 to 1992: Women are obliged by the IOC to submit to what is often, as it is in my case, a once-in-a-lifetime sex-verification test. A cheek swab is taken from all female athletes arriving at a major competition who don't already have a sports-issued certificate. The cells in the swab are tested for a Barr body (an inactive X chromosome), the presence of which is assumed to identify a multiple-X-chromosome, or XX, female.
- 1976 to today: Women and men have to submit to random anti-doping tests designed to detect elevated levels of testosterone and the presence of other banned substances in and out of competition. This is far more intrusive than any cheek sex swab and, of course, is mandatory.
- 1992 to 1999: Women are asked to submit to genetic testing designed to detect the SRY gene located on the Y chromosome. If it is there, the athlete is deemed to be male. At the Atlanta

Olympics in 1996, eight women test positive for the SRY gene but are still allowed to compete.

- 2003 to 2015: Women's sport is no longer ring-fenced for female athletes after the IOC allows males identifying as women access to female sports two years after sex-reassignment surgery, including a gonadectomy, or removal of testes, and a certificate confirming the sex reassignment.

- 2015 to 2021: It's open season in female sport. Surgery is no longer required for male athletes who identify as women to compete with female athletes. We look at that game-changing decision by the IOC in Chapter 8.

- November 2021 to December 2022: The IOC replaces all previous 'statements' and rules on inclusion with its 'Framework on Fairness, Inclusion, and Non-Discrimination on the Basis of Gender Identity and Sex Variations'. This calls on international federations in each sport to 'develop the criteria that are applicable to their sport'. The guidance is non-binding and there is no specific IOC rule on inclusion of transgender athletes.[22]

- December 2022: After a year of controversy and debate over the IOC's November 2021 statement, a 'position statement' is issued by a team of academics linked to the IOC. It reiterates much of the 2021 statement but makes no mention of the word 'female'. The IOC clarifies that its framework 'does not preclude the possibility that certain individual athletes could be subject to participation restrictions or exclusions where an unfair and disproportionate advantage and/or unacceptable safety risk is clearly demonstrated and cannot be mitigated via reasonable accommodations', but its update also notes: 'The challenge before IFs is to find ways to develop eligibility pathways that are fair and non-discriminatory and that provide opportunities for inclusion in an athlete's preferred category wherever possible, while also continuing to take meaningful action on gender equality.'[23]

The combination of the random anti-doping tests used from 1976 and the SRY-gene testing used between 1992 and 1999 worked well for the vast majority of women, but the IOC was deaf to what women wanted. A 2000 study involving researchers who worked with the IOC suggested existing sex test methods were objectionable to female athletes.[24] In fact, it was more proof that women's voices were being ignored.

As the study noted, a survey of female athletes at the 1996 Atlanta Olympics asked whether they thought the testing of females should be continued in the future and whether or not testing procedures made them anxious. The result: of the 928 athletes who responded, 82 per cent felt that testing should be continued and 94 per cent indicated that they were not made anxious by the procedure. Forty-six athletes were made anxious by the testing requirements that preceded their competitive events.[25]

So, the overwhelming majority of female athletes wanted the screening to continue. The IOC concluded that the methods were too time-consuming and costly, and that they caused too much emotional and social injury to a tiny number of athletes.

In summer 1999 the IOC conditionally rescinded 30 requirements for on-site gender screening of all women entered in female events at the Olympic Games. Then, in 2003, Olympic bosses leaped from a traditional ring-fencing of female sport to a place in which male transsexuals or transwomen who had undergone full legal and surgical sex change were allowed into female sport regardless of any male advantages that had been retained.[26] In 2015 it went much further, as we'll see in Chapter 8.

The IOC simply ignored the voices of female athletes. Cathy Devine, an independent scholar, joined other leading researchers in a November 2022 paper entitled 'When ideology trumps science':

The total disregard for female athletes' voices is similarly apparent in the discussion of the historically intrusive sex (not gender) verification of female athletes, which, if reinstated, would now involve the minimally intrusive, once in a lifetime, cheek swab/buccal smear. The evidence we have shows that a large majority of elite female athletes, when actually asked, support sex testing.[27]

I think it was a mistake to remove sex-verification tests. For me, it was just a quick, painless cheek swab on the inside of my mouth. It was once in a lifetime because the cells on the inside of your cheek will remain the same throughout life, no matter what you do or what surgery you might have. We got a little card and you were approved for female racing. That was it.

It wasn't at all intrusive or humiliating. And it's no good people saying that these things are not reliable or that DSD people are affected. The test is to show who is biologically female. You can't say it's fair if you don't test for doping. You can't say it's fair if you don't test to see if anyone in the competition has male physiological advantage.

Categorisation is another one of those topics subjected to trans gotchas. Here's one: if Michael Phelps has long arms and enjoys an atypical and astonishing rate of recovery between races, then why does it matter if transwomen have advantages too? Name me a sport in which the physiology (not disability) of an individual has ever been used to give them their own category? There are, of course, none.

They single out Michael and the natural advantages he's put to great use in the pool while insisting that none of us even have a right to mention that they are dragging natural male hormone advantage into female sport to produce artificial results. And as we've already pointed out in Chapter 6, Michael beat his main rivals by tiny margins (far less than 1 per cent) in the majority of his battles, whereas the average gap between best men and best women in swimming is 11 per cent.

In any case, for safety purposes, distinctions are made within the spectrum of each sex in contact sports like boxing, such as to determine weight categories, because it would be dangerous to have a heavyweight and a lightweight in the same ring. Trans athletes surely get that, but at the same time they cheered when Hannah Mouncey, a 6' 2" Australian rules football and handball player weighing 15 stone and 7 pounds, crashed into much smaller female opponents. They rallied round Fallon Fox when the ex-marine and biologically male mixed martial arts fighter boasted of enjoying fracturing a woman's skull, too.[28]

No amount of sophistry and attempted 'gotchas' by the trans lobby can change the facts. Humans are sexually dimorphic, and being biologically male confers massive performance advantages. That's why there must be a clearly enforced system of categorisation within sporting competition based on sex.

The rules have long been interpreted in precisely that way, and sports history shows us why that's important if pledges made in the Olympic Charter are to be upheld. Yet since 2015, the IOC has actively sought to tear down one of the key pillars of Olympic sport and sex-based equality. Female athletes have been the target of injustices now unfolding as a result.

8

THE GAME CHANGER

THERE are moments in history that shame Olympic bosses: the GDR fraud and the IOC's reaction to it; the Nazi salutes at the 1936 Games; Coubertin's antics.[1]

In 2016, a new episode was added to this inglorious history: the demolition of the only hurdle high enough to prevent a rush of male advantage into female sport.

Between the Olympic years of 2004 and 2016, transgender athletes were obliged by the IOC to have genital sex-reassignment surgery if they wanted to compete in the category opposite to their biological sex. Men identifying as women had to have their testes removed to stem the tide of testosterone that had built them from boy to man.

Then, in late 2015, the IOC agreed a new policy that was highly questionable on ethical grounds.[2] The obligation to go under the knife was removed. Of course, making athletes have life-changing surgery did not exactly paint the perfect picture of sport as a healthy pursuit, but taking down that barrier to biological males without having a worthy replacement policy at the ready was pure folly.

In terms of women's sport, the IOC had one job: to ensure that female and sex-based equality rights were preserved in whatever new inclusion rules they came up with. They failed. The IOC not only bought into the false notion that hormone-reduction therapy would be enough to ensure fair play when they gave biological males a ticket to female sport, but in doing so they imposed challenges and conditions on female athletes that male athletes never have to face.

There was no chance of any biological female identifying as male beating the best men in the world, and that's why many transmen and non-binary females choose to live out their sports career in the category of their biology. However, female athletes no longer had an automatic right to the same degree of fair play as men enjoy. The IOC's new policy of self-identification backed by evidence of hormone-reduction therapy guaranteed the flood of biological males we've witnessed in women's sport in the past few years. There are many times the number of transwomen in women's sport than we'd seen before.

Statistics show that men are far more reluctant than women to have any form of genital surgery during transition. Many of those transitioning don't want their genitals removed or mutilated because they remain sexually attracted to females.

Surgery would also put an athlete out of action for a fair while, so it's only an option for those who don't have serious sports performance targets in mind, who intend to make a lifelong choice and who are unlikely to change their mind next month or next year. A huge life-changing decision.

The United States has some of the highest levels of gender surgery in the world among trans people, despite the costs and barriers of insurance. In a 2019 paper, New York researchers estimated that 25–50 per cent of transmen (females) went in for genital surgery in a ten-year study period.[3] The rate for transwomen (males) was 5–13 per cent and fell to 1 per cent among those describing themselves as non-binary.

Rates are estimated to be smaller in Europe, where 26 out of 28 countries, including the UK, don't allow surgery before 18 years of age. In 13 of those countries, there is a blanket ban, while in the other 13 parents have to consent. In all but one country, Slovenia, surgery is not permitted under any circumstances before 15.[4]

As a result, far more trans people saw Olympic sport as a viable option the moment the IOC removed the surgical hurdle and put up a sign telling biological males to 'roll up for a ticket to the female locker room'. All they needed was to self-identify as a woman and then keep testosterone levels to an arbitrary and misleading level well above that of biological females.

WOMEN WAKE UP TO THE THREAT TO FAIR PLAY

As we said in Chapter 7, the IOC basically declared open season on women's sport. The whole thing was done with such stealth that the Rio Olympics in 2016 went by without many even noticing the new ruling, which didn't come in time for anyone affected to qualify for the Games.

Many of us around the world only saw the obvious danger for female athletes when trans weightlifter Laurel Hubbard, born a boy named Gavin, hit the headlines in 2018 after making a comeback as a contender in women's sport the year before.[5] In 2017, Samoan female lifter Iuniarra Sipaia was among the very first athletes to speak out about the situation. After defeat in the +90 kilogram competition at the Australian Open Weightlifting Championships, she told the *Samoa Observer*: 'I felt that it was unfair because all in all, Laurel is still a male... we all know a woman's strength is nowhere near a male's strength no matter how hard we train.'[6]

Even then, the news was low key. Many didn't truly wake up to it all until Hubbard made the New Zealand Olympic team on their way to becoming the first openly trans Olympian in history at the Tokyo Games in 2021.[7]

It was 2003 when the Medical Commission of the IOC established three conditions of eligibility for transgender athletes:

sex-reassignment surgery, including changes to external genitalia, such as gonadectomy; proof of legal recognition of their new gender (identity, not biology); and two years of hormone therapy.

That's what trans cyclist McKinnon/Ivy had in mind when suggesting it was untrue to say that transwomen athletes had an unfair advantage because 'it's clear that they don't' and the numbers since 2003 proved the point.[8] The activist wrote in a *New York Times* commentary in 2019: 'Since the 2004 Athens Olympics, there have been over 54,000 Olympians. Not one of them has been openly trans... No openly trans woman has set an open elite world record in any sport... No openly trans woman has won an elite world championship in any sport, let alone a medal.'

McKinnon/Ivy conveniently made no mention of the surgical barrier in place between 2004 and 2016 when adding: 'If there were going to be mass gender fraud, we'd have seen it by now.'[9]

That was disingenuous: the gateway to female sport was only thrown wide open in 2016 and too late for any impact at the Rio Olympics that year, so any reference to numbers in the period before that is obviously misleading. It's easy to muddy the waters if your audience isn't given the facts.

The cyclist's wheels were spinning too fast when it came to the implication that there simply wasn't an issue: history had already shown us that women had been denied by biological males, some of whom knew they were men, others possibly not.

Germany's Dora Ratjen, fourth in the high jump at the 1936 Olympics, set a world record for the women's high jump at the 1938 European Championships, but suspicions led to an inquiry, and Ratjen was declared a man. Ratjen, who may have had a DSD, later took the name Heinrich and lived the rest of his life as a man.[10]

After sex testing was introduced, the IOC barred Austrian 1966 female world champion downhill skier Erika Schinegger from the 1968 Winter Games in Grenoble because they'd found that the skier had internal male sex organs. Erika later became Erik and lived life as a man.[11]

It's true to say that relatively few males did go in for surgery before the 2016 rule change. I've spoken to a couple of ex-international athletes who were elite men before their transition. They have gender dysphoria and it was imperative for them to have surgery. They also tell me they don't think transwomen should be in female sports because it's unfair.

One of the world's most famous transwomen, Olympic men's decathlon champion Bruce and now Caitlyn Jenner, believes in fair sport and, naturally, understands elite sport. Caitlyn has always maintained that biology matters in sport and has had hate thrown at her from the trans community because she's spoken the truth, much as I have.

We're not alone. There was widespread agreement with the speech from Dr David Gerrard we quoted in Chapter 5. He said: 'We cannot ignore irrefutable biological science in a debate so frequently over-whelmed by anecdote, emotion and pure subjectivity. As an Olympian, a physician, and a male, I stand unashamedly supportive of every natal female athlete, whose voice I believe deserves to be heard.'[12]

Frankly, it's infuriating that so many women in sport feel the same way but were never asked for their opinion before the IOC removed the need for surgery. When I spoke up, I was told to pipe down. It is extraordinary that they took their decision knowing that they'd already removed sex tests, the other key barrier to male advantage in female sport. Ideally, those tests should be brought back. Problem solved. A simple swab to the inside of the cheek, once in a lifetime. And, if necessary, as appears to be the case, they could rename the category 'natal female'.

Here's what the official IOC decision of 2016 looked like, with their adoption of pronouns reflecting the politics of feelings rather than actual biology – and with my thoughts in italics:

1. Those who transition from female to male are eligible to compete
   in the male category without restriction.[13]

*Stop the clock: firstly, the terms 'male' and 'female' describe sex and biolog-
ical reality. Humans cannot change sex and no one can change from male
to female or vice versa. Transitioning from male or female is identifying
as the stereotype of woman or man that society is presenting.*
*In addition, this rule is a clear admission that trans inclusion in
men's sport is no threat to men. If biological females want to identify
as men and race the blokes, we all know that it won't make any
difference.*

2. Those who transition from male to female are eligible to compete
   in the female category under the following conditions:
2.1. The athlete has declared that her gender identity is female. The
    declaration cannot be changed, for sporting purposes, for a
    minimum of four years.

*Stop the clock: Olympic leaders are quite prepared for trans athletes to
switch from biological sex to self-identified gender and back to biological
sex in the way that an athlete can change countries, though not quite as
fast. The four-year rule suggests that IOC leaders are keen not to have
anyone gaming the system. They don't spell it out like that but what other
reason could there be? Is that also four years of identifying before they
first race? And if not, why not? Who's checking, and what happens if they
change their mind? How can we prove they are living as a woman? What
does that mean? Will there be allocation of medals if someone changes
their mind? Places on teams missed by females who should have been
there can't be reallocated.*

2.2. The athlete must demonstrate that her total testosterone level in
    serum has been below 10 nmol/L for at least 12 months prior

to her first competition (with the requirement for any longer period to be based on a confidential case-by-case evaluation, considering whether or not 12 months is a sufficient length of time to minimize any advantage in women's competition).

Stop the clock: as we learned in Chapter 7, this measure is nonsense and bound to fail female athletes if the purpose is to remove all male advantages and deliver fair play. The level of the wonder steroid that propels men to be, in the words of the Olympic motto, 'faster, higher, stronger' than women is set at 10 nanomoles per litre, but the female testosterone range is 0.52 to 2.4 nanomoles per litre. The vast majority of females, including myself as an elite athlete, are under 1 nanomole. How can that be fair? It means that transwomen get to benefit from full male levels of testosterone through all the crucial development years, then they get to be at least four times the highest levels of females while competing (and women with levels at that level often live with conditions like endometritis). If I was still competing they'd be allowed to have ten times my levels! This is all the more shocking when one be in in mind that testosterone is on the WADA banned list and tested for at the Olympic Games to catch cheats.

2.3. The athlete's total testosterone level in serum must remain below 10 nmol/L throughout the period of desired eligibility to compete in the female category.

Stop the clock: There's no robust testing system in place anyway that's independently funded and checked.

2.4. Compliance with these conditions may be monitored by testing. In the event of non-compliance, the athlete's eligibility for female competition will be suspended for 12 months.

Stop the clock: 12 months? Yet women get a four-year ban if they test
outside a permitted range of testosterone far lower than that set for trans-
women. This is transparently unfair.

DOUBTS OVER DR HARPER'S RESEARCH

The IOC simply got it wrong. But it gets worse. It turns out that the
IOC ruling was at least partly based on a single study of eight older
athletes, including the Canadian doctor and transgender researcher
who has the ear of Olympic bosses.[14]

Dr Joanna Harper, a Canadian medical physicist specialising in
radiation oncology (not, as one might expect, sports science), ran a
fine marathon as a young man before self-identifying as a woman
at the age of 47. As a transwoman, albeit well beyond peak athletic
years (the average age of Olympic marathon runners is just under
30[15]), Harper noticed a drop in personal running performance after
taking the female hormone oestrogen. Would it be possible to prove
that males might be able to compete fairly with females under the
right chemical conditions?

What happened next is described by kinesiologist Dr Linda
Blade as a 'scientifically dubious home brew research project' that
would change the world of Olympic sport for women.[16]

Harper spent three years searching social media platforms for
other male long-distance runners who self-identified as women
and were willing to share performance data. She found seven and
decided to make her own case the eighth sample. None of them were
elite Olympic-level athletes and all were of an age when you would
expect performance to drop off regardless of sex or gender identity.
All data was self-reported. There was no clinical data control.

Each athlete had a baseline personal-best time as a man, followed by a series of runs while identifying as women over a period
of between two and 30 years. The point was to show that the

transwomen's performances had dropped off and come much more in line with women's.

There's an obvious problem: over three decades one's performance will inevitably drop anyway. My last Olympics was 30 years ago. Funnily enough, now, in the 2020s, I am slower.

Could it have something to do with the fact that I haven't trained five or six hours a day in the pool through all those years? Or perhaps becoming a mum to three kids took a toll. What could it be? Time, perhaps. They say you should never ask a lady her age but I'm happy to tell you that I've kept fit all my life, made a comeback and turned 30 as a world-class swimmer before being one of TV's Gladiators in the years that followed my second retirement from Olympic sport. At 60, I consider myself in the kind of fitness range most forty-somethings would be proud of. I've also known for decades that I'd never see my Olympic-best times or British and Commonwealth record speeds again. No one in their right mind would have expected me to.

So, in Harper's study, it's hard to say what might have been behind a drop in form, beyond ageing – notably the impact of time passing on cardiovascular health, muscles and joints – and obvious stuff like putting on five stone, suffering illness or serious injury and other variables in a long life, such as variations in training regimens. These things can go both ways: I know swimmers in their fifties who train more now than they used to when they were teenagers. Perhaps they were lazy back then or they're just much more dedicated now – or maybe something else is happening. Who knows?

The point is, none of that stuff feels very controllable in the context of Harper's long-term study. The control was a World Masters age-grading system that allows comparison with times calculated on a percentage of fall-off from the top runner for a given age and sex category.

Harper claimed to have shown that the people in her study were as far off the pace of the best man in their age group when they raced as men as they were behind the best woman in their age group after transition. Harper acknowledged that it only applied to distance running. That alone would rule out applying any finding of mitigation of male advantage to other sports, particularly power sports, but Harper concluded that 'the study does make a powerful statement in favour of such a position'. I beg to differ.

Everyone I've spoken to about it seems to agree that Harper's original model was statistically unreliable, that the sample was alarmingly small, and that the control was not much more scientific than me racing four laps of the pool at 13, 17, 29 and now and trying to remember my times.

Hilton and Lundberg made this serious assessment:

Factors affecting performances in the interim, including training and injury, were uncontrolled for periods of years to decades and there were uncertainties regarding which race times were self-reported vs. which race times were actually reported and verified, and factors such as standardization of race course and weather conditions were unaccounted for. Furthermore, one runner improved substantially post-transition, which was attributed to improved training. This demonstrates that performance decrease after transition is not inevitable if training practices are improved. Unfortunately, no study to date has followed up these preliminary self-reports in a more controlled setting, so it is impossible to make any firm conclusions from this data set alone.[17]

Enough for us to be highly sceptical – but not the IOC, which didn't even commission other independent studies before changing its policy.

In her analysis of Harper's work, Blade notes that sample no. 7 was the older athlete who actually ran faster as an older transwoman than as a younger man. Obviously that would run counter to what Harper was trying to prove. And here's the bit I find truly outrageous: Harper dropped it from the results as an outlier. An outlier in a tiny sample. Is that ethical? Is it scientific? Whatever it may or may not be, one thing is obvious to me: the IOC should never have based the future of women's sport on such a flawed exercise – but they did.

In early 2023, Harper, an adviser to the IOC's Medical Commission, was in the process of more research on whether women's sport can remain fair or even meaningful if transwomen with irreversible male advantages are allowed to compete against females. The new work, backed by the IOC and being carried out at Loughborough University in England, hit a bump in the road in February when it emerged in an article in *The Times* that a sample of just four trans athletes was down to one, believed to be the British trans cyclist Emily, née Zach, Bridges.[18] Harper confirmed that three participants had left the programme.

It was not clear whether the research could continue with such sparse participation, but it is clear to me that we shouldn't have science led by a researcher with an interest in a particular outcome; we shouldn't have leaders who lend weight to one side of the argument; we should have ethical standards in science and any conflicts of interest must be declared. Studies should be reviewed by peers before research is validated, let alone used to form a policy likely to have a serious impact on legions of females at all levels of sport around the world.

The IOC had a duty to listen to independent counter-argument before making its move in late 2015. Whatever 'meaningful competition' means, it would always have to entail a commitment to sex-based equality and to blocking any form of unfair advantage, otherwise what's the point of any WADA drug-testing programme? A little bit of cheating is still cheating.

DIFFERENT DEAL FOR MEN

How would that trans-inclusion debate have gone had it been something that affected men's sport? Do you think men would have tolerated losing out on medals and awards if inclusion looked like someone with a strong advantage likely to end in victory for the newcomers? The speed of resolution in disputes affecting men provides the answer.

When a new Nike shoe threatened world records the debate was done and dusted the minute men thought it could be bad for them.[19] It was the same with the arrival in swimming of non-textile 'shiny suits', called that by Craig because they were stretched so tightly they looked like a polished mirror. They were like surfboards, and 43 world records fell in eight days at the 2009 World Championships. Craig led a campaign to sink the suits and give swimming back to swimmers. It wasn't just the performance enhancement. A standard suit cost several hundred dollars – even though the new luxury items burst like a balloon if they got snagged by a fingernail. Many athletes and parents just couldn't afford them.

Swimming nations voted to get rid of the suits but leaders dragged their feet on setting a date for a ban, so Bob Bowman, coach to Olympic great Michael Phelps, said that the star swimmer would not attend any FINA events until the day the ban was named. The first of January 2010 was made official just hours later.[20]

The crisis was all over in less than two years and a new system of suit checks and licences, and a related money-making industry, was introduced. The very same thing happened with the carbon footwear that broke records. Men can sort things when it affects men.

When it came to the debate over the impact of trans inclusion on women's sport, the men in charge were silent, barring the constant, quiet, irritating and false mantra of 'There's a lack of research to tell us' – and so can't we all #BeKind, #BeWelcoming until trans researchers have worked out what 'meaningful' competition looks like?

That approach raises questions from a dark chapter of Olympic history. Given what we know about the live experiment of GDR doping, has there been any talk from IOC bosses of lessons learned from that era? No. Has there been any acknowledgement from them that any research must be conducted away from the live environment of women's sport? No. It should never enter the IOC's collective mind to think any research in the live-competition environment is acceptable given the damage done by the laboratory that scooped up the bulk of prizes in my sport and others in the 1970s and 1980s.

It was left to women to raise the red flag and fight all over again for truth and rights.

DR HILTON ON THE TRAIL OF
THE IOC'S MISSING SCIENCE

When the IOC made its disastrous 2015 decision, it said that it had based its inclusion criteria on 'available information', such as Harper's unhelpful contribution. Hilton raised an eyebrow and set off in search of what research there actually was out there.

She took off on a systematic search of the science leading back to 2003, when the IOC introduced a requirement of genital surgery for anyone aiming to compete in the gender category opposite to their biological sex.

I was one of the speakers at the Woman's Place UK conference in 2019, where Hilton, an unpaid director at science-based campaign group Sex Matters, produced a review of her findings, which you can watch on YouTube in full.[21]

Hilton, who studies aspects of human genetic disease, told the conference that in 2003 the published information available to the IOC was somewhat sparse. It consisted of just five studies on bone density covering around 120 transwomen up to three and a half years after gonadectomy. None detected any significant or enduring difference in bone density compared with reference males.

It looked like that was it, until Hilton spotted that one of the experts present at the IOC's 2003 inclusion meeting later published data in a research paper on muscle changes in transwomen. The time frame of the study, 'Transsexuals and competitive sport', was three years, and there were clear indications in the paper that the data had been presented at the 2003 IOC meeting ahead of publication in 2004.[22]

Louis Gooren had studied changes in muscle area in 19 non-athletic transwomen and shown that, after three years of hormone treatment, muscle area had decreased but remained significantly higher than in the study's control females. It was also noted in the study that the height of athletes remained the same.

Those findings came as no surprise to the human-development biologist because males are stronger than females, males out-compete females in sports, and transwomen do not lose bone mass or magically get shorter and retain significantly larger muscle area compared with females even three years into transition.

Summarising her journey to 2014 in her conference talk, Hilton noted that up to that point 'the body of information available to the IOC comprised four studies showing that transwomen, even five years past transition and their testes long gone, retain more muscle mass and remain much stronger than reference females'.

By the time the IOC removed the need for trans athletes to have genital surgery for eligibility, there had been six more studies of bone density, confirming little to no change in skeletal structure when males transition.

The last one, in 2015, tracked 44 non-athletic (and non-athletic is important, of course, because they are not training to maintain muscle mass) transwomen from pre-transition through two years of hormone treatment. Compared to reference males, transwomen had lower muscle mass and more body fat, and were weaker across measurements of grip strength, bicep strength and quad strength.

But why would you want to compare them to males when they wanted to compete against women? As Hilton put it in her talk: 'The authors of these two studies, and perhaps the IOC, were concerned with how much weaker these transwomen were compared to males. I calculated how they compared to females. Well, they're still stronger, a lot stronger, especially in the upper body.'

Leaving Hilton's trail for a moment, there was also a study that reviewed the medical and fitness records of 29 transmen and 46 transwomen who started gender-affirming hormones while in the United States Air Force between 2004 and 2014. The researchers concluded:

> The 15–31% athletic advantage that transwomen displayed over their female counterparts prior to starting gender affirming hormones declined with feminising therapy. However, transwomen still had a 9% faster mean run speed after the 1 year period of testosterone suppression that is recommended by World Athletics for inclusion in women's events.[23]

By 2019, a further eight studies assessing transwomen's physiology had been published. Two of them tracked the effects of transition in around 100 males before or shortly into puberty, to around 20 years of age. Males as young as 12 were treated with puberty blockers, followed by hormone treatment at 16 years old, with some opting for gonadectomy after reaching 18 years of age. Despite the early intervention, their grip strength 'remained far higher than in age-matched reference females', Hilton noted at the conference.

In all her systematic searching, only 11 papers contained 'any data most relevant to sporting performance', and of those only four contained any direct measurements of performance, only three were 'good science' and only two were available to the IOC in 2015. And both of the papers that Olympic bosses had access to 'demonstrate that transwomen retain far superior muscular architecture and strength that would favour competitive advantage', she said. Neither of those papers, she added, supported 'the premise that transwomen can be fairly included in female sports'.

Hilton noted that Louis Gooren, who first established that transwomen have significantly higher muscle mass than females, told the IOC in 2004: 'Depending on the levels of arbitrariness one wants to accept, it is justifiable that reassigned males compete with other women.'

One would hope that no level of arbitrariness would be acceptable when it comes to eliminating the fundamental distinction that created a male category and a female category to compete fairly in those two distinct categories in sports.

As Hilton said in her speech:

> I go back to this recommendation a lot, and I still can't believe that the first formal attack on female sport was so openly acknowledged as arbitrary. Sex segregation in sports does not exist for arbitrary reasons and it should never have been compromised for arbitrary reasons. The IOC and other sports federations are pursuing a social principle, and female athletes are considered collateral damage. We must continue to fight this.

We did and we will until women's sport is for females only.

For more detail on the studies that show male advantage survives transition, see Appendix 1. All of these studies support the case for ring-fencing the women's category for female athletes only.

THE FIGHT IS ON

The IOC has a responsibility to state clearly that its job as a governing body is to protect female sport as much as it is to protect male sport. It should be saying, 'Here's our Olympic Charter with fair-play provisions – no discrimination against females.'

As they have, in fact, ignored the mountain of scientific evidence that shows that only sex-segregated categorisation does that, they have to be persuaded to change tack. So, in 2019, Paula Radcliffe and I rallied as many World Champions and Olympic medallists from Team GB as we could in a rush. Over just one weekend we got more than 60 names, men and women, to sign a letter calling on the IOC to suspend the transgender guidelines pending further transparent scientific study and analysis.

The letter was sent on 5 September 2019 from Fair Play for Women to Thomas Bach, the IOC president and the executive board (see Appendix 4).

Only my signature appeared on the published letter. The other names were redacted. It is disappointing that more of those names have not spoken out openly. A few have done so over the years, on Twitter and the like. They are all household names who could do so much good, but most stay silent. They didn't want their identities known openly when signing, but their names were visible to the IOC. Fear of repercussions is a common curse in Olympic sport, impact on earning capacity being one of the main reasons.

Athletes, coaches, parents and friends have to contend with trans extremists on social media. The culture of a male-dominated sports governance system built for self-preservation has also faced accusations of ostracising those who are not on board, as my co-author Craig knows to his cost. Leaders of Olympic sports spend money seeking to discredit critics who reveal the truth. Look at the criticism levelled at the *Sunday Times* journalist David Walsh over the Lance

Armstrong affair.[24] But the stories were right all along. The net effect is that a lot of people never put their heads above the parapet.

When I see that happening in women's sport, the very place where I and many other women were denied by unfair play, it instructs me to do the opposite: speak out and encourage others to do so. In early 2019, before we sent our letter to the IOC, Fair Play for Women's Director Dr Nicola Williams, a research scientist specialising in human biology, was accused by McKinnon/Ivy of spreading hatred when she noted on behalf of all of us that claims of transphobia were wild and unfounded.

I agree with Dr Williams. They're just a tool used to shame women into silence. We only want to have a discussion that leads to sports bodies implementing policies that are fair to females. I've lost work for speaking out and I know that current athletes fear loss of sponsorship for simply telling the truth and supporting women's sport. It affects their careers, livelihoods and capacity to pay their mortgages and fund their training.

Invited to take part in a BBC discussion with Williams in early 2019, McKinnon/Ivy refused to participate in a panel that included any woman from Fair Play for Women. The BBC agreed and asked Williams to join the programme after the activist, sparking criticism of the broadcaster.[25] But if there was anyone who ought not to have been given a platform it was the extreme activist who tweeted they wanted to see women die in grease fires.

Meanwhile, 12 days after our letter was sent to the IOC, we received a reply from Dr Richard Budgett, the IOC's medical and scientific director. He said an IOC working group was developing a new framework that balanced fairness, safety and non-discrimination and allowed 'the realities of each sport to be considered'. He claimed they'd spent four years consulting 'affected athletes, lawyers, scientists, medical doctors and human-rights experts' and would broaden that consultation process further.

He was able to say that athletes had been consulted because they had. Just not the right ones. As many athletes on in-house committees at global sports organisations will tell you, such bodies all too often reflect the views of the governors and not those of athletes when it comes to the huge issues.

Canadian Beckie Scott quit the anti-doping athletes' commission at WADA in 2019, saying that she hoped 'voices that challenge or dissent will be heard and taken into consideration, rather than undermined and dismissed'.[26] She said that balance and independence had to be restored to the top tables of governance 'so that all interests and priorities here are aligned with equality of opportunity and fairness, rather than the business of sport'.

Athletes have often told journalists like Craig and his colleagues that they are unaware of who sits on athletes' committees and say they were never consulted. You know there's a serious problem when an athlete like Britain's Olympic swimming champion Adam Peaty, in the middle of a storm of protest over Chinese cheat Sun Yang, can tell the media, as he did in 2019, that he's never met anyone on a global athletes' committee and call on them to engage and provide a 'more streamlined service' that serves athletes.[27]

And that's the experience of a leading man. Go back to those shiny suits for a moment. Craig did a survey of leading women at the time. It involved more than 50 top names. Not a single one of them had been asked by anyone in authority for their opinion about whether they wanted to wear equipment that many found deeply uncomfortable and could take 20 minutes to squeeze into.

Those of us who organised the letter to the IOC in 2019 had a small window in which to have our voices heard. We were invited by Budgett to a conference call. There was me and Nicola Williams of Fair Play for Women from our side. They listened and Budgett said he believed it was up to the whole international sports movement and particularly the international federations to make sure they protected women's sport. And then he went and spoiled it all by saying something stupid like the IOC had spent a hundred years promoting women's sport and that transwomen are women.

In June 2020, Save Women's Sports, our sisters in North America, also sent a letter to Christian Klaue, the IOC's director for corporate communications and public affairs, raising all the same issues. He replied to confirm what Budgett had told us, that there would be no change of policy before the Tokyo Games because to do so would be 'neither fair, nor ethical or legally admissible'.

Linda Blade from Save Women's Sports told Klaue in response that the IOC had signalled to the global sports community that the human rights of everyone except female athletes took precedence in the minds of Olympic leaders.[28]

Klaue was reminded that the IOC's guidelines on trans inclusion contravened the international treaty obligations of the 189 states that had ratified the Convention on the Elimination of Discrimination against Women (CEDAW; see Appendix 2) since its inception in 1979.[29]

THE HUBBARD AFFAIR

The IOC stuck to favouring trans inclusion over female rights, and, at the Tokyo Games in 2021, delayed by Covid, the Olympics got its first transgender athlete, a biological male competing in women's weightlifting for New Zealand.

Gavin Hubbard was a New Zealand men's champion and national record holder in his youth, but his form declined and his career plateaued. Then, at 34, he decided to become Laurel and start hormone-replacement therapy. At 41, after a period of retirement, Laurel Hubbard made the national women's team for the 2019 Pacific Games. What happened next is part of a trail of tears, damage and discrimination suffered by female weightlifters.

Feagaiga Stowers, of Samoa, was 17 when she won the Commonwealth title in 2018. After victory, she shared her story of a traumatic upbringing with the *Samoa Observer*.[30]

An abuse survivor, she was afraid of the outside world and thought 'everyone was just as evil as the people who hurt me'. She was cared for by the Samoa Victim Support Group (SVSG) in 2013 and the only person she felt she could trust was 'Mama Lina', the SVSG president Siliniu Lina Chang. Stowers was one of the female survivors of violence who took up weightlifting as part of their rehabilitation programme in 2015 through a partnership with the Samoa Weightlifting Federation.

Through weightlifting, she found a way to release her anger and her sense of hopelessness, and hoped her journey would inspire other survivors to seek help and find ways to build a new life. She set her heart on the Olympic Games in Tokyo.

Selection would be guaranteed by victory at the Pacific Games in 2019, and Stowers arrived a title favourite, but Hubbard took gold for New Zealand. The Olympics had its first openly transgender woman and the Samoan champion was out. Stowers bowed her head on the podium and accepted her loss gracefully. Her dreams had been shattered.

Samoa Observer journalist Mata'afa Keni Lesa eloquently summed up the problem on 15 July 2019.

> We are talking about sports here. One of the values of sport is fairness. We cannot say that allowing a transgender to compete against women is fair. It is grossly unfair for women like Stowers, or all women, for that matter… It will be a tragedy of gigantic proportion for sport when this… is allowed. We talk a lot about empowering women, this does not empower women. If anything, it is taking power away from them. It is robbing them of what rightfully belongs to them.[31]

Like generations of women denied by steroid-fuelled opponents in the 1970s and 80s, Stowers had been let down. Sports bosses looked the other way back then and have done so ever since. Now the nightmare is happening to female athletes all over again. The parallels with the past are unavoidable.

THE STATE OF THE IOC AND OLYMPIC SPORTS GOVERNANCE

In truth, the apparent indifference of the IOC to women's sport shouldn't surprise anyone. It links to the wider IOC culture, which is characterised by a complete lack of openness and accountability, a general indifference to athletes' interests, and a pervasive 'boys' club' mentality that hasn't changed much since the days of Coubertin.

The opening ceremony at the Sydney Olympics in 2000 suggested that the wind was changing. Australian Olympic great Herb Elliott handed the Olympic torch to Raelene Boyle and then a great relay of other legendary female athletes from the host country: Betty Cuthbert, Dawn Fraser, Shirley Strickland and Shane Gould passed the torch in turn before Cathy Freeman lit the cauldron.

Under the lights of a glorious night at the opening ceremony, things finally seemed to be heading in a better direction. Our calls for truth in the case of the GDR fraud had been rejected, but could it just be that the blokes in blazers might finally be willing to do justice to women?

No. The IOC members were all men. Not a woman in sight, apart from those invited to join the wives' tour of highlights down under while their husbands got on with Olympic business and politics. As one man put it just weeks before the Games in 2000, the highest achievement of a woman is to be a good corporate wife.

In the years running up to Sydney, investigative journalist Andrew Jennings exposed the IOC and its culture in a series of books.[32] He depicted a secretive and elite domain where self-serving decisions are taken behind closed doors. There's no athlete voice at the table and money is blown on five-star lifestyles for leaders and spin doctors. Some of it is siphoned off to offshore bank accounts, far from the reach of athletes.

Olympic bosses had one last chance to redeem themselves with women. They blew it. As Jennings reported, the IOC created five new positions on the ruling committee for 'honour members'.[33] Again, all were men, including Henry Kissinger, the American diplomat, Gianni Agnelli, the former head of the Fiat motor company whose winter sports facilities near Turin made a mint from the Winter Games of 2006, and Yoshiaki Tsutsumi, the Japanese billionaire whose hotel chain and ski runs around Nagano profited when taxpayers were forced to contribute hundreds of millions of dollars to build a bullet train and expressway from Tokyo to the Winter Olympics of 1998.[34]

The other two picks were men, too, but did you spot the conflict-of-interest questions raised by Jennings? They are just a few of many such connections in the Olympic realm, with members of boards in a wide range of sports connected to businesses that make millions from contracts with Olympic sport.

If such things should be open to greater scrutiny and questions about possible conflicts of interest, then the trains of Tokyo in 1998 remind us of more recent events connected to Olympic business in the same city. In February 2023, prosecutors arrested a former operations executive with the Tokyo 2020 organising committee and three others over bid-rigging allegations.[35]

As we noted in Chapter 1, Olympic sports bosses, bizarrely, describe themselves as 'volunteers'. What could they mean? In 2015, the Associated Press reported: 'IOC presidents and members are considered volunteers and do not receive a salary, but their travel, housing costs and other expenses on Olympic duty are covered.'[36]

The focus of its reports was this gem: 'In what it described as a vital show of financial transparency, the International Olympic Committee on Thursday disclosed how much its members receive in allowances and per diem payments – including an annual 225,000 euro ($242,000) sum for President Thomas Bach.'

The IOC's media statement noted that executive board members and commission chairs would receive $900 daily on Olympic business, 'including the day before and after meetings to cover travel days', regular IOC members would receive $450 a day 'at meetings and at the Olympics', and members could also receive an annual sum of $7,000 for 'administrative support'.[37]

Such volunteers exist in all Olympic sports federations and they can receive between $150 and $750 per day, depending on rank, from lowly committee to top table, when on federation business. The standard definition of a per diem is an allowance paid to employees for lodgings, meals and incidental expenses incurred when travelling. I know this from personal experience. We get them when travelling and working for the BBC. But they are always the bare minimum needed to cover a basic meal, with no alcohol. Fair enough – we're there to do a job, not have a party. But in Olympic sport the volunteers have no expenses. Their four- or five-star hotel is covered, and their flights, including for the upper-echelon folk in first and business class, are already paid for. All their food is on the table each day without a bill, and there are gifts and goodies on top. Useful incentives, perhaps, when a vote comes round.

Craig describes the hoard of presents showered on members of the FINA Media Committee when he attended a meeting just over a decade ago: a tailored suit, for which they'd even asked for measurements in advance, for the annual photo, a pair of brogues, a FINA blazer, two pairs of sports trousers, two polo shirts, one baseball cap, a sports bag, a watch, a tie, two notebooks and a pen.

What for? Nothing, says Craig: 'I was just there to advise them on the working environment and information journalists need to do their jobs at major championships. We helped them write an update to the media provisions that ended up in contracts for event hosts.'

Still, the maid must have been very happy when he left. Craig kept the cap and a shirt and left the rest behind. On a more serious note, all of that stuff was in the gift pack of every committee member, more than 400 in all. At one meeting of the 'executive volunteers' every member of the ruling bureau got a laptop.

Craig tells me that the per diems to committee members were paid in cash for many years. Since it wasn't officially registered as a return of costs against receipts, I wonder how many declared the income on their tax returns? Some of the gifts made it home in the form of luxury items bought for partners and children and stored away in luggage. All of it should be absolutely 100 per cent transparent, of course, but it hasn't been that way.

THE SORROWFUL SOUND OF SILENCE

Transparency has not been an Olympic strength. *Omertà*, the code of silence operated by the Mafia, can be found far and wide in Olympic sports, the work of Jennings and other investigative journalists suggests.

And where silence is encouraged, bad things happen. Take the USA Gymnastics (USAG) scandal. How could it be that for 18 years, Larry Nassar, the team doctor of the US women's national gymnastics team, managed to exploit, deceive and sexually assault hundreds of children and young women?[38]

He repeatedly sexually assaulted at least 265 female athletes under the guise of medical treatment. Some of the abuse took place while the mothers of athletes were in the room, so potent and poisonous was the control that Nassar and those running gymnastics had over the athletes. The depth of depravity in gymnastics is captured in the deeply disturbing and award-winning documentary *Athlete A* (2020).[39]

Nassar's various sentences of up to 125 years were put together in one pot. He's gone to jail for life, without parole. Great that they caught him. But what about the guardians of sport who took their eye off the ball? What about the children who suffer from their incompetence?

In January 2018, the *New York Times* looked at the fallout from the Nassar case and trawled through a range of authorities that could have raised a red flag but didn't.[40] Earlier the same month, USAG announced that its entire board had stepped down, including its chairman, Paul Parilla, vice chairman, Jay Binder, and treasurer, Bitsy Kelley.[41]

The head of the United States Olympic Committee (USOC), Scott Blackmun, had threatened to decertify USAG if its entire board did not resign, but he also faced heavy criticism, given that the boss of Olympic sports in America ought to have known more about what was happening on his watch. In 2019, when he stepped down citing ill health, Blackmun received $2.4 million in severance pay.[42]

In his paper 'Sports ethics beyond the rules', Dr Ram Gopal states: 'The health, safety and well-being of children and young athletes are the number one priority. Children must not be treated as young adults and all those concerned must be fully aware of the physical and psychological changes that accompany their development and how these influence sporting performance.'[43]

Despite this, it was not until 2021, three years after Nassar's conviction, that the IOC launched its 'Safeguarding Officer in Sport' certificate with specific guidance and instruction on safeguarding policies for children. The many references in the rule book to 'all athletes' when it comes to safeguarding and welfare miss two key factors in abuse: an adult may give consent to sex whereas a child cannot do so, under any circumstances, under the law in most countries; and Olympic sport is populated by a vast number of children.

It is a major shortcoming that the IOC does not have specific and obligatory 'child protection in sports' rules that all sports federations must recognise. More often than not, it's female child athletes who suffer the most.

In March 2022, more than 500 Canadian gymnasts spoke out about the toxic and abusive culture they said they had endured.[44] The survivors of what are alleged to have been cases of rape, sexual assault and other crimes called on the Canadian government to initiate an independent judicial investigation into rampant child abuse. To date, those calls have been ignored. Similar calls have come from athletes involved in winter sports, who have made allegations of misogyny and institutional bullying.

USA Swimming's list of the permanently banned or ineligible for membership runs to more than 340 people, the vast majority men registered for sexual offences against minors.[45]

Abuse survivors allege that the list is incomplete. Among those who still face allegations is coach Paul Bergen, accused of sexual abuse of minors by the women he trained in his programmes as teenagers. The abuse was first reported to police authorities in the 1970s. It came up again during meetings of USA Swimming's Abuses Committee in 1991 but never resulted in an inquiry or any action.[46]

Allegations of abuse by Bergen have been widely reported since Olympic gold medallist Deena Deardurff-Schmidt made a damning statement in 2010 confirming what she had told others in the sport on many occasions down the years.[47] The 1991 Abuses Committee noted her case and made a long list of 'Safe Sport' recommendations. It was 2010 before USA Swimming adopted some of them as part of its own new 'Safe Sport' measures.[48]

Deena's case is an example of how women were treated by police and legal authorities back in the 1970s, when it was not uncommon for those reporting sexual abuse effectively to be told to go home and deal with it so it wouldn't be embarrassing for your family – which is what they said to Deena. Bergen's only comment down the years was in answer to a question from the Associated Press. He simply said: 'It's a misunderstanding.'

No sports or legal authority has found a way of dealing with it, and, because of that, Deena, an Olympic gold medallist for the United States in 1972, has never been inducted into the International Swimming Hall of Fame (ISHOF). However, Bergen is an 'honor coach'.[49] It's time he wasn't, in my opinion, and that ISHOF recognised Deena for the Olympic and World Championship medals she won and global standards she set in the pool for the United States very much against the odds.

Deena has never given up the fight. She was among those who successfully campaigned for the adoption of a game-changing athlete-empowerment Act in the United States. The campaigners called themselves 'Team Integrity' and included advocates such as 1984 Olympic 100 metres freestyle champion Nancy Hogshead-Makar, coach advocates for Safe Sport such as Dia C. Rianda, and victims of abuse, including the US gymnasts who helped jail Larry Nasser, as well as a who's who of Olympians from around the world.[50]

In October 2020, the US House of Representatives matched the Senate's unanimous vote in passing transformative Olympic reform legislation – the Empowering Olympic, Paralympic, and Amateur Athlete Act (S2330).[51] It was a landmark moment that may one day burst the bubble of the IOC's self-proclaimed autonomy.

In the past, the IOC has suspended nations if it perceived political interference in matters such as selection (or deselection) of NOC officials. The S2330 legislation makes that IOC approach illegal in the United States. Will the IOC ban the United States if one day the American government were once again to find fault, as it did in recent years, with the leadership of the United States Olympic and Paralympic Committee (USOPC)? It seems unlikely, to put it mildly. On 7 May 2014, the IOC awarded NBCUniversal the US media rights for the Olympic Games through to 2032 for $7.65 billion.[52]

The bill gives athletes far more rights, while holding the NOC to a higher standard of care. It would be great to see similar bills passed in countries around the world, sending a message to the IOC that where they fail athletes, others will protect them.

Nancy sums it up well: 'The Olympics are a unique treasure for us. Striving for excellence, to be the best-of-the-best, reflects our American identity... Our quest remains: to fix a broken sport governance system on behalf of those most vulnerable in the Olympic Movement, and those most impacted by the Sports Act.'[53]

Without reform to fix this entire culture, it's difficult to see the injustices meted out to women within the context of the trans debate ever coming to the surface.

9

THE SWIMMER WHO PROVED THE SCIENCE

We shouldn't have to wait decades for the IOC to get it right or until unfair play reaches the Olympic Games before we cry foul and stop it in its tracks. Yet that's what it feels like we're fighting against. Thankfully, some examples of what happens when males get a ticket to female sport make the issues so obvious, the discrimination so clear, that they can't be ignored. That hasn't stopped many federations sticking to the wrong road, but every time a case such as that of Lia Thomas comes along, it makes the flawed arguments of regulators ever weaker.

THE LIA THOMAS CASE

In 2022 Lia Thomas became the first trans swimmer to win an NCAA title, in the 500 yards freestyle, ahead of three female Olympic silver medallists in the United States. In men's racing, neither biological male Lia Thomas nor pre-transition Will Thomas would have stood a chance of qualifying to race at the NCAA championships, let alone make a final or win a medal.

Will Thomas raced for the University of Pennsylvania's men's team for three seasons before transitioning in 2021 and becoming Lia. Will was never a champion in the relatively tame waters of Ivy

League Championships, while Penn – as the university is known – has just one NCAA champion in the long history of men's racing: Chris Swanson, in the 1,650 yards freestyle in 2016.

As Will or Lia, the Penn swimmer's best 100 yards freestyle times are 47 seconds. That's inside the top-tier qualification time for NCAA Division 1 for women by more than three seconds, a relative ocean over 100 yards freestyle. But 47 seconds was a massive five seconds shy of the qualification target in the men's race in 2021–22. Will's best pace pre-transition wasn't good enough to rank him in the best 10,000 performances over 100, 200 and 400 metres (assuming a generous conversion from swims in yard pools). He was a good club and non-elite college swimmer, but very far from the world of Michael Phelps and others who make the world's top men's swimming team in international competition.

But where Will would not have even made the championships, Lia beat three female Olympic medallists from the world's no. 1 swim nation.

It's even more egregious when you consider that Will was a distance swimmer while Lia has won top college races in sprint events. Male physical advantages make their greatest impact in power events. Even in competitions that Will didn't take part in, Lia can defeat women. Will was a 1,650 yards specialist, chosen by his Ivy League coaches for distance freestyle because that was where his natural abilities were at their best. Lia winning college sprint events felt as strange to me as it would be to watch a male Olympic 10,000 metres champion transition and then win the women's Olympic 100 metres sprint title.

In short, we all know that Lia Thomas won the 500 yards title at the women's NCAA championships in 2022 not because of the swimmer's athletic ability but because of the male advantages that the transitioned Will brought to the female race. By late 2021, Will was gone and Lia was racing for the Penn women's team. The season

began with Thomas claiming three victories as the first trans swimmer to do so at the Zippy Invitational in Akron, Ohio, in December,
breaking two women's meet records with efforts that suggested an
athlete capable of rattling the best women swimmers in the country,
and therefore the world (this is the world's top swimming nation,
remember).[1]

A swimmer we'd never heard of before was suddenly in headlines
around the world and the backlash was keen. In an interview on
trans inclusion in sport, boxer Mike Tyson, when told that Thomas
had a penis, said: 'Well, you got the penis, you can't play, baby.'[2]
Michael Phelps left it at: 'I believe that we all should feel comfortable with who we are in our own skin, but I think sports should all
be played on an even playing field.'[3]

An official for USA Swimming for three decades, Cynthia
Millen, quit in protest, saying: 'Bodies swim against bodies. Gender
identities don't swim.' She added: 'And nothing that Lia did by
taking a year off to take testosterone suppression drugs – that does
not change Lia's body. This is grossly unfair. I can't support this.'[4]

Save Women's Sports had an army of protesters outside and even
inside college competition venues. Both qualification events and the
NCAA finals were marked by angry clashes between campaigners
for fair play in women's sport and trans activists denying science and
demanding access to female sport for biological males.

Thomas was booed before and after several races as feelings ran
high among athletes, families, fans and protesters on both sides.
Female athletes were told to keep quiet or face consequences,
stretching to losing their places at college for expressing concerns
at having to see male genitalia in their changing rooms.[5] The threats
came from the very guardians of women's college sport, the NCAA
and other college authorities.

On 1 February 2022, a letter was sent to police and legal authorities in Philadelphia reporting a potential and alleged violation of

the laws on indecent exposure by Thomas in the women's changing rooms at Penn.[6] Lia is a 6' 4" transwoman who, swimmers reported, was still sexually attracted to females: it's hardly surprising that there was discomfort.[7]

Campaign group Women's Declaration International (WDI; see Appendix 2) drew up their letter after female athletes at Penn told journalists they had expressed concern about being exposed to Thomas's male genitalia in the women's changing room but had been told by college authorities to 'accept this harassment and indecent exposure'.[8]

Nothing came of it in law, but the female athletes got their message out without college authorities being able to identify them or punish them. Citing media reports and the Pennsylvania Code of Law, WDI USA president Kara Dansky and US director of the campaign group Keep Prisons Single Sex (KPSS) Amanda Stulman claimed in their letter that women swimmers had been forced into silence under threat of penalties that extended to being 'kicked off the team'.[9]

THE YARDSTICK OF A CRISIS

In swimming performance terms, the situation became impossible to ignore on 19 February 2022, when Thomas crushed female opponents over the last 50 yards of a 200 yards freestyle race. Some sports media suggested that Thomas had been 'holding back'.[10] It wasn't hard to see why. We won't dive too deeply into the nerdy world of swimming splits, but look at the following two lines showing the times (in seconds) of each 50 yards of the race and the overall result (in minutes and seconds):

- 25.12; 27.02; 25.94; 25.04 – 1:43.12, Lia Thomas, Penn, gold
- 24.94; 27.25; 26.70; 26.93 – 1:45.82, Samantha Shelton, Harvard, silver

Thomas was playing with Shelton over the first 100 yards, it seems, and I can't recall a single time in the history of 200 yards (or metres) racing at elite level where a swimmer raced faster over the last 50 than they did over the first, with the advantage of a dive! It's unprecedented. A negative split is where the second half of a race is faster than the first. That's not what you'd expect to see in any sprint race. It looked like the controlled and tactical pace of aquatic alpha-maleness in the female pool.

Both Lia Thomas and coach Mike Schnur at Penn know swimming well but were happy to say that Lia had broken no NCAA rules and had a right to be there. Lia dismissed the suggestion that being male explained the success.[11]

USA Swimming, the American regulator, understood what it was looking at too, and, before the NCAA finals, it rushed through new rules that would have excluded Lia Thomas from the finals on a number of grounds.[12] College authorities opted to ignore the national rules.

Despite the protests and the controversy surrounding the athlete, Lia Thomas appeared to be thriving on more publicity than that of any woman on any swim team that NCAA season. A feature headlined '"I am Lia": the trans swimmer dividing America tells her story' was the Sports Illustrated 'Daily Cover' story online on 3 March.[13]

It was a huge piece, and on the eve of the NCAA finals a petition was launched with almost 6,000 signatures, among them 3,000 athletes and 300 members of USA Olympic, Paralympic and National Teams, calling for authorities to acknowledge that sex matters in sport.[14] I signed the petition, as did a who's who of swimmers and coaches from the United States and around the world.

Organised by the Women's Sports Policy Working Group and the Champion Women advocacy group founded by Nancy Hogshead-Makar (see Appendix 2), the petition argued that 'we should not be teaching our daughters to be gracious losers to athletes with unfair, insurmountable, biological advantage in their competitive sports'.[15]

Three days later, Lia Thomas claimed the 500 yards NCAA crown by beating Olympic silver medallists from the United States women's swimming team in Tokyo. Olympic 400 metres medley medal winner Emma Weyant took silver, Erica Sullivan bronze, and Brooke Forde was left off the podium in fourth.

Will Thomas had not been good enough to get to race at a national championships in an Olympic 50-metre pool and so we have to convert his and Lia's best yards times. Erring on the side of caution by opting for the slower end of likely conversion times from a 25-yard pool to an Olympic pool, Thomas would not have made the best 10,000 performances in the world over 400 metres freestyle among men in 2019–20, but among women the swimmer's status changed dramatically. Lia Thomas was right to think of a place on the USA Olympic team for Paris 2024 alongside Katie Ledecky.[16]

It was all so uncomfortable to watch. One photo of the start has become iconic in swimming: it shows Thomas diving high above the females in the other lanes on a trajectory you'd expect to see among men. It highlights the stark difference in power between athletes of opposite sexes diving off their blocks. The race also highlighted that victory relied on strength, not technique, which was poor.

The podium looked uncomfortable as 6' 4" Thomas towered above the rest. The protests and the TV coverage of male advantage in female sport reached well beyond the pool. A Republican senator for Alabama, Tommy Tuberville, a former sports coach, took the matter up on the floor of the US Senate and referred to the '*real* March Madness' (the name for NCAA finals season at the same time every year).[17]

We'd witnessed women being beaten to a prestigious national title by a biological male in one of the big three Olympic sports, swimming, which is in the top tier of IOC funding alongside athletics and gymnastics. Bigotry, cried trans activists, but they had no answers to key questions, such as whether the Lia Thomas case could be cited as one that showed mitigation of male advantage.

The truth was all too clear: the opposite had been proven. Female swimmers had been cheated out of rightful rewards by an average male athlete, something that did not escape the notice of international regulators, who had already called together a task force of experts to come up with recommendations on models of inclusion, as we'll see in Chapter 13.

The facts were undeniable. Lia raced women while having greater height, bigger hands, bigger feet, larger and longer limbs, a breast-free angle of buoyancy, a male Q-angle-powered leg kick, larger lungs and a larger heart, to name just a few irreversible male advantages Will had developed with the levels of testosterone nature grants males but not females.

Some people say that it's not Lia's fault as she was just following the rules. I don't see it that way. In my opinion, Lia carries more guilt on that score than the abused ranks of East Germans. Most of them had no information and no choice in the matter, but Lia grew up swimming in the West, fully informed and fully aware.

The fact is that Will Thomas was more average in swimming than my much-loved co-author, Craig, a national finalist and county champion in Scotland and England in his day. He takes pride in having his name on the Grampian 200 metres butterfly trophy next to that of Ian Black, a triple European champion for Britain and Commonwealth champion for Scotland before Craig and I were born.

In some races – not all – Craig was faster than me. When recalling that, he gives away his feelings about it and his status as a world-class expert in my sport: 'Faster – but not better,' he says. Thank you, Craig.

That's because he and every other man I've ever swum alongside in training and in competition warm-up, every person who appreciates and understands why many sports are divided by biological sex, would find it embarrassing to even suggest that competitive comparison between female and male athletes is valid.

CYCLING IN A SPIN

Cycling is a sport seemingly cursed by a lack of decent, robust governance and at war with stakeholders in several countries with strong cycling traditions.

After watching the toxicity of events at the National Cyclocross Championships in Hartford, Connecticut, in December 2022, Mara Yamauchi, former elite marathon runner (on a sizzling 2.23:12), two-time Olympian, coach, commentator and warrior for women, took to Twitter to say: 'At what point do all these male-inclusion rules just boil down to allowing what [would] otherwise be crimes? Collisions in sports – assaults. Naked males in women's changing rooms – indecent exposure & voyeurism.'[18]

In 2022, the American cycling scene looked like a dark comedy that included:

- Male on female physical violence in races that went unpunished
- An online 'Transphobe/TERF Tracker' used to keep a head count of leading names who oppose male advantage in female sport[19]
- Women who object to biological males in female races being reported for 'abuse' to the US Center for SafeSport, the outfit largely needed because women have long been the key target of sexual abuse, violence and discrimination
- Gun club members in a country with a firearms crisis showing up in black balaclavas and shades to hide their identities to provide 'support' for trans athletes coached by a member of a national cycling organisation.[20]

Cycling has a sorry history when it comes to equality for women. It was 1984 when women got to compete in cycling for the first time at the Olympics, 88 years after men cycled as pioneers at the inaugural Games in Athens.

The Tour de France remains a man's world despite the progress women have fought for. A token female race was held in 1955, and then women were allowed a limited race for the first time in conjunction with men in 1984. By 2013, outraged by the lack of further progress, former pro cyclist and filmmaker Kathryn Bertine joined forces with cyclists Emma Pooley, Marianne Vos and Chrissie Wellington to launch Le Tour Entier (the Whole Tour).

A petition they submitted to Tour de France director Christian Prudhomme was signed by 98,000 people and noted: 'While many women's sports face battles of inequity, road cycling remains one of the worst offenders: fewer race opportunities, no televised coverage, shorter distances, and therefore salary and prize money inequity.'[21]

Bertine, whose film *Half the Road* (2014) tells the story of gender inequity in professional cycling, told the media at the time of the cycling petition in 2013 that some athletes who were supportive were concerned about retaliation if they spoke out publicly. 'Many were afraid to rock the boat because they were nervous that their own contracts with their teams could be (in jeopardy),' she told NBC. 'A number of women reached out to us and said, "I'm behind you 100% but I have to remain quiet because I'm worried about my job."'[22]

Tour de France organiser the Amaury Sport Organisation (ASO) eventually created 'La Course by Le Tour de France', a one- or two-day women's race that was held annually between 2014 and 2021. Women are supposed to be thankful for small mercies from men, but, as pro cyclist Lizzie Deignan put it: 'I think being grateful is one of the worst things we could be. That's the trap that a lot of women fall into... you have to sometimes be brave and be bold and be outspoken. It's not always comfortable.'[23]

Currently, the Tour has eight stages for women, 21 for men, which means women have gone backwards, because back in 1984 women raced 18 stages to the men's 23.

Now there's a new adversary and a barrier to overcome.

The 'Transphobe/TERF Tracker' started out by compiling 161 entries from cycling alone. We've no idea who's behind it, because although they're happy to name and shame the people they list as 'transphobes' and, hilariously, 'suspected transphobes', they'd rather you didn't know who they were in case they get named and shamed themselves.

High-achieving cyclists like the UK's Nicole Cooke and Katie Archibald and marathon runner Mara Yamauchi are named as transphobes by the tracker. It wouldn't be a surprise to find cyclists Inga Thompson, US multiple national champion, world medallist and Olympian, and Alison Sydor, Olympic medallist and multiple world champion from Canada, there too. We can't tell, because some entries on the tracker are 'redacted', identified only as 'Olympic cyclist'; other 'positions' listed include 'government official' and 'US Olympic Committee'. The guilty include sponsors, officials from sport and government, coaches, journalists, shop owners, sports directors and managers, teachers, parents, bike mechanics and bicycle reps.

The 'behaviour' column is largely empty.

The 'Transphobe/TERF Tracker' names Orion Coaching, run by Nate Llerandi, former college swimmer turned triathlete who is now a Masters cyclist and coach. He rejected the transphobic slur as a patently false accusation. He took to Twitter to liken the tracker and its activists to the Salem witch trials, with those backing biological women's claim on the women's sex-based category as witches and trans activists as the accusers with absolute power.[24]

That's precisely how it feels. Accusations are flung by bullies, and regulators afraid of appearing unsympathetic jump on the #BeKind bandwagon with the sword of cancel culture hovering over their decision-making heads. Narcissists get what they want at great cost to a common-sense majority, who are told their views count for less than those of a so-called oppressed minority.

Nate is one of many who feel a need to take to social media to push back the lies and assault on established practices in sport, including the need for categories designed to mitigate unfair play.

Inga Thompson is also among those who refuse to bow down to the bullying of female athletes. For that, she's one of dozens of women who have been reported to the US Center for SafeSport, the authority established because women face horrendous abuse in sport.[25] It's truly sickening that female athletes are being reported to an organisation established to protect them from abuse because sports authorities largely run by men are advocating policies that create more opportunities for biological males and fewer for biological females.

The US Center for SafeSport was set up in 2017 to ensure that there could never be a repeat of the Larry Nassar scandal in gymnastics that included allegations that female athletes reported abuse to officials who covered up the abuse.[26] In its first survey, SafeSport asked nearly 4,000 athletes in more than 50 sports about their experience. Results released in July 2021 found that an astonishing 93 per cent of respondents, largely females, had suffered sexual harassment or unwanted contact during their careers but did not report it.[27]

That's largely because they had no confidence in a sports system that has consistently failed women. Movements like #MeToo and the courage of high-profile athlete sex-assault survivors have contributed to a better picture. While 300 abuse reports were received in 2017 in the United States, the number rose to nearly 3,000 in 2020, the year the Empowering Olympic, Paralympic, and Amateur Athlete Act was passed by the US Congress.

Inga was one of more than 30 people reported to SafeSport by a group of campaigning activists in 2022 on grounds that she wanted women's sport preserved for females. Such reports are likely to meet a tall barrier called the First Amendment, but filing false claims of abuse is unacceptable, a bullying tactic that should be stopped dead in its tracks.[28]

Inga told me that trans campaigners even claimed to have influence inside federations to effect changes to inclusion policy, one of the activists having let it be known that she had a lengthy list of 'shitty and transphobic coaches'.

Perhaps that came from one of those responsible for the tracker, but it doesn't matter who it is: the fact is that it appears that lobbying to smear women is going on behind the scenes, away from proper scrutiny and accountability.

GUN CLUB OF MASKED TRANS SUPPORTERS IN THE SADDLE

When the women's racing came to a close at the National Cyclocross Championships in Hartford, Connecticut in December 2022, retired Canadian Olympic medallist and multiple world champion Alison Sydor told us that transwomen accounted for 6 per cent of all entries and had 40 per cent of all top-five places in women's racing, while over on the men's side there were zero transmen entries and therefore zero top-five places.

USA Cycling claimed that an inclusion policy that allows biological males into female races is designed to maintain fairness and equal opportunities. The reality, however, is that wherever you look there are transwomen winning races and finishing in the prizes. There are far, far fewer transmen, and you'd be hard-pressed to find a single one who's finished in the top five among men, let alone won races.

In Hartford they even awarded a bronze medal to a transwoman who was filmed trying to shove a female rider off her bike. Austin

Killips, a biologically male rider, was caught on camera trying, it appears, to push Hannah Arensman to the ground. Observer Tom Pearman, the father of a female rider, exposed the film on Twitter and said that it represented one of three similar moves to block Arensman.[29] Even though the actions seemed very obvious, the race ended with Killips taking bronze just 0.02 of a second ahead of Arensman, and was won by defending champion Clara Honsinger ahead of Raylyn Nuss. USA Cycling launched an inquiry only after the film was drawn to its attention, but by then the medals ceremony had taken place: Killips had celebrated alongside two female athletes, while a third was locked out of the prizes and the opportunities that flow from podium places in sport. Killips described accusations that Arensman was shoved as 'ridiculous', but, shortly after the event, Arensman retired, saying that there was no point in competing if males were allowed to be in female races.[30] If that carries on, more and more women will quit sport because there's no point in entering unfair competition.

The IOC talks about the need for the human rights of transgender athletes to be upheld in keeping with international standards, but they say nothing when international standards explicitly invoke sex-based rights, such as in the UN Convention on the Elimination of Discrimination against Women (CEDAW), which disallows

> any distinction, exclusion or restriction made on the basis of sex which has the effect or purpose of impairing or nullifying the recognition, enjoyment or exercise by women, irrespective of their marital status, on a basis of equality of men and women, of human rights and fundamental freedoms in the political, economic, social, cultural, civil or any other field.[31]

How do such rights fit in with masked members of a self-proclaimed gun club being asked to attend a national championship organised by USA Cycling to provide 'support' for transgender athletes? You'd imagine the IOC might ask USOPC to reassure the Olympic Movement that no 'gun clubs', with or without weapons and masks, will be invited to line up outside Olympic venues when Los Angeles hosts the 2028 Olympic Games.

Social media exploded when images of masked gun-club members in shades and carrying rainbow flags and anti-female slogans at championships in Hartford began to appear. Inga took screenshots of a series of tweets that appeared to show that USA Cycling official Adam Myerson had had contact with the gun club member and even thanked them for being there. Inga called out Myerson, a member of USA Cycling's cyclocross committee, who denied it but also acknowledged that he had spoken to the gun club and welcomed their presence. Call me old-fashioned, but the only kind of gun club I'd want at a sports event are the athletes showing up for a shooting event.[32]

NO BUILDING BRIDGES WHEN FEMALE RIDERS ARE FORCED TO RACE MALES

Female riders in Britain have also had an uphill battle against the decisions of their national federation, British Cycling.

In October 2020, British Cycling issued a new transgender and non-binary participation policy. It was business as usual for men; women, move over and make way for biological males who don't feel like men. Philippa York, who publicly announced transition from the professional male cyclist Robert Millar in 2017, was among those consulted. York praised British Cycling in its statement because it 'has been setting the benchmarks for performance in sport and now they are doing the same for inclusion by having a policy which is easily understood'.[33]

We understood instantly: it was brazen discrimination against female cyclists. After all, it was issued with a clear threat to women.

British Cycling's policy stated that members should 'accept all participants in the gender they present' and that anyone breaching the guidelines, including by demonstrating 'stigmatisation or discrimination' against a competitor, will face 'appropriate action'.

It's British Cycling's job to look after female well-being just as much as male well-being. The very least they could have done was listen and work with females and the actual science, which they must have understood, given that the study of how male and female bodies work is part of the preparation of world-class cyclists.

If their policy wasn't bad enough, hearing that York had anything official to say in cycling, let alone playing any role in formulating policy, churns the stomach. In York's past, Millar tested positive for testosterone.[34] A cheat, he was caught and punished with a three-month suspension for taking a substance that can land an athlete a four-year ban in the World Anti-Doping Code produced by WADA these days.

York's story also reminds us of the wholly inappropriate use of pronouns in attempts to rewrite sports history. On Wikipedia, we read: 'Philippa York... initially began riding for Glenmarnock Wheelers cycling club and quickly established herself as a leading amateur road racing rider'; 'she was a relatively small man'; 'she moved to France in 1979'; and: 'As Millar, she married a French woman.'[35]

Ludicrous. Robert Millar was the boy who began riding for Glenmarnock Wheelers and moved to France in 1979, and he was Mr Millar, a man, when he married a Frenchwoman. None of Millar's big professional cycle-tour results, or the doping ban he served after a positive test during the Spanish Vuelta race, belong to anyone but a man called Robert Millar, who in 2017 declared himself a transwoman called Philippa York on the cusp of turning 60 years of age.

Whatever choices anyone makes, you cannot change the past and an entire sports career belonging to a man. Such fibs feed into the falsehoods shaping the kind of sports policies that have put fair play for female athletes on life support.

Meantime, federations seem to find it very hard to consult females on matters that directly affect them, but whoever they consult they should never ever take advice from a caught cheat.

British Cycling did not have to wait long to see the consequences of its misguided policy. The arrival of Emily Bridges in 2022 prompted Ross Tucker to say that federations were placing a bet that they would not have a good enough male come along to show the 'fairness and inclusion compromise' up as a false promise. Now we could see what happens when that good-enough male did come along.

In youth, Bridges, when Zach, set the British junior 25-mile (40.2-kilometre) record in just over 47 minutes (the women's record is two minutes slower), and was still racing as a man while on hormone-reduction therapy as part of transition when he claimed gold in the points race and bronze in the team pursuit at the British University Championships in Glasgow in February 2022, racing for the University of Birmingham.[36] Bridges and male teammates were ten seconds faster than the British quartet of Katie Archibald, Dame Laura Kenny, Neah Evans and Josie Knight when they took silver behind Germany at the Tokyo Games in 2020.

Just weeks after the university competition, in April, Bridges was preparing to take on Dame Laura, the five-time Olympic champion, at the National Omnium Championships in Derby, racing among females for the first time. Global regulator the Union Cycliste Internationale (UCI) stepped in to call a halt and tell British Cycling that Bridges had not met its international eligibility conditions.[37] Dame Laura backed a statement from teammate and two-time Olympic champion Katie Archibald setting out her objections to the presence of Bridges and any other biological males in female racing.[38] British Cycling's head of Olympic programmes, Sara Symington, agreed and signed a letter to the UCI calling on it to guarantee fairness for female athletes by ring-fencing the women's category.[39]

In a further blow to Bridges's plans, a June decision from the UCI halved the upper limit for testosterone for transwomen to 2.5 nanomoles, meaning that Bridges was out of women's racing – for the time being at least.[40]

In late November 2022, Bridges appeared in an ITV Wales documentary about transgender athletes.[41] The tone was clearly meant to garner sympathy for Bridges. It is telling that there has not been one single documentary covering the plight of female athletes being forced to give up their dreams in their own category of sport.

ROWING INTO CHOPPY WATERS

In October 2022, British Rowing chair Mark Davies urged World Rowing to update its inclusion policy. His message was clear: follow FINA's decision four months earlier and preserve the women's category for female rowers only.

World Rowing's policy allowed transgender women to enter female competition if they kept their testosterone below a level at least five times above what I had as an athlete in the middle of the standard female range. Davies told the World Rowing Congress in Prague:

> World Rowing is less protective of women's sport than some other international sports federations like FINA, which has adopted a policy of having open and women's categories, where open is for anyone who went through male puberty – recognising limiting testosterone levels fails to counteract the lasting impact of that. Might rowing look at its policy out of concern that there is a threat to hard-fought-for progress in women's sport, and consider following FINA's lead?[42]

World Rowing president Jean-Christophe Rolland said it was all under review, and in March 2023 a further update to bye-laws barred any athlete from the female category at international level if they had experienced male puberty (see Appendix 5). In the meantime the lack of guidance led to uncertainty and poor outcomes for women at domestic level, as seen in the United States when USA Rowing issued an inclusion policy that was met with widespread objection.[43]

However, extraordinarily, when it came to mixed relays, they had to be made up of only four biological males and four biological females in the racing eight.

Surely not because the men in those races object to having biological males identifying as women against them in relays? Or perhaps it's because the sound principle has been accepted after all: biological males should not be competing with or taking up places and opportunities allocated to females in sport.

USA Rowing responded to criticism on social media with a tweet that read: 'While we encourage open dialogue and discussion, our top priority is creating a safe, welcoming community for all. Comments constituting hate speech, bullying or transphobia will be reported, and corresponding accounts blocked.'[44]

USA Rowing's policy recommended that 'all athletes be assigned to share accommodations based on their gender identity'. How could that be compatible with sex-based SafeSport polices and rules, particularly since transwomen in sport are often significantly older than the female athletes they are competing alongside?

In part as a result of the poor, non-binding guidance handed down by the IOC, there are mismatches between international and domestic federations in many sports.

World Triathlon requires transgender women to demonstrate a reduced testosterone level that is still well above the female range for two years and put up a further barrier when they ruled that four years had to pass before a male could appear in female racing. But I'm extremely proud to say that British Triathlon cut through all that when it announced that its events will be held under the 'female' and 'open' categories from 2023.

Federations are not the only ones in a mess on inclusion policy. The Canadian Centre for Ethics in Sports (CCES) is a case in point, as highlighted by Dr Linda Blade and Barbara Kay in their book *Unsporting: How Trans Activism and Science Denial Are Destroying Sport* (2020).

It was 2014 when the CCES set up the Trans Inclusion in Sport Expert Working Group.[45] The experts told the authors that no male advantages that had been shown in transwomen were 'so significant that they merit policy exclusions'.

Those were the words of Professor Bruce Kidd, working-group member, former Olympian for Canada in running at the 1964 Olympics and a sports professor at the University of Toronto.

We are back to categorisation, and we all know that if anyone were to suggest that able-bodied people could now compete in the Paralympics there would be outrage. It was a point Mark Tewksbury, the 1992 Olympic swimming champion for Canada, made when the LGBTQ+ advocacy group Egale Canada held a webinar on inclusion in sports.[46]

Mark pointed out that the sex-binary model defined all categories in sport, and asked what panellists would recommend in its place if it were to be scrapped? There was silence, and viewers were left with the feeling that the only policy they had in mind, as Blade and Kay put it, was: 'Let's destroy the house first and decide what to replace it with later.'

When the CCES published its guidance to Canadian sport in a 2022 paper entitled 'Creating inclusive environments for trans participants in Canadian sport', it topped the work with a quote from Canadian sociologist George Dei, who said: 'Inclusion is not bringing people into what already exists; it is making a new space, a better space for everyone.'[47]

In which case, the CCES should have burned the rest of its paper and started again, given that women's sport is clearly not a better space for having biological males invade it.

In reviewing the work, British sociologist Dr Jon Pike said the CCES was 'sponsoring and publishing pseudo-science and intellectual dishonesty to the Canadian public, at the expense of the same Canadian public, up to and including misrepresentation of academic peer-reviewed research.'[48]

His stinging rebuke added:

> This report is frighteningly bad... it fails to meet minimal standards of intellectual debate. The report's authors do not understand what it would take for inclusion of male-bodied transwomen to be fair, and present mutually inconsistent accounts. It misreads and mischaracterizes the history of sport. The literature review is partial, shoddy, and dishonest. It is sometimes wrong, but often doesn't rise to the threshold of even being wrong.[49]

The CCES is perhaps one of the most egregious examples of what we have seen over the past decade: sporting authorities all over the world – with a few noble exceptions like World Rugby and World Aquatics – abrogating their responsibility to deliver fairness and safety for women.

10

THE ONSLAUGHT
AGAINST WOMEN

WHY are we not learning from the mistakes of the past? Whenever athletes dared to speak out in the 1970s and 1980s or raised concerns about freakish GDR performances and the obvious cheating, we were shut down.

It's been similar with the trans assault on women's sport, but the bitter attacks are on a different scale.

The attempts to silence women who have spoken out have been ruthless. Kim Jones, campaigner for the Independent Council on Women's Sports (ICONS; see Appendix 2), criticised American college bosses who had told female swimmers expressing concerns over fairness and safety that if any trans athletes committed suicide on campus the blood would be on their hands.[1]

Silencing women with truncheons and threats didn't work in the nineteenth and twentieth centuries and it won't work now.

Sadly, many women have been bullied and scared off by death threats and have lost work through cancel-culture campaigns. We hear of butch lesbians being scoffed at and ridiculed by biological males declaring they know better what it is to be a woman while wearing ridiculous sexual-stereotype clothing and caked-on make-up. Sex is not a narrow stereotype enforced by societal trends. It is a biological reality. It's something you experience because of that biology and because of the rules and laws often set and applied by men. In countries like Iran, it means that just being a female is dangerous. In China, female babies were aborted or abandoned for many years under the one-child policy.[2] Females do not get to opt out of being females in those countries.

Lesbians are accused of transphobic bigotry if they won't have sex with a transwoman.[3] It's sexism and homophobia all wrapped up in one. And, largely, it's about women fighting a men's movement that conflates femininity with a societal version of femaleness and wants to muscle in on our sex-based rights, police our thoughts and rewrite our language in a way that brings falsehood, menace and danger to women's lives.

People have come up to me so many times in the street and at events and whispered that they're 100 per cent behind me and support everything I've been campaigning for. But we have to whisper it. How have we got here?

Thankfully there's a large number of us in a global network who will not let up until female sport is ring-fenced from male advantage, and transwomen are included in a category that does not disadvantage others knowingly.

This book is dedicated to all those who have stood up to the deniers and bullies. Who have shone a torch of truth straight back at them. They include athletes, coaches, scientists, academics, kinesiologists, human-development biologists, politicians, lawyers, women's rights campaigners, investigative journalists and media not afraid to call a transwoman a transwoman.

They're among those leading the way when it comes to finding courage and determination to have the truth told, to have women's voices heard and our rights upheld. I hope many more will join them as awareness grows of the damage being done.

WHAT WE'RE ANGRY ABOUT

A BBC poll in December 2022 led to an article headlined 'Are women getting angrier?'[4] It noted that when it comes to negative feelings in particular – anger, sadness, stress and worry – women consistently report experiencing these more frequently than men.

Ironically, the very same article cites the BBC's own '100 Women' list for 2022, designed specifically to honour inspiring and influential women and their achievements, but fails to mention that it includes biological males.

The truth is that we have no choice but to get angry. When my friend and Olympic teammate Daley Thompson came along to the London conference 'A Woman's Place is on the Podium' in July 2019, there were trans activists screaming 'transphobes' at us as we were trying to get through the door. And all because we just wanted to talk about peer-reviewed science and equal opportunities.

I've had death threats on social media like a lot of others campaigning to save women's sport and safe spaces, but I've never had anybody get physical with me yet. I know people who haven't been so lucky. They've been hit, spat on and menaced up close. You don't have to look far to find pictures all over the internet of trans activists wielding baseball bats and wearing T-shirts with 'Kill a Terf Today' all over them. They call themselves trans activists, but in reality they are nothing more than unpleasant men looking for a reason to hate on women.

Research has made the link between use of social media and the huge mental-health issues affecting our young people. On average 37 out of every 10,000 girls self-harm each year in the UK. There are areas where the figure is alarmingly close to one in every 100 girls aged 13 to 16.[5] There are some schools where one in five girls was found to have self-harmed.[6]

The biggest front line is online. Women feel obliged to defend themselves on Twitter against falsehood every single day. We face tidal waves of bitter exchanges over pronouns, feelings vs facts, sexual stereotypes as an expression of gender identity and boundaries being challenged in the very places which laws such as the Equality Act 2010 in the UK single out as sex-based spaces that are legally reserved for those born female.

I largely ignore stupidity and wilful ignorance on Twitter, but some things are impossible to overlook because they involve respected academics with influence over decision makers. Surely an academic should never place ideology ahead of the facts. How do we quantify a feeling?

THE BIG DIVIDE: INCLUSION VS INVASION

Fairness and inclusion have been made opponents in a clash of rights, which must be resolved in the best interests of the vast majority in sport. We must call transwomen transwomen and give them the respect and space to be who they wish to be but in harmony with others.

Sadly, regulators have been getting it wrong for almost 20 years and bowing to pseudoscience for the best part of a decade now. They made a 2015 decision based on the false notion that male biology can be reversed enough to make competition between male and female athletes fair. Female athletes were not consulted. Some of the science the IOC relied on was never put to robust peer review.

Permitted levels of testosterone and the time period required for males to show a consistent dip in hormone levels before being eligible to compete with females have both shifted like sand over the years because sports bosses have made policy on the hoof and without a single shred of solid, peer-reviewed study to back up their decisions.

There is no evidence that a best-in-class male has ever, due to reducing testosterone levels, fallen back from proven performance advantages of between 10 per cent and more than 160 per cent to anywhere remotely close to parity with best-in-class females in the same sports or events. At the same time, there is plenty of evidence that average males have enjoyed a radical change in their status on post-transition entry to the women's category, and a growing number of them have now won titles, medals and prizes in competition with the best females.

The obvious conclusion is that sports organisations have to ring-fence women's sport for female athletes and create an 'open' category. That will be the case in at least two sports and probably a few more in 2023, but has already been slammed by trans activists citing false media headlines as a 'trans ban'!

Not a single trans athlete has ever been stopped from taking part in sport. They have simply been asked to take part in the category of their biological sex until a decision is made on new categories for those who don't want to compete with others of their own sex.

Trans activists are not prepared to wait. They want access to female sport while more research is undertaken for as long as it takes for their ideology to become the norm. By all means conduct as much research as you want, but female athletes should refuse to be lab rats in a live experiment on the women's category. The IOC and other sports organisations should not be funding research aimed at proving that women are wrong to want their own category, safe spaces and sex-based rights upheld.

MEET THE OLYMPIC INCLUSION SPECIALIST

One of the biggest opponents of fair play for females in sport works at the highest levels of the Olympic Movement.

Madeleine Pape ran in the preliminary heats of the 800 metres for Australia at the 2008 Olympic Games, and after graduating in sociology at home got her doctorate at the University of

Wisconsin–Madison in 2019. Within a year, she'd joined the administrative side of the Olympic Family when she was engaged by the IOC as its 'inclusion specialist' to support the rollout of their 'Framework on Fairness, Inclusion, and Non-Discrimination', the one in which Olympic bosses handed decisions on trans inclusion back to international federations with the dubious notion that there should be 'no presumption of advantage' in any athlete.[7]

Pape has the ear of the IOC on how to regulate eligibility in elite women's sport. Some of her work is supported by the Olympic Studies Centre, and her passion, she explains on her website, is looking into

> how notions of 'biological sex' and 'sex difference' become embedded in gender equity projects in sport and biomedicine, and with what consequences. By examining how policymakers, scientists, and (certain) feminists seek to enact 'sex', I show how 'it' emerges as elusive and ambiguous and always entangled with gender, race, nation, and other socially meaningful forms of difference.[8]

But no matter how much academic jargon you use to try to obfuscate the truth, sex is a biological reality and it matters greatly when we're dealing with a real physical activity like a race.

I watched Pape's lecture titled 'Biofeminism: the epistemic [a person's beliefs about knowledge and knowing] politics of inclusion in women's sport', delivered virtually at a conference held by the School of Kinesiology and Health Studies at Queen's University in Kingston, Ontario, in January 2022.[9] It was hard going, a sales pitch for gender identity. The participants took a few swipes at that nasty opponent 'sex' and mocked scientific studies that suggest that gender dysphoria in children fades away past puberty because they obscure 'the dynamic nature of both gender and sex'.

Pape started by naming me, developmental biologist Dr Emma Hilton, chair of Fair Play for Women Dr Nicola Williams and British cyclist and coach Victoria Hood among speakers at the 2019 conference for women organised by Woman's Place UK.

In her presentation, Pape said that we 'don't know a helluva lot' about how Fair Play for Women and Woman's Place UK are funded – but Fair Play for Women have said that they are a

voluntary group who have come together because we share a single purpose: to defend the sex-based rights of women and girls. We have no formal membership. Our supporters come from all walks of life, with a wide range of professional expertise and real-life experiences to offer. Some supporters prefer to remain anonymous, while others openly support us.[10]

Madeleine is supported by various organisations named on her website but just how many dollars she receives from advising and advocating on inclusion issues at the IOC is not made clear, so tit for tat. At the same time, she makes a point of saying that crowdfunding helps pay for a full-time job at the helm of one of the women's campaign groups.

It's striking that Madeleine had her time as a female athlete without having to suffer the possibility of being disadvantaged by competing against biological men, but is now advocating for inclusion and what amounts to an unfair playing field for women. Would she have given up her place happily, after all the years of hard work, to a male who decided to identify as the opposite sex the year before Olympic trials? Surely no one can say that who hasn't been presented with that stark choice and challenge in real time. Some of the opportunities Madeleine now has in the sports world have come from the chance she had to represent her country on the biggest stage. She even refers to that as granting her an edge in her academic work. She's now using that to influence policy that denies other females the same chance she had.

She forgets the scientific arguments of 18 peer-reviewed studies (by spring 2023) that showed that male advantages remain truly significant in sport even after years of hormone-reduction therapy.[11] Instead, she claims that 'the research on this topic is considered to be widely limited and insufficient at this stage'.[12] This is simply untrue. The research we do have shows that there is no mitigation of male puberty anywhere close to the point of fairness for females.

The IOC has placed more weight on the studies' sociological side of the argument in its favouring of an inclusive approach and policy that is anti-science and at the cost of fairness to women athletes. It might have listened to alternative scientific and philosophical arguments like those of doctors Jon Pike, Cathy Devine and Miroslav Imbrišević.[13] Rarely do far more successful female athletes with the opposite view have their voices heard at the Olympic top table.

Pape, in her presentation, noted that Hilton and Williams attended the World Rugby meeting which concluded with an announcement that the women's category in the sport would be for females only (Pape calls it a 'trans ban') because of the physical differences in the sexes. She does not mention the overriding reason that matters: the safety of women and their protection from injury and harm.

Listening to Pape's 'Biofeminism' lecture presentation, it felt like she objected to World Rugby's approach, which involved daring to listen to women who disagree.[14] Rather than engage with the substance and the significance of sex, not gender identity, in sport, she spouts sociological jargon and goes a long way to implying that campaigners for women's sport are funded from questionable sources. She does not spell out the nature of her concerns over funding.

What Madeleine has done, however, is sign an open letter in support of Athlete Ally, the LGBTQI+ advocacy group campaigning for biological males to have access to female sport.[15]

Madeleine finds herself in an awkward situation, in agreement with Athlete Ally but out of step with some of the IOC top brass. In April 2023, when World Athletics issued a new inclusion policy that largely ring-fences the women's category for females only, the LGBTQI+ campaign group told *Newsweek* that it was 'beyond devastated to see World Athletics succumbing to political pressure'.[16] In a welcome and unusually robust move, World Athletics, led by IOC vice president Lord Coe, hit back at what it called 'a number of problematic statements' from Athlete Ally.[17]

THE SAFETY OF WOMEN IN SPORTS

Safety is of critical importance in combat and contact sports. When Fallon Fox boasted in a tweet in 2020 about two fights, she wrote: 'For the record, I knocked two out. One woman's skull was fractured, the other not. And just so you know, I enjoyed it. See, I love smacking up TEFS (trans-exclusionary feminists) in the cage who talk transphobic nonsense. It's bliss!' The tweet was subsequently deleted but campaign group Save Women's Sports captured it.[18]

It certainly wasn't bliss for Tamikka Brents. Fox's opponent suffered concussion and needed seven staples to hold her head together. Fox later said it was a common fracture, nothing unusual. It was for Tamikka, who considers herself an abnormally strong female and emerged from treatment to say: 'I've never felt so overpowered ever in my life.'[19]

When World Boxing decided in 2022 that it would create a fight category only for transgender athletes, it did so partly because male boxers refused to fight transmen on grounds that they did not want to be responsible for causing serious harm, or worse, to biological females.

In July 2022, England's rugby union and league governing bodies banned transwomen from any female games because of the physical threat their male size and strength posed, yet over in Ireland in the same month Gaelic football witnessed extraordinary events that suggested governors had given the whole inclusion issue far too little thought.

When the Na Gaeil Aeracha girls LGBTQ+ inclusive 16 years squad turned up to the 2022 Ladies Junior J. Shield Cup, the players on the opposite team included a biological male who looked to me to be about twice the size of the girls in the game, was approaching 40 years of age and wearing the no. 21 shirt. No one appears to have raised the player's age. The manager of the opposition team objected to the presence of a man and the referee told Na Gaeil there was a problem with no. 21, but the male was allowed to play to half-time (having been taken off and put back on the field after an injury), before being substituted.[20]

The player was Giulia Valentino: when not in the thick of girls' Gaelic football, Valentino identifies as a 'trans dyke' and performs at fetish clubs around Europe as 'DJ Mav', according to promotional links to social media and websites cited by Reddux.com. For pointing out that Valentino was male, women got suspended from Twitter.[21]

How does that square with modern safeguarding standards in sport? Parents have a right to be informed about the environment their children are being exposed to. We need to hear far more from the IOC on what they think about such things and what their specific guidance is.

One thing we can all be clear on is this: women who do dare to disagree don't tend to get given cushy jobs and platforms within major international sporting organisations like the IOC. In fact, some of them get dismissed for raising critical issues. A good example of this is Nancy Hogshead-Makar.

NANCY'S STORY OF COURAGE
AND ADVOCACY AGAINST THE ODDS

Former Olympic swimmer Nancy Hogshead-Makar has dedicated her life to gender equality while fighting sexual abuse in sport. In 1984 she claimed three gold medals at the Olympic Games in Los Angeles. The Soviet-led boycott of that year gave athletes like Nancy a brief respite from the GDR onslaught in female swimming – and she capitalised on it.

Shortly after her Olympic success, she joined the Women's Sports Foundation (WSF), an organisation set up by Billie Jean King in 1974 to promote equal opportunities for women in sport and fight sexism and discrimination.[22] She rose through the ranks and over time became the WSF's president, legal adviser and director of advocacy.

Among other things, it was her own experience of sexual violence that prompted her lifetime of activism and advocacy. Some years before her Olympic success, when she was 19, Nancy was out jogging near the campus of Duke University in North Carolina where she was reading law. She was attacked and raped by a stranger.

In one of several interviews on advocacy with Craig, she said: 'I felt profoundly broken… I was scared all the time and I thought that I could overcome it by willing it away. That was part of the post-traumatic stress disorder I had for months after the attack.'[23]

Her healing was not helped by media reports at the time. One headline read: 'Female student raped while running alone'. No mention of the criminal male. When it came to blame, the raped not the rapist was singled out for attention. To Nancy, the implication was that she was to blame because she'd been out 'running alone'.

'I didn't talk about it for 20 years because I would have started to cry; I wasn't quite healed enough,' said Nancy, who was encouraged by human-rights activist Richard Lapchick to talk publicly about her experience as a rape survivor.[24] She recalled:

It made me a better advocate. It's something that sports leaders and trans activists don't appreciate in this whole assault on female sport. Women are particularly vulnerable. I know. I was raped by overwhelming violence without a weapon. And it happened when I was at my strongest. I was in the top 1 per cent of strongest women and the whole idea that what we women have to do is take a self-defence class is just insulting.

It was the same argument with the GDR and now it's back again with trans activists telling us we just need to be stronger, we just need to swim faster, we're just not shaping up the way we could if we really tried. It's deeply insulting, it just doesn't recognise who women are, who I am, that I am built perfectly for what women were designed to do. This is the reality for women: a 5' 10" male can run in our neighbourhood and on college campuses and be perfectly safe. Women are not.

My male teammates in swimming were 10–11 per cent faster than me in the pool. Average male punching power is 162 per cent greater than females, with the least powerful man still stronger than the most powerful woman. Don't tell me there's no evidence to show biological males have big and unfair advantages over females in sport.

Nancy wasn't always on the same side as me in the trans debate. She says:

I was on a radio interview with Sharron several years ago and I was like, 'Come on, they're just so few, it's never going to happen, they're not going to get all the way to the Olympics or anything like that.' But she was right and I was wrong on about ten different counts. I'd been told and sold on them being given affirming hormones that would make it fair and they could just move laterally from the men's competition. But I soon realised that was just not true.

Nancy started to read the reports of Emma Hilton, Tommy Lundberg and Ross Tucker, and she listened to presentations by Mike Joyner.[25] When she listened to Senate hearings on the US Equality Act, the penny dropped:

> In the hearings they were saying that there should not be a carve-out for sports, that sex discrimination and gender-identity discrimination are the same thing, but if that was so it meant there is actually no sex discrimination because gender identity is more important and trumps women's rights. I was like, whoa, no way! We'd fought for decades to have Title IX rights to equality in college sport and that law reaffirmed.[26]

In response, she and others formed the Women's Sports Policy Group to campaign for better laws and raise awareness of where the clash of rights was headed.

Nancy feels immensely grateful that the boycott stopped her from having to face East German dominance. The GDR years taught us all that numbers don't matter. It took just a few GDR girls on each sports team to dominate the podiums. Cheating demotes every athlete down the ranks but Nancy homes in on gold and says:

> Go ask an Olympic champion what it means to win that medal. It's for the rest of your life. It's more meaningful than any honour or degree or doctorate. It made me and gives you opportunities for the rest of your life. All those beaten by East Germans for 20 years missed out and my heart goes out to them. Sharron was one of those cases of a swimmer being denied what she'd worked for. It just wasn't right. When that happens to athletes, the medal is stolen, the moment is gone and the consequences are for life, especially when the IOC just looks away. The rules

said one thing, the result shows that cheating pays off. That's not what the Olympic Charter had in mind.

What has happened to Nancy as a result of her tireless advocacy for women in sport and her determination to stand up for fair play? Has she been promoted and funded by the IOC? Has this rape survivor and fearless defender of women's sports been given the respect and place at the table she deserves from sports authorities?

No.

In October 2021, Nancy told her followers on social media: 'After 30 years with the Women's Sports Foundation, my renewal contract had a paragraph forbidding me from advocating for athlete sexual safety on TeamUSA.' The story was broken by the Californian newspaper the *Orange County Register*.[27]

She refused to accept one of the most vile and pernicious aspects of abuse in sport, where victims, survivors and advocates find themselves silenced and shut down on issues that have a direct and excoriating impact on women's lives.

The offer of contract renewal stated that she should

not discuss, opine, or participate, either verbally or in writing, as an advocate, expert, or spokesperson regarding sexual abuse, sexual harassment, sexual allegations, or any other issue related to sexual conduct in any manner, shape or form, whether said participation is done as an individual, as a private citizen, as a spokesperson for any party, on behalf of WSF, or on behalf of any other party or organization.[28]

Nancy was also told that if she wanted a settlement payment, she would have to hand in any materials she'd ever worked on while at the WSF. Not even her family would be allowed to keep copies.

In response to the WSF's loaded 'take-it-or-leave-it' offer, Nancy left it and walked away.

In her valedictory statement, Nancy cited the courage of American gymnasts Maggie Nichols, the first known athlete to report Larry Nassar's sexual abuse to USAG in June 2015, and Aly Raisman, who, on 19 January 2018, was one of several leading athletes to read moving impact statements at Nassar's sentencing to 175 years in jail.

Her message was clear: if Maggie, Aly and others among the 265 girls and young women abused by Nassar during the 18 years he served as the US Olympics gymnastics team doctor found the courage to speak out, so could and should all other women.

The *Orange County Register*'s headline on 12 October 2021 asked 'Did Women's Sports Foundation try to silence a leading voice fighting sexual abuse in sports?'[29] I recommend reading the answers provided in the article.

An organisation representing women asked a survivor of rape and safe-sport advocate not to mention sexual abuse.

Nancy told the newspaper that the women's group had given in to pressure from USOPC at a time when it was steeped in accusations of inaction and cover-up at USAG over Nassar.

Nancy walked away from the WSF with her fine reputation, her professional integrity and her honesty and advocacy for women intact. She set up Champion Women (see Appendix 2) and carried on her advocacy. She tells us: 'There's been this idea that sports organisations don't have to do anything with sexual abuse because the police will deal with it. It's one of three things Champion Women focuses on, along with equality for women in college and now the transgender issue.'

THE CANCELLATION OF CAROLE HOOVEN

She isn't the only one with courage to stand up for women's sport who has been at the sharp end of trans attacks.

Dr Carole Hooven, who we met in Chapter 5, has been one of the most prominent scientists defending the truth: that testosterone gives biological males a massive and irreversible performance advantage in sport. The best-selling author of *Testosterone: The Story of the Hormone that Dominates and Divides Us* and lecturer in human evolutionary biology at Harvard was invited onto a TV news programme to discuss her book in summer 2021.

She was asked about an article written by the journalist Katie Herzog on the pressure some professors felt to back away from referring to 'males' and 'females' and 'pregnant women' when teaching.[30] Hooven knows her science and pointed out that sex is binary, male and female. She then added:

> The ideology seems to be that biology really isn't as important as how somebody feels about themselves or feels their sex to be, but we can treat people with respect and respect their gender identities and use their preferred pronouns, so understanding the facts about biology doesn't prevent us from treating people with respect.[31]

That seems all very reasonable and honest to me. But Hooven felt the full blast of the trans lobby and those in its grip.

A graduate student, Laura Lewis, tweeted out a thread, representing herself in her official capacity as director of the 'Diversity, Inclusion and Belonging' task force at Hooven's department. She was 'appalled' by Hooven's 'transphobic' and 'dangerous' remarks, which, she said, allegedly interfered with the task force's efforts to ensure that the department was a 'safe space' for people of 'all gender identities and sexes'.

Hooven received a sanction but Laura Lewis did not, even though she was the one who had actually broken Harvard Free Speech guidelines, which say: 'Because we are a community united by a commitment to rational processes, we do not permit the censorship of noxious ideas. We are committed to maintaining a climate in which reason and speech provide the correct response to a disagreeable idea.'[32]

Challenges to truth and science do many trans people no favours. Many actually disagree with the activists and say they feel less safe in the hostile environment sparked by false accusations of transphobia.

In her 2022 paper 'Academic freedom is social justice: sex, gender, and cancel culture on campus', Hooven provides excellent advice to Harvard, reminding those kowtowing to ideology what academic integrity looks like.[33]

She suggests that academic freedoms must be frequently trumpeted and that the foremost mission of a university is the pursuit, preservation and dissemination of knowledge. This cannot happen without academic freedom. Sadly, universities around the world seem to be a hotbed of ideology and virtue-signalling.

RILEY GAINES TAKES A STAND

Perhaps one of the most striking examples of the threats and bullying meted out against women who take a stand against the madness happened in the context of the Lia Thomas saga.

In the 200 yards freestyle final at the NCAA Women's Championships in March 2022, something unexpected happened: Lia swam below best, sparking more speculation about deliberate holding back. The title went to Stanford's Taylor Ruck, a Canadian Olympian. Thomas finished equal fifth with Kentucky's Riley Gaines, after which the medals presentation was another insult to the women in the race. The NCAA had not anticipated ties and there was only one fifth-place trophy. It was handed to Thomas, while Gaines was told to hold the sixth-place award 'for the photo', and that her fifth-place trophy would be mailed to her at some point.

It had been just 'one slap in the face after another', said Riley.[34] Thomas had come from nowhere. It wasn't just us in Britain and the rest of the world who'd never heard of Will Thomas. Americans like Riley didn't know them either. As Will, they were ranked outside the top 500 in the United States over 200 and 500 yards freestyle. When Riley heard that Lia was actually Will she felt a sense of relief, but she and her coaches then felt a sense of shock, she said, when they understood two weeks before college finals that the NCAA had given a green light to what was 'wrong and unfair'.

After the post-200 yards podium insult, Riley felt so incensed with the NCAA's treatment of female athletes that she put a plan to train as a dentist on hold to keep up the fight for fair play for women.

Riley had experienced 'extreme discomfort' when sharing a locker room with Lia Thomas. At a summer 2022 rally for the new 'Our Bodies, Our Sports' movement to celebrate the 50th anniversary of Title IX, she told the crowd, above the noise of an 'antifascist' trans-activist protest shouting her down, that she had been moved by the 'tears shed' by her female teammates and opponents at the NCAA championships, not only because they'd been forced to race Thomas's male advantage, but also because they'd had to face his exposed penis when changing. There was, she added, 'no one in authority who was willing to intervene and says this is wrong'.[35]

Sport needs many more women to find the courage to speak out, but Riley notes the reason why they don't: 'Women are intimidated by their universities. They're told they'll lose their places, that they can forget graduate school, that jobs will be hard to get. It's emotional blackmail.'

Some swimmers in 2022 spoke to American media anonymously to say that they'd even been told that they would be 'solely responsible' if there were any suicides among trans students on campus. For adults at university to shut down truth with a weapon like that was a blatant attempt at moral blackmail.

With tears in her eyes, Kim Jones, a former All-American tennis player and mother of a Yale swimmer, told the crowd at the 'Our Bodies, Our Sports' rally in early 2023 that NCAA and Ivy League officials, often men, had 'tossed aside' female athletes. 'This is not the world that I want for my daughter,' said Kim, who co-founded the Independent Council on Women's Sports (ICONS).[36]

Over in Britain for a conference in 2022, Kim told me about the appalling bullying and threats that women swimmers had been forced to endure in NCAA competitions from authorities that serve as the regulators of rules that forbid such behaviour in others.

Riley graduated and felt no need to hold back. Others who must still complete their college courses and risk losing funding and places were more cautious when it came to telling their stories beyond the cover of anonymity. At the 'Our Bodies' rally, skateboarder Taylor Silverman urged women to keep speaking out. A constant wave of women's voices was one of the biggest weapons in the fight, she suggested. Taylor had lost prize money at one contest against a biological male opponent but refused to stay quiet while women are 'being made to feel unimportant in a space created for us.' That's pure sex discrimination and restriction of trade.[37]

This is the treatment female athletes can expect in the twenty-first century: being denied the moment to celebrate and be photographed on the podium with your trophy because the privilege was given exclusively to the biological male you tied with; being bullied, threatened with loss of college places and morally blackmailed into silence by governors at academic institutions.

11

THE GENDER INDUSTRY

JUST as it is important to understand the motivation and the politics behind the systematic abuse of young athletes in the GDR, it's useful to consider the backdrop against which the inclusion crisis has unfolded in women's sport.

In the decade since the WHO decision to remove gender dysphoria from its list of mental-health conditions, a gender industry backed by extremely wealthy individuals and corporations has grown astronomically into a multi-billion-dollar global business.

That economy now includes transgender-campaign backers and big brand names allocating budgets to transwomen hired to endorse and promote products aimed at the predominantly female market.

The headline-grabbing but insulting parody of a sportswoman by transwoman Dylan Mulvaney skipping around in a sports bra as a male without breasts was infuriating for many including me, as both a woman and a professional female athlete.[1] Athletes spend decades becoming coordinated and strong to be able to do their job on the track, pitch or pool. It may come as a shock to Mulvaney and Nike but females use sports bras as an athletic support relevant to our anatomy long after we all started to move away from the old cliché of 'running like a girl'. It's hard to imagine women ever being hired to advertise jockstraps.

In a pinned comment to Nike's verified Instagram account, the company instructed customers to 'Be kind, be inclusive... Encourage each other.'

The phone never stopped ringing with journalists wanting to know what female athletes thought about Mulvaney and Nike. I didn't officially call for a boycott, but I did say on a TV interview that I would vote with my wallet and simply stop buying the products of companies that can't understand why a sports bra should be marketed to women by women. In 2019, Allyson Felix penned a column in the *New York Times* in which she stated that Nike wanted to renew her contract at 70 per cent less after she got pregnant.[2] She left and set up her own shoe company.[3] Nike responded to the backlash by making changes to its company maternity policies.[4]

Dylan Mulvaney was also used by Bud Light to advertise its brand; after an uproar, parent company Anheuser-Busch was reported to have lost more than $6 billion in market capitalisation, while two Bud Light executives were subsequently put on leave.[5]

The lack of understanding or respect shown to females by some big brands and marketeers is particularly galling when you consider that less than 1 per cent of sports sponsorship budgets go to women. In 2020, the figure for the United States was put at a minuscule 0.4 per cent.[6] Just let that ridiculous bias sink in!

Business engagement with transwomen to advertise women's products coincides with the growing influence of the Corporate Equality Index (CEI), a report published by the Human Rights Campaign Foundation as a tool to rate American businesses on their treatment of gay, lesbian, bisexual and transgender employees, consumers and investors. The CEI is similar in some regards to Stonewall's Diversity Champions Programme.[7]

Meanwhile, in 2021, the American Civil Liberties Union (ACLU) launched its 'Jon L. Stryker and Slobodan Randjelović

LGBTQ & HIV Project' after the couple gifted the union's foundation $15 million. The ACLU, which is heavily involved in bringing legal challenges to court over models of trans inclusion in sport in the United States, described the donation as the largest LGBTQ+ rights-focused gift in its 101-year history.[8]

Such funding has been used by ACLU to challenge and win cases favouring trans inclusion in female sports even though such decisions are unfair and discriminate against girls and women. Related battles have been particularly prevalent at state level, as we note later in this chapter when we consider the impact on women's rights and sex-based legislation in the United States.

And the growth in the gender identity market continues apace. The Gender Mapping Project organisation estimates that there are now thousands of gender clinics around the world.[9] The Global Market Insights research firm has estimated that the market in genital surgery, with all its complications, will grow by 25 per cent by 2026 and take profits in the sector to $1.5 billion in the United States alone.[10]

Among the many questions that medical intervention raises for sport is the meaning of manipulation, which already stretches to relatively new challenges such as gene doping. It was 2008 when a Chinese doctor was caught by Germany's ARD television doping investigations team trying to sell stem-cell treatments to an official posing as an American swimming coach.[11] Various forms of manipulation that afford a performance advantage are ruled out of sport in the WADA anti-doping code.

At a time when we spend millions every year fighting to keep drugs out of sport it runs against the grain to bring in new regulations on testosterone levels for males so they can compete against females. The whole premise of sport is to be the very best you can be, not to deliberately impair your performance. We should be using sport to be the healthiest we can be.

We've established that the inclusion of males opens a potential new loophole for rogues in sport. The penalties faced by females who cross a red line for specific drugs offences are no longer the same for everyone allowed to compete in the women's category. How can that be fair? If we allow physical manipulation of humans through medical procedures that specifically confer performance advantage, where will that lead us and what outcomes might we expect?

Meanwhile, more basic questions are being asked of politicians and policymakers prepared to set aside long-established sex-based rights in sport in favour of prioritising inclusion over safety and fairness.

THE CHALLENGE TO BIDEN ON TITLE IX AND DISCRIMINATION AGAINST WOMEN

The pressure being brought to bear by the gender industry, LGBTQ+ lobbyists and their political allies has legal consequences. In January 2021, soon after being sworn in as president of the United States, Joe Biden signed a number of executive orders. Among them was one entitled 'Executive order on preventing and combating discrimination on the basis of gender identity or sexual orientation'.

The order noted that the word sex in Title IX means 'gender identity'. It cited a 2020 Supreme Court case involving employment-law precedent, known as the 'Bostock case'.[12] Even though the Supreme Court went out of its way to specify that Bostock was strictly limited to protecting citizens from losing a job based on sexual orientation or the clothes they wore, the Biden order sought to use it as a way of overwriting 'sex' with 'gender identity' in Title IX. It could be seen as a direct attack on females and their specific, biological, sex-based rights.

A month later, Biden formally nominated Rachel Levine as assistant secretary for health.[13] Levine, a four-star admiral in the US

Public Health Service Commissioned Corps, had spent most of their life as Richard, a married man with two daughters, before he divorced his wife in 2013 around the time he transitioned. The presence of Levine, a strong advocate for trans rights, gave opponents to males in female sport little hope that Title IX's original purpose of equality between the two binary sexes would survive without a legal fight.

Title IX became law in 1972, and states that no one shall, on the basis of sex (not gender identification), 'be excluded from participation in, be denied the benefits of, or be subjected to discrimination under any education program or activity receiving Federal financial assistance'.[14] That means, for example, schools, colleges, university courses and their sports programmes.

The intent was very clear: protection of and equal rights for females. When Title IX was born, only 7 per cent of high school girls in the United States participated in sport. By 2014 more than 41 per cent of girls, that's 3.2 million, engaged in sport. That's still small compared to males, but Title IX had a great impact.

The benefits of Title IX extended well beyond the United States, because the college system in America invites female athletes on scholarships from all over the world, many of whom go on to make Olympic teams for their own countries. I myself accepted one at Berkeley in San Francisco while on a tour of Californian universities in late 1980.

Why would any American administration wish to ruin that? When Biden's order threatened all of that it was a body blow to the rights of females in sport. Clearly, they would now have to contend with male advantage, and potentially trans-identifying males being awarded scholarships that were designed to offer female equality in further education, which in America is very expensive.

Hypocrisy is never far away when politicians interpret the word 'sex' differently for different circumstances. Despite a pledge to keep transwomen out of the military draft and the fact that women are not eligible, the president mandated that transwomen must register for service because the law states that anyone assigned male at birth must do so.[15] So transwomen are male when it comes to war but they're not male when it comes to sport?

Sport must battle it out in court, meanwhile. By 2023, legal challenges to keep males out of women's sport had been successful in almost half of all American states.

On 5 January 2023, US district judge Joseph Goodwin ruled in favour of a state law passed in West Virginia in 2021 to keep a transgirl student out of female sport. Heather Jackson filed her complaint in federal court in May 2021 on behalf of her child, Becky Pepper-Jackson, then 11. To cut a long story short, the male-born youngster had wanted to race in her school's girls' cross-country and track teams, but after state laws had been passed preventing boys from participating in girls' sport, Becky's request was denied.

Judge Goodwin said that no one wished to deny Becky the right to live as a transgirl but that that status challenged the 'entire structure of school sports'. 'Ultimately, [Becky's] issue here is not with the state's offering of girls' sports and boys' sports,' Goodwin wrote. 'It is with the state's definitions of "girl" and "boy." The state has determined that for the purposes of school sports, the definition of "girl" should be "biologically female," based on physical difference between the sexes… [Becky] seeks a legal declaration that a transgender girl is "female."'[16]

He added:

Title IX authorizes sex separate sports in the same manner as HB 3293 [the relevant state law], so long as overall athletic opportunities for each sex are equal. Despite her repeated argument to the contrary, transgender girls are not excluded from school sports entirely. They are permitted to try out for boys' teams, regardless of how they express their gender.[17]

In February 2023, a federal appeals court reinstated a challenge to Connecticut's policy of allowing transgender girls to compete in girls high school sports.[18]

Four female runners filed a lawsuit in 2020 against the Connecticut Interscholastic Athletic Conference, the state's high school sports governing body, as well as several local school districts. They sought injunctions to bar enforcement of the state policy and to remove records set by transgender athletes between 2017 and 2020 from the books, as well as money damages for the harm caused. The case challenged the inclusion of transwomen athletes such as Terry Miller and Andraya Yearwood in female high school competition.[19]

In December 2022, a three-judge panel upheld the transgender-inclusion rules, but the Second US Circuit Court of Appeals in New York City decided in February 2023 that the full court will rehear the appeal of four female runners who said they were unfairly forced to race against biological males in high school competition.

Christiana Kiefer, a lawyer at Alliance Defending Freedom (ADF), which represented the four female runners, said: 'Every woman deserves the respect and dignity that comes with having an equal opportunity to excel and win in athletics, and ADF remains committed to protecting the future of women's sports.'[20]

At the time she spoke, 18 states in the United States had passed laws blocking transgender women or girls from female sport on grounds of unfair advantage.[21] One of those went a step further in February 2023: Kansas became the first state to pass a 'Women's Bill of Rights', which defines 'woman' as someone who is 'biologically born a female', a move aimed at preserving single-sex spaces such as public toilets, school sports, prisons and shelters.[22]

The challenges for female athletes are far from over in North America, however. Just before Christmas 2022, a bill that would have banned biological males from playing on girls' sports teams in Ohio failed to pass in the state's General Assembly.[23] In late 2022, civil rights lawyer Nancy Hogshead-Makar pointed to the many legal processes under way in the United States and predicted many more.

A passionate defender of Title IX, she says it's 'criminal' to exclude female voices from the decision-making processes that affect women in sport. She estimates that the equality gap in the sports market in the United States means that the opportunities men have that women don't are worth about a billion dollars every year.

She insists that 18- to 22-year-old women at college in the United States 'can go in front of a judge and get all that changed' by insisting that Title IX sex-based provisions be upheld by a court.[24] It's one of the big legal and political battlefronts in the transgender debate in the United States, and by extension the world. If women don't stand up for what the law entitles them to and the rules are based on ideology, they will lose female sport to biological males, says Nancy. Very important given that, as we've shown, throughout history opportunities in sport to earn a living for females have been far fewer than for males – and this is still the case today. To then lose the ones we do have seems so terribly wrong.

She explains why she believes women will win the argument: 'I've never met a single female athlete that couldn't list the ways they're getting second-class treatment as compared to male football or basketball players.' Over the past four decades, 'the unwritten rule [in US college sport] is that women's sports can exist, so long as not a single male is harmed by women's inclusion, yet now, women are expected to graciously roll over and let trans athlete-inclusion change what the women's sports category means, what rights it conveys,' Nancy tells us.[25]

She also says, as I have, that it would be nice if more of our male sports peers spoke out, too – although they are beginning to do so. They are all very aware of performance difference and should be standing with us to remind regulators why the rules and categories of sport were sex-based in the first place.

The legal battles in the United States moved the arguments beyond women's sport in March 2023 when a Minnesota state judge put an entire sport on notice. If USA Powerlifting did not allow transgender athletes to compete in the sex category of their gender choice, then all powerlifting in the state would cease, for men and women.[26] USA Powerlifting announced that it would appeal the decision and was investigating relocating competitions out of Minnesota. Powerlifter JayCee Cooper sued the regulator in 2021 after USA Powerlifting barred biological males from female competition. The court found that the organisation's policy violated state anti-discrimination law.[27]

Meanwhile, the 'Protection of Women and Girls in Sports Act', introduced to Congress in February 2023 by Greg Steube, a Republican congressman representing part of Florida, seeks to amend Title IX with a clarification that recognises sex as that which is 'based solely on a person's reproductive biology and genetics at birth'.[28]

This is the third time that Steube has introduced the legislation, but the first under the new speaker of the US House of Representatives, Kevin McCarthy, also Republican, who is supportive. On 20 April 2023, shortly before our book went to press, House Republicans voted to ring-fence women's sport for females only.[29] They passed the Act, amending Title IX protections to reinforce sex-based categorisation in sport, by 219 to 203 votes. No Democrats supported the measure, which then faced a vote in the Senate. President Biden had indicated that he could veto any vote in favour. I can't fathom why any president would want to discriminate against females in sport.

This is something I've been trying to do with our own Equality Act in the UK: get clarity that sex, as a protected characteristic, actually means biological sex. By March of 2023 over 100,000 people had signed a petition asking the movement to do exactly this and debate it in Parliament, while the chair of the Equality and Human

Rights Commission, Baroness Falkner, has recently written that they have recommended to the government that it consider adopting a biological definition of sex.[30]

UK POLITICAL CHALLENGES

Labour was the first political party in Britain to support female suffrage, back in 1912. Equal rights became one of the key reasons why many women have voted for Labour ever since.

Yet here we are in 2023, and the Labour leader in opposition, Sir Keir Starmer, a barrister and former director of public prosecutions, positions whose work relies on clarity of meaning, can't give a straight answer to the simple question 'What is a woman?'

The question was put as the Labour leader prepared to go on the local-election campaign trail in Bury in March 2022 just a few streets away from the route of an official 'Suffragette's Tour' of Manchester, where women were thrown to the ground and beaten by police under orders from male politicians opposing equal rights just a century ago.[31]

Sir Keir was surely aware of all of that history, but in an interview with *The Times* in March 2022, he said: 'A woman is a female adult…' Excellent. Sadly, he didn't stop there, adding: 'and in addition to that, a minority of people who are transwomen, are women.'[32]

Asked by LBC radio's Nick Ferrari, Sir Keir said: 'Of course we can be called on to defend women's rights. I spent a lot of my working life dealing with violence against women and girls first hand, and I know from that experience just how important it is to fight for women and fight for equality.'[33]

Ferrari pressed on and asked: 'So a woman can have a penis?' Sir Keir couldn't – or wouldn't – answer, because he wanted 'respectful' and 'open' discussion. Something that's been sorely missing so far.[34]

I think it's impossible to have either of those things in the absence of truth and the ability to spell out basic differences of biological

THE GENDER INDUSTRY 207

sex, such as the facts that a male has a prostate, a female has a cervix, only females menstruate or give birth, there is not and never has been a human hermaphrodite, there is no third sex, only small or large gametes, and there's no such thing as non-binary because sex is binary, even with a DSD diagnosis.

There are, of course, infinite personalities that inhabit the reality of a biological human body. Those should be celebrated and accepted. It seems so strange to me, at a time when society has worked so hard to try to move away from strict stereotypes, that we are back to putting people in boxes and adding labels to how we present our personalities. As Germaine Greer told Channel 4: 'Female is real, and it's sex, and femininity is unreal, and it's gender. For that to become the given identity of women is a profoundly disabling notion.'[35]

As Germaine notes in that interview, biological females make up half of society. That half of everyone may well decide not to vote for elected policy- and lawmakers who feel they can't look after that 50 per cent. I'd rather not vote at all than vote for any party that cannot describe what a woman is – and what a woman is not. If you can't describe it, you can't protect it.

Politicians have a mandate to represent all of us, but in the rush to #BeKind to one side of the transgender debate it's clear that women and children are being put at risk. Sadly, bad people take advantage of bad laws. History shows us that over and over again – and we'd be wise to remember that with every passing victim of crimes that such regressive 'progressive' decisions as allowing biological males into female spaces and races facilitate.

Biology matters in many areas beyond sport, like medicine, but also crime and its statistics.

In 'Evidence and data on trans women's offending rates', submitted to the UK Parliament's Women and Equalities Committee in 2020, three female professors cite a Swedish study that considered patterns of crime in a controlled population of transwomen. It concluded: 'male-to-females... retained a male pattern regarding criminality. The same was true regarding violent crime.'[36]

The study was described by the three professors as a 'methodologically robust, peer-reviewed, large-scale comparative source'. An extract from the evidence to Parliament notes: 'MtF [male-to-female] transitioners were over 6 times more likely to be convicted of an offence than female comparators and 18 times more likely to be convicted of a violent offence.'[37] Those findings are part of a large library of reasons why we can't slap a '#BeKind' badge on discussions and pretend the truth is irrelevant.

The Swedish study is all the more striking because it considered only transwomen who had undergone genital surgery, so the sample was much more tightly defined than a population based solely on self-ID, a hot topic in many countries.

The submission also cites Dr James Barrett, president of the British Association of Gender Identity Specialists, in his report to the government's Transgender Equality Inquiry in August 2015. He noted that there had been an 'ever-increasing tide of referrals of patients in prison serving long or indeterminate sentences for serious sexual offences', and raised several red flags:

> These vastly outnumber the number of prisoners incarcerated for more ordinary, non-sexual, offences. It has been rather naïvely suggested that nobody would seek to pretend transsexual status in prison if this were not actually the case. There are, to those of us who actually interview the prisoners, in fact very many reasons why people might pretend this. These vary from the opportunity to have trips out of prison through to a desire for a transfer to the female estate (to the same prison as a co-defendant) through to the idea that a parole board will perceive somebody who is female as being less dangerous through to a [false] belief that hormone

treatment will actually render one less dangerous through to wanting a special or protected status within the prison system and even (in one very well evidenced case that a highly concerned Prison Governor brought particularly to my attention) a plethora of prison intelligence information suggesting that the driving force was a desire to make subsequent sexual offending very much easier, females being generally perceived as low risk in this regard.[38]

So that question of Nick Ferrari's doesn't seem so unimportant after all. A woman does not have a penis. She cannot legally commit rape. A transwoman very likely will have, as very few have surgery – and yes, it is important to say so. Crime statistics must be sex-based so we can make informed decisions about safeguarding, as we've seen in the UK with recent prison rules relating to sexual and violent transwomen prisoners. We must not put vulnerable females in even more dangerous positions.

Sir Keir told Ferrari that he's an 'advocate of safe spaces for women', including the exemption of refuges for female domestic-abuse victims that is set out in the UK Equalities Act. But as this book heads for the printers, Labour, among others, has yet to make clear what its actual policies are. Sir Keir and shadow secretary of state for justice Steve Reed indicated their support for amendments to the Act that would safeguard safe spaces for women and mean that transwomen would not be allowed on female-only hospital wards.[39] There remained significant opposition in the Labour ranks to the proposed changes, even though in April of this year it was reported there were over 6,500 sexual assaults in just the last four years in UK hospitals.[40] The Labour leader has certainly honed his thoughts on the subject of self ID and reforms since events surrounding the controversial Gender Recognition Reform Bill (Scotland) turned sour but Labour's position remained unclear heading into May 2023.[41]

The saga over the Scottish bill was a warning to Starmer about the political price to be paid for failing to listen to the views of a large voting constituency.

Championed by Nicola Sturgeon at the time she was Scottish first minister, the Gender Recognition proposals would have allowed children to self-identify as the sex opposite to their birth sex from as young as 16, with no medical diagnosis. It would also have cut the wait to get a gender-recognition certificate (GRC), during which you are supposed to live as the opposite sex, from two years to just three months. What does that actually mean? Does it mean that, if you are a male, you have to put on a skirt and lipstick every time you leave the house? As a woman, I don't do that. And who's checking anyway?

It passed a Scottish parliamentary vote on 22 December 2022, even though polls indicated substantial voter opposition.[42] I was among women who went to Scotland to give evidence on how it would affect sport, but was not given the chance to speak. Women's rights campaigners condemned it. On 16 January 2023, prime minister Rishi Sunak and the UK government blocked the Scottish legislation that would have made Scotland the first part of the UK to introduce a transgender self-identification system.[43] The block was imposed using section 35 of the Scotland Act 1998 for the first time.

After months of controversy over the Gender Recognition Reform Bill and weeks of argument over Sunak's popular triggering of section 35, Nicola Sturgeon resigned as Scotland's first minister on 15 February.[44] She said she no longer had the stamina to continue in the highly pressured and demanding role. In the days that followed, some celebrated her departure as a female leader who had failed to stand up for women's rights and represent their voices.

One of those who challenged Sturgeon was J. K. Rowling, who responded to a lack of support for female-only rape shelters in

Scotland by founding and funding Beira's Place, 'a sexual violence support service for women – run by women'.[45] As a safe space for women, it excludes all biological males.

In the face of death threats and cancel culture, the author has continued to speak up in support of women and their sex-based rights. She explains why in a great podcast series called 'The Witch Trials of J. K. Rowling'.[46]

SHIFTING LEGAL RIGHTS BY STEALTH

It often feels to me as if the rights and legal protections of women have been undermined by stealth.

Cathy Devine, an academic expert on the impact on female sport of transgender-inclusion strategies, has highlighted the phenomenon of 'policy capture': that is, powerful players seeking to reshape, re-define and reinterpret existing rules and conventions without debate, let alone democratic consensus and agreement.

During the UN's '16 Days of Activism against Gender-Based Violence' in late 2022, Volker Türk, the United Nations High Commissioner for Human Rights, called for transgender women to be accepted as women in the face of violence.[47] He failed to mention the violence of some biological males now able to access female spaces simply by self-identifying as women.

Cathy reminded him that women's and girls' rights in all UN conventions are based on sex. She responded to Türk's suggestion that 'gender equality can only be achieved if all women, in all their diversity, are included', including transwomen, who 'face particularly high levels of violence', by noting: 'This is policy capture pure and simple. All the core human rights instruments explicitly protect the human rights of girls and women on the basis of sex. Not gender identity. Yet here is the UN High Commissioner for Human Rights advocating for gender identity to overwrite sex.'[48]

Whether it relates to current bending of the law or future political challenges, the message is clear. We have to take up this fight on a political and legal level. Without clear sex-based protections in domestic and international law, women's sport will be under threat even if there is progress within sports governing bodies.

The damage to female sport cannot just be viewed through the prism of elite, world-class sport. Allowing biological males into the female spaces and races is harmful at every level of sport, from the grass roots upwards.

12

WHY GIRLS' SPORT MATTERS

A T its best, sport is a force for good. It's a place where parents introduce their children to a healthy environment and where trustworthy teachers and coaches commit to helping athletes get the best out of themselves.

Everyone should have the chance to participate in sport and benefit from physical and mental fitness, as well as the dedication, determination and discipline required and the lifelong friendships formed in communities, clubs and competitions.

Whether competition is part of our sport or not it should be about fun, health, resilience and the development of skills and mind-sets we need to cope with life's challenges. Research has also shown the beneficial effect of exercise and sport on schoolwork, behaviour and organisational skills.[1]

The UK Government Equalities Office claims that girls lose motivation to play sport after the age of seven, often as a result of self-consciousness and loss of confidence.[2] Perception is a common problem, with many girls considering boys' sports to be rough, while boys believe that girls lack skill. The lack of female sporting role models also has a negative impact.

A 2012 study for the Women's Sport and Fitness Foundation in the UK noted that more than half of girls are put off by PE classes.[3] The report found that only 12 per cent of 14-year-old girls get enough physical activity each week, whereas twice as many boys do.

Girls want to be active and healthy but are discouraged by their poor experience of sport. Barriers include:

- spaces dominated by boys
- girls being self-conscious about being seen exercising and getting hot and sweaty, in particular in the presence of boys
- a perception that being sporty is not aspirational for girls
- higher expectations at home that girls will help out around the house and do 'female' chores while the boys go off to sport.

The foundation concluded that barriers are deep-rooted and entrenched, particularly around notions of femininity, pressures to be thin (as opposed to fit) and perceptions of sport being a man's world and only of value if competitive. That's been compounded by a lack of deeper understanding about the nature of sport.

Yes, the medals and prizes are a key reason why people compete, but there's much more to competition than that, including self-improvement and all the lessons learned from setting goals and working to achieve them.

Sport also teaches resilience, one of the most important life skills. It's about learning to be able to get knocked down but then to rise, train harder and go again. This has been invaluable to me throughout life. I have been well served by sport and my passion for it. I was a Devon senior champion in swimming at ten years of age and made my England debut at 11 when I was still in primary school. The best girl, often by a big margin, I still wasn't as good as the boys were at that age.

My experience in sport ever since tells me that, from grass roots upwards, we've taken the wrong turn. At a time when it's already hard enough to keep girls in sport, there's a serious risk things are

going to get much worse because of the overtly discriminatory policies being advocated and adopted by authorities.

My daughter Grace was told at the age of 11 or 12 that she could
no longer play with the boys because it wasn't safe from that age –
but apparently it's perfectly OK for a transgender woman who is a
biological male to play with the girls at any age. I've had parents of
young girls who love youth rugby tell me they've been told to stay
quiet when they see powerful transgirls show up on opposing teams.
Their only option is to withdraw their daughters from the sports
they love. That's tragic for women's sport.

In her book *Irreversible Damage: The Transgender Craze Seducing
Our Daughters*, Abigail Shrier asks why it is always girls and women
who need to be more accommodating than boys and men.[4]

It's what Linda Blade describes in *Unsporting* as: 'Men: As you
were. Women: You need to sacrifice.'

It breaks my heart to think that women have fought for decades
only to find the young women of today now suffering from new and
in some ways more virulent forms of sexism.

That's very close to home for me. My mum was of a generation that
fought and worked hard for rights many take for granted these days.
She was 78 when she passed away in 2017 after a battle with cancer
rooted in a hepatitis-C viral infection caused by a blood transfusion
during an operation in the 1970s. It was a big scandal that affected a
lot of people. Effectively, the drugs she had to take to fight the virus
eventually caused her liver cancer, we were told. The legacy she left me
included part of the proceeds from my parents' first house together.
Mum was told she couldn't have her name on the first mortgage
secured with her own money. She believed very much in the family
and being a wife, but she had an independent career and fought and
worked her way up in life. That was fine progress back then.

After my parents divorced she paid all her own bills, finished
raising my two younger brothers alone and had her own mortgage

eventually. When she died she owned her own home after decades of working as a civil servant in the Ministry of Defence. Her generation had fought very hard for independence, acceptance and equality, and made massive strides that subsequent generations benefited greatly from. Now, I feel we're genuinely going backwards.

I was never a vocal feminist, to be honest, because I never felt I was persecuted. Nor did inequality seem to be a big thing to me back then, because I was a young athlete and all of us, men and women, trained, travelled and raced on the same teams. I had a good, strong role model at home, and a dad/coach who had instilled resilience and confidence in me through my sport.

In some ways there's more sexism now because it's hidden. I never thought we'd ever again see the kind of treatment female athletes experienced in my prime years in sport because of East German doping. Tragically, the discrimination faced by women today not only runs parallel to events in elite sport all those years ago but reaches all levels of sport, grass roots to Masters. In many ways it's worse and affects more people.

WHAT HAPPENS WHEN YOU TAKE COMPETITION AND SEX-BASED CATEGORIES OUT OF SCHOOL SPORT

Two of the most critical aspects of grass-roots sport have come under attack of late. On the one hand, there's been a move to remove competition from school sport altogether, while on the other there's been a drive to strip sport of sex segregation.

Sport can only be fun if no one is left disappointed or feels like a failure, we're told by those who want school sports day to be an uncompetitive affair.

In Inverness in 2018, a primary school scrapped separate races for boys and girls so that any prepubescent children who might end up opting for transition wouldn't feel excluded.[5] What about all the other kids there? Don't they matter? In January 2023, the same school made headlines once more after parents said that it was asking children as young as five if they were gay or transgender.[6]

It's even happened in schools where there may be no trans-gender kids but decision makers have opted to impose policies that discriminate against girls. In the United States, the ACLU, which has become, in effect, a trans lobby group, runs a campaign against 'outing' in a number of states with legislation that ensures trans-parency, because they want to keep details of biological sex private. Their website states: 'School officials may think they're doing the right thing, but revealing a student's sexual orientation or gender identity to their parents not only violates the student's privacy rights, but can open an LGBTQ+ child to hostility, rejection, and even violence from their parents.'[7]

How would that be managed? Should a trans pupil wish to play sport and share locker rooms with pupils of the opposite biological sex, wouldn't the other pupils and their parents have a right to know and then raise any concerns they have about a clash of rights, fair-ness and safety? Or should girls, like those at the NCAA swimming championships in 2022, wait to see a penis in their changing rooms before being properly informed about what that particular model of inclusion looks like? Binary sex status is not hidden, but the ACLU argues that trans pupils who are 'outed' may suffer negative or harm-ful consequences at school or at home from that disclosure, despite the fact that they would have chosen to live their life identifying in the gender opposite their actual biological sex.

Meanwhile, local authorities are under pressure from campaign-ers who say that 'stereotyping means making assumptions about children because of their gender', in the words of the campaigning organisation Not Only Pink and Blue. In an article on its website, we read: 'One suggestion to improve gender equality in school sports is to encourage more mixed-gender sports. Not only would this allow girls more equal access to sports, but would also help support non-binary students to feel comfortable in pursuing the sports they love to do, too.'[8]

That represents a total misunderstanding of why little girls want and should get a chance to race other little girls. It's frustrating to hear from senior officials involved in school sport that heads are being told to drop separate competition for boys and girls to avoid having to deal with any parents insisting their children be given a ticket to sport with the opposite sex.

Parents of young females who love rugby tell me that they're pulling their daughters out of the sport because they're turning up on match day to find opposing teams lining up with teenage males identifying as girls who are physically much stronger and more aggressive. The risk of injury is real. That's why World Rugby ruled in 2020 that only female athletes could enter women's matches.

Tanni Grey-Thompson is a multiple Paralympic champion and an athlete who understands the value and nature of categorisation. Now Baroness Grey-Thompson and a peer in the House of Lords, she told a women's conference in December 2022 that 50 per cent of teenage girls don't feel good enough to take part in sport. Tanni sent me the full transcript of her excellent speech. She nailed it when she noted:

> Girls are not born under-confident but are immediately and consistently exposed to the narrative that they will not be good at sport or as active as boys. These limiting stereotypes mean that girls go into secondary school with much lower self-belief than boys. And then come new challenges of managing brutal changes to their body during puberty and the onslaught of social media. As a result 1.3 million teenage girls in the UK alone have fallen out of love with sport. Until we crush these limiting gender stereotypes society will continue to steal girls' self-belief, forcing

girls to the sidelines and in so doing contributing to spiralling anxiety, self-harm and eating disorders.

Inspiration, confidence, self-belief and opportunity all play a key role in sport. The Paralympics is a manifestation of that for both women and men and transforms lives and alters perceptions of people with disabilities.

The assault on female sport is happening far and wide. I had a very distraught tweet sent to me by a mother who told me that her 11-year-old daughter came home from her own primary-school sports day saying that not a single girl had won an event, so what was the point of her entering? Her mum was livid, and asked me to carry on fighting for our daughters. I said I would.

It's little wonder that, in 2020, a 'systematic review' on 'Trends in physical fitness among school-aged children and adolescents' by a team of researchers from universities in Germany, Portugal and Montenegro, which studied more than 1.7 million children and adolescents from 14 countries (China, Finland, Sweden, Belgium, New Zealand, Denmark, Spain, Norway, Mozambique, Poland, USA, Lithuania, Portugal, Canada) over the period between 1969 and 2017, showed that there had been a constant decline in strength and endurance.[9]

In other words, we're going backwards in our physical abilities. That's a very worrying trend when we also know childhood obesity rates are rising.[10]

International federations deal with the elite end of sport but their member federations don't only do that. School sports days, as well as local club and country competitions, are all part of the performance pathway that can lead to Olympic dreams.

The direct link is nowhere more visible than in the United States, where local swim leagues for kids have been a competitive birthing pool for generations of Olympic champions, including greats like swimmer Katie Ledecky.

Progress from little league to Olympics doesn't follow a straight line upwards. On a graph, that line looks more like a roller coaster for many – and, significantly, the trajectory for females is very different to that for males. Experience in swimming shows us that junior females often improve between puberty and the transition from girl to woman, when their form plateaus as they adjust to the physical changes as their body matures.

Brooke Hanson, the Australian breaststroke specialist who claimed a record six gold medals at the World Short-Course Championships in 2004, at the age of 26, told Craig:

> It was only after a few years of those changes that I started to get stronger again as my body got used to the new, adult me. We have a different development cycle to the men and a lot of girls just quit when they couldn't improve around the age of 19 to 22–23 but I'm here to tell them to stick with it, persevere. You'll come through it and you'll be stronger for it. Your best years are in your mid-twenties upwards. That plateau is just a part of who you are as a woman.[11]

There's scant research into that side of female development in swimming (perhaps the IOC should invest in scientists seeking budgets to work on projects aimed at finding out more about what affects women). Even so, we know the female plateau is real and Brooke's advice to girls is golden. Of course, you have to have the girls stick with the sport at 12, 14 and 16 first.

If you dump sex-based categorisation in favour of a melting pot, boys win and girls learn that in sport they will always lose and never win. So why bother at all? In that climate, it isn't only swimming, running, cycling, netball, football, tennis, rugby and much else that girls lose but the myriad lessons in life that sport can teach us.

That includes the difference between womanhood and femininity. I don't believe that a male can actually understand what it feels like to be female, or vice versa, because a large part of being a female is dealing with hormones and the biological processes that bring challenges. It's also about learning to take extra precautions at night because females feel vulnerable. It's so much more than an outfit or toys young kids want to play with. I grew up climbing trees and competing with my two brothers, always on a bike, short hair, jeans and smelling of chlorine. I was a tomboy but not once did I think I was in the wrong body. I was in 'my' body.

My daughter Grace, like lots of young women, went through her teenage years crying, it seemed, just as I had – she is super sensitive! It was an emotional roller coaster. How can anyone born male know what that feels like? Males have their own challenges. My 16-year-old son is at a grunting stage and breaking out in spots everywhere because of high levels of testosterone. When his voice broke it was a big deal. Puberty is a really hard time. I think we are wrong to say that we can delay or stop it, or change the natural processes that have to happen before a young person emerges into adulthood and finds out who they are: we have to help them through it instead.

Humans are designed to go through puberty – it's a massive part of our development, both mentally and physically – so we can make better decisions at the end of it. If it's deemed children aren't old enough to drink, smoke, drive, get married or vote – to name just a few things out of bounds for them – how can they be deemed mature enough, with enough life skills, to take hormones that could make them infertile or give them potentially huge medical issues in years to come?

Taking testosterone as a female changes your voice, gives you an Adam's apple, shrinks your womb painfully, thins your hair, grows hair on your face, builds a different body shape and more. Much of that cannot be totally reversed if a person in transition changes their mind. Medically transitioning is a massive step, especially for females. Testosterone takes over when oestrogen is removed in a male, so males stand a better chance of changing their minds and resuming normal male body appearance and function. Females who change their minds will be left with visible changes that they will have to live with for the rest of their lives.

Then there's pregnancy and carrying a child. There's no transitioning on that one. A male can say he feels like he's pregnant and he wants to get pregnant. But he can't! It's impossible. You can't carry a baby and you'll never know what that feels like as a male. We have to be realistic about this. Society's become a place where #BeKind means telling lies – and telling them to our children, too. It's a fantasy that causes harm and we shouldn't encourage it, neither in our children nor in society in general. Sport is one of the realms that reinforce the message that one can't change sex, that feelings and self-identity do not address issues of safety and fair play and that we should not only be realistic but acknowledge the harm done to others if we fail to tell the truth.

WHAT SPORT AND COMPETITION TEACH US

If we're serious about equal opportunities for males and females, then the answers cannot include banning the competitiveness of sport, nor allowing biological males into female races. Life is incredibly competitive, and we're doing our kids no favours by pretending otherwise, so we have to explain the merits of competition for all, first to last.

In a debate about it in 2017, psychologist Amanda Hills echoed my long-held view when she said: 'This business of saying that sports days need to be politically correct, with no element of competition, to me that's absolute nonsense. It doesn't teach children anything useful, because life is competitive, and they have to learn to lose as well as win.'[12]

She says it's unfair not to celebrate the achievements of a sporty child. I agree. Kids have a multitude of talents and we must appreciate all of them. We should also remember that even the greatest athletes lose sometimes and many of them and their coaches cite the losing moments among the most important of their careers. Improvement starts at the point where you identify what you might have done better, while losing feeds the champion mindset with hunger, drive, motivation and the determination that serves discipline and dedication.

I also think that losing teaches children the values of humility and stoicism, both of which are valuable virtues to cultivate.

That's a point made by Adrian Rădulescu, the coach to David Popovici of Romania, who drew comparisons with legends of his sport such as Australian Ian Thorpe and American Michael Phelps in an extraordinary 2022 season that included an unprecedented sweep of world, world junior, European and European junior titles in the 100 and 200 metres freestyle. In an interview with Craig in Rome on the eve of David winning the world 100 and 200 metres freestyle titles at just 17 years of age, the coach recalled the value in teaching children how to lose well.[13]

The swim coach wanted to teach his pupil that failure = opportunity to prove virtue and improve as a person.

In sport, feelings of nervousness can be just the body and mind getting you ready for fight not flight. But fear of failure, the judgement of others, sends young athletes to their blocks like a bag of negative nerves sometimes, and it's hard to get the best out of yourself in those circumstances.

Adrian pointed David to the ancient Stoics to teach him such lines from Epictetus as: 'There is only one way to happiness and that is to cease worrying about things which are beyond the power of our will.' The coach explained to the swimmer how such an approach would free him from 'pre-race fear, the fear of failure, the fear of being embarrassed', Rădulescu told the World Aquatics Development Conference in Lund, Sweden, in February 2023.[14]

My dad would always say that losing a race is an opportunity to get better, because we analyse our defeats more than we do our successes. Teaching our kids to be proud of themselves if they give the very best of themselves, regardless of the outcome, is a positive thing – but easier said than done in a world of instant likes and airbrushed virtual gratifications. So, we need more lessons in resilience, more lessons for life taught through sport. Another curse of our times is that children are being wrapped up in cotton wool and rarely exposed to the rough and tumble of life. Every rock of the boat is a crisis waiting to happen.

All great athletes arrive in elite sport from local community, club and school backgrounds. The foundation years are critical and the lessons learned do not only apply to those destined for greatness.

Fun can be about setting goals and following a step-by-step process of self-improvement, getting the work done each and every day for months and years, so that no matter what place you finish on race day, there's something to celebrate, take pride and learn from. That goes for Olympic podium placers and finalists just as much as the child who finishes fifth on school sports day.

The result matters, of course, but the question, even in an Olympic final, is not just 'Did you win?' The learning curve of sport means that we ask whether a performance exceeded, matched or fell shy of what the competitor had set as a goal and believed themselves capable of. Learning follows.

But what do girls learn if they get to sports day and find that all their races and competitions are won by male classmates? What do they learn if they look at the world and understand from an early age that they are destined to be officially and systematically discriminated against?

The difference between boys' and girls' sports starts earlier than advocates of all-in-one-pot school sports days would have us believe.

The USA Track & Field (USATF) website lists national records from '8 & Under', a category in which male advantage already shows up in running, jumping and throwing events.[15]

The performance gap between girls and boys in a variety of sports, including swimming and running, is not as great at that age as it will be post puberty, but there's no denying that significant differences have already started to show. Children develop and mature at different rates, but at around 12 to 13 years of age, as puberty kicks in, the picture changes dramatically and it is much harder to find any girls who remain competitive with the best boys in sport. There's just one overriding reason: their sex!

Whatever the truth of any performance gap in any given pre-pubescent population, boys and girls will soon understand why males and females are segregated into competition categories in sport.

Rules written specifically with equality, safety and fair play in mind are part of sport and its cultural references. I see no reason to change that and many reasons to reinforce it.

As Baroness Grey-Thompson pointed out, if you don't have races for boys and girls and you consistently expose girls to the narrative that they can't win at sport and will never be good at sport 'like the boys are', you'll get a self-fulfilling prophecy: far fewer girls in sport. I'm sure, sadly, that that also translates into life in general.

The issue also spills into the experience of women in the workplace. The 'Voice of Women Working in Sport' report published in February 2023 by sports market-research company Sporting Insights and the not-for-profit organisation Women's Sport Collective included some alarming findings. Fewer than 1 per cent of women working in sport believe there is gender equality in the industry, while women rate the sector as 4.63 out of ten in terms of gender equality, 51 per cent believe they are paid less than men for the same work, 36 per cent say male gatekeepers in sport restrict their career progression and 44 per cent call on male allies in the sector to let their voices be heard and be more visible in defence of their female colleagues.[16]

SAFETY FIRST

My friend and former Olympic teammate Daley Thompson, who won back-to-back decathlon golds in the 1980s, is among the men who have stood up and supported women on this issue. We need more men to stand up and be counted. It is their fight too: they have daughters, mothers, sisters and wives. They train with females; they know the truth just as much as women do.

Never one to hold back his opinion, Daley told the media that it was depressing to see biological males in women's sport 'because it has the potential to put an end to women's sport. Theoretically I can identify as a lady and go and compete.' Daley summed up the IOC relaxation of inclusion rules by saying: 'A lot of people said, "Let's be as inclusive as we can," and didn't think about the unintended consequences. We are sleepwalking into a minefield.'[17]

I know there was terrible sexism when I was growing up, but because I was tall and pretty robust and had a strong character, men would be wary about trying it on. They knew I'd be among those saying very loudly things like 'What did you just say!?' and 'Take your hand off me!' I would certainly have dealt with it there and then. It's important we teach young girls not to accept abuse, physical or mental – and to speak out and report immediately.

I met Jimmy Savile several times.[18] I never felt comfortable in his presence. It turned out he was even more vile than anyone other than his victims could have imagined. He didn't try it on with me. Weak, disgusting men like him choose their victims very carefully: they pick on the vulnerable and seek out the moments and circumstances when they know their target will find it hard to fight back.

Crime statistics prove that we must have preventative measures in place. Young women are surely vulnerable if inadequate policies and rules catering for trans athletes, coaches, venue staff and others under-mine single-sex spaces in sport for girls. Bad men all through history have taken advantage of bad laws. That's not speculation, it's fact.

We know that grooming is on the rise in the internet age, as are self-harm and other mental disorders affecting young girls and women, like anorexia.[19] Sport is no more immune than any other section of society.

According to new research by the children's commissioner for England in January 2023, one in ten children in England (similar statistics exist for other countries) have watched pornography by the time they are nine years old.[20] The commissioner, Dame Rachel de Souza, noted the harmful effects of exposure to violent pornog-raphy. Astonishingly, half of the 16- to 21-year-old boys who took part in her survey assumed girls either 'expect' or 'enjoy' sex which involves physical aggression. These are all very alarming issues and cover early-development years when the guidance young children get sets their pathway in life.

It's important to understand that in a sport like swimming, which has had its fair share of sex-abuse scandals down the years, squads often have kids around the age of puberty right through to adults in their twenties and thirties training in the same pool and using communal changing rooms.

There are safeguarding and privacy issues that must be taken into account if biological males, not only athletes but potentially coaches, pool staff and parents, are allowed to be in the female locker room and showers. If we're to have rules and inclusion in sport, then it's only fair and proper to ask sports venues to create extra changing facilities or reallocated space so that single-sex spaces are preserved for females. Such spaces should not be open to biological males, regardless of how anyone feels or identifies.

WHY WOMEN ARE QUITTING SPORT

At grass-roots level in the UK, girls and women, including pensioners, are quitting community and recreation sport because they are being forced to face male opponents identifying as women. Fair Play for Women compiled a dossier of cases in January 2023. Its director of sport campaigns, Fiona McAnena, said: 'If you think this is a very small problem, think again. This issue is hitting women's sport right across the UK, and sadly it is pushing some women to completely drop out.'[21]

She was speaking in response to an interview in which cyclist Bo Novak, aged 55, said she had stopped attending women-only road-cycling sessions after a transwoman started to lead the group she joined in south-west England. The sessions had been advertised as 'leisure rides for women in small groups led by a woman', but the lead cyclist turned out to be a biological male who was much stronger than the rest of the group, and much faster too.

The Fair Play for Women case file included a female hockey player in an amateur London league who walked off the pitch after being tasked with marking a transgender opponent. The athlete said:

> The person was 6ft 4in and had an Adam's apple. Every time I was going for the ball, the transgender woman was far faster and after a few minutes I just took myself off. I was in tears. I came to play against a female opposition and there was a male on the pitch. I just felt the sense of fairness was not there.[22]

She said that she felt unable to complain in case she was branded a 'transphobe'. I understand how she feels, but urge women everywhere to stand shoulder to shoulder and refuse to put up with being bullied into silence.

Fair Play for Women also notes that a parent and cricket coach from the south of England expressed concerned about the safety of girls, one as young as 12, after his team was asked to play against opposition that included a transwoman. He said: 'As father to these girls [aged 14 and 16] I find that unacceptable, uncomfortable and dangerous, both morally and physically.'[23]

It's disturbing to think that human-rights advocates, sociologists, sports leaders and politicians lecturing us about being 'kind' are among campaigners for the inclusion of biological males in female sport when they surely know what it means for women, of all ages. How is it being kind to them? Why does kindness only seem to go one way?

There's only one response. We're not going to be bullied by activists into giving up rights for females so hard fought for. As Nancy Hogshead-Makar put it in an interview with us for this book: 'It's just sexism 101 running through the whole movement, Olympics to local little league. They're saying to girls that it doesn't matter in high school sports because that's all about participation not competition. Nobody's saying that to the boys in soccer, basketball, American football or any boys' sport.'

Regulators should have been on the ball. Instead of making trans inclusion add up to open season on female athletes, they should have confirmed the reason why sport has sex-based categories and ring-fenced the women's category for females. They should then have found a home for transgender athletes in an appropriate category, not one chosen by the athlete, where they get the biggest advantage.

No transwoman should ever have been allowed into the women's category at any level of sport until thorough inquiry and research had shown it to be fair and safe. There is no such evidence – and that matters. I've always spoken up for myself and other women where there's injustice and I'll continue to do so. Sport is still a man's world. Time for change.

It's been a very hard road for women. The deafness of sports' leaders to women's voices is appalling.

THE POWER OF LEADING SPORTS VOICES

Caitlyn Jenner, who claimed the Olympic men's decathlon title for the United States in 1976 as Bruce Jenner, is a case in point. Caitlyn speaks from the perspective of both a supreme male athlete and a transwoman.

While she has 'one hundred per cent' respect for swimmer Lia Thomas's wish to live life 'authentically', she says that that should not come at the expense of women in sport. Transition, said Caitlyn, 'comes with responsibility and some integrity. I don't know why she's doing this. It's not good for the trans community. We have a lot of issues in the trans community that are very difficult and very challenging.'[24]

She advocates a model of inclusion in sport that has first to be fair to female athletes. Biological males do not belong in women's sport, she believes, noting the truth about Lia Thomas: 'She was born as a biological boy. She was raised as a biological boy.'[25]

A growing number of leading sportswomen are becoming braver. In February 2023, surfer Bethany Hamilton announced that she would not compete at World Surf League (WSL) events if the federation stuck to a new policy of allowing transwomen into the female division. In a video posted on Instagram Bethany asked: 'Is a hormone level an honest and accurate depiction that someone indeed is a male or female? Is it as simple as this? Who is pushing for this huge change?'[26]

Patricia Spratlen-Etem, a former US Olympic rower, is also speaking out. She was denied her place at the Games in 1980 by the American boycott, and pointed to a painful history when she described President Biden's trans-inclusion stance as an 'awful threat' to Title IX. Patricia likened the 1980 boycott and her shot at rowing gold to what young girls and women face in sports today because of bad transgender-inclusion policies.[27]

To add insult to injury, the University of Pennsylvania nominated Lia Thomas for the NCAA 'Woman of the Year' award in July 2022. Tennis legend Martina Navratilova tweeted in response: 'Not enough fabulous biological women athletes, NCAA?!? What is wrong with you?!!!!!!!?'[28]

Ultimately neither Riley Gaines nor Lia Thomas made the final NCAA shortlist for the Woman of the Year honour, but swimmer Brooke Forde, one of those beaten by Thomas in the 500 yards, did.

The 2022 season marked the end of Lia Thomas's college career, but, in an interview on *Good Morning America*, Thomas implied that it was fair to have biological males in female racing because some women had 'more testosterone' than others.[29] Thomas did not mention rules that allowed her to have ten times the testosterone than an average female has.

Thomas said: 'I don't need anybody's permission to be myself. I intend to keep swimming. It's been a goal of mine to swim at Olympic trials for a very long time, and I would love to see that through.'[30]

The truth is that such goals had only become remotely realistic as Lia. Will was never an athlete with even a tiny chance of getting anywhere near Olympic trials, let alone on a Team USA Olympic swimming team.

Whether Thomas gets to race at the US Olympic trials in 2024 remains to be seen. One thing is for sure, however. Thomas will no longer be eligible to race in the women's category, thanks to a vote on 19 June 2022, when FINA, as part of a reform process that also led to a name change to 'World Aquatics', delivered cathartic and heart-warming news.

13

GREEN SHOOTS – AND SWIMMING
TURNS THE TIDE

Nᴏᴛ all international federations are as blind as the IOC.
When World Rugby bosses believed their own eyes and
listened to the science in October 2020, they barred biological males
from the women's game on grounds of safety.[1] The risk of injury in
contact sports had been obvious to anyone who had seen the likes
of trans player Kelly Morgan fold an opponent 'like a deckchair',
but World Rugby followed an exemplary process before making its
landmark decision.[2]

Female athletes celebrated the decision along with everyone else
who noted that safety and fair play were already promised in sports
rules as a precondition of inclusion for all.

All aspects of safety, including the right to safe spaces and privacy for female athletes, are essential in all sports. Injury is a big part
of the picture in general, with sport accounting for 20 per cent of
all non-fatal injuries in the EU in 2012.[3] In the United States, 3.5
million young athletes under the age of 15 receive medical care each
year for injuries sustained in sport, and two-thirds of those cases
require care in emergency units. And in Africa, 23 million adolescents are estimated to suffer sports injuries annually.[4]

Rugby is high up the league of injuries associated with contact
sports, and there are grounds for suing any federation that fails to

deliver adequate prevention and mitigation measures in competition rules. In 2019, rugby referees told the *Sunday Times* that they were quitting the sport because they were afraid of being sued by females injured by transgender women in games.[5]

The referees had been warned not to challenge bearded or heavily muscled players on women's teams even though the rules of rugby state that a referee is the sole judge of fact and of law during the match and must remove a player who presents a danger to themselves or others. One referee that season had seen five different players with beards in women's matches in a matter of a few months. Another told the paper: 'Being forced to prioritise hurt feelings over broken bones exposes me to personal litigation from female players who have been damaged by players who are biologically male. This is driving female players and referees out of the game.'[6]

Against that backdrop, World Rugby took decisive action in February of 2020 when it invited key stakeholders and experts, including women's rights groups, trans players and advocates, doctors, kinesiologists, sports scientists, developmental biologists, human-rights and ethics specialists, lawyers and insurers to a series of brainstorming face-to-face presentations and discussions.

It was great to see the federation of a leading sport welcome Dr Nicola Williams, head of Fair Play for Women, and biologist Dr Emma Hilton, whose efforts as global pioneers in the struggle to save women's sport have been heroic. They attended groundbreaking consultations at World Rugby with doctors Jon Pike, Tommy Lundberg and Ross Tucker, the federation's chief scientist, which acknowledged that injury to female athletes increases by a minimum of 20 to 30 per cent when they're forced to play against males.[7]

The science and the research that produces those facts should play an obligatory part in any decision-making process on inclusion issues at sports organisations. You can't base safety and fair-play rules on feelings. Common sense prevailed in global rugby, however, and after listening to all the experts and advocates, the council announced in October 2020 that the women's game would be for females only – because 'a balance between safety, fairness and inclusion could not be provided for transwomen playing women's contact rugby'.[8]

At last we had a decision that took into account the well-being of female athletes. Trans activists complained that rugby had made the decision on the basis of a few incidents in a contact sport, as if safety rules can be set on the assumption that any injury sustained by a woman overpowered by a biological male is acceptable. It's not. Sports organisations have a responsibility to be proactive where there is a risk of preventable harm.

As Tucker has often suggested, sports governors must do the right thing, not the reactive thing. I couldn't be more grateful for the work of Tucker, Hilton, Pike, Lundberg and their colleagues bringing the science to light and showing how it matches the reality unfolding in front of our eyes as biological males prosper in a wide range of female sports.

Dr Linda Blade deserves praise, too, for outstanding efforts in the fight for women's sport. Linda and Barbara Kay, the journalist who worked with her on *Unsporting*, have put to the fire the feet of weak governance in Canada, a country that flies the woke flag highest but that has one of the worst abuse records in recent sporting history. Linda and Barbara are part of a sorority that's refusing to back down in the face of infuriating hypocrisy and what we see as intentional sexism at sports organisations largely run by men.

Thanks to their tireless campaigning with women's advocacy groups (see Appendix 2), the message is being heard over the noise of those telling us that being a man or a woman is nothing to do with sex but all about feelings. And feelings that count for more than ours because trans people are an oppressed minority that couldn't possibly be wrong when insisting that there's no such thing as male advantage in sport and that standing up for safety and fair play is bigotry and hatred.

Athletes, coaches and parents know what's fair, but it's not uncommon in sport for their opinions never to be courted. They're just stakeholders, after all, and athletes are just the people there to entertain us.

Beth Stelzer is founder of Save Women's Sports. She's a powerlifter who faced the aggressive and obnoxious protest of a male lifter demanding a ticket to the female category at the Minnesota State Powerlifting Championships, which she ran, in February 2019.[9] Beth faced the wrath of trans activists but stood her ground and prevented the damage that would have been done to an event she'd worked hard to stage.

She held a successful rally in Washington DC in June 2022 under the banner 'Our Bodies, Our Sports', while Save Women's Sports lobbied the IOC and its supporters staged peaceful demonstrations inside and outside venues at sports events across the United States at various levels, including NCAA championships.[10] Without such consistent efforts, female sport would have been pushed over a cliff edge by now.

We need more good people in positions of authority to find the courage to do the right thing. Beth's federation, USA Powerlifting, has Dr Kris Hunt as its medical director. His presentation at the 2019 USA Powerlifting meeting on transgender policy provides some fine tips for other sports still struggling with science, fact and reality. Dr Hunt's comprehensive explanation of the science and the justification for female-only women's sport ought to form part of the IOC's literature on the subject.[11]

After noting that the Court of Arbitration for Sport (CAS) and IOC make no distinction between sex and gender and that therefore Olympic bosses expect federations to 'accept that transwomen, born male, are actually female and the data on sexual dimorphisms and physiological differences is irrelevant', Dr Hunt adds:

Our counterclaim to this argument is that identifying as one
sex does not defy the factual physical differences between sexes
that exist regardless of sex reassignment or hormone suppression. The assertion of gender choice, although legal to change
in parts of the world, does not erase the dimorphic differences
of sex, formalised at birth and continually developing throughout the lifespan, that have direct implications to performance
advantages. Although gender may best be understood on a
continuum, designation and consequences of biological sex
do not.[12]

A court overturned the USA Powerlifting decision and legal
counter-challenges are promised. Even so, those truths are slowly
being heard in various sports the world over and all the more so after
the IOC issued sexist, non-binding guidance in 2021.[13] A year later,
an update from the IOC sought to explain that it was committed
to fairness in women's sport, but at the same time reinforced all the
reasons why we need to keep up the fight until women's sports is
saved for female athletes.

I've had meetings with Cabinet ministers and Members of
Parliament, as well as in the House of Lords, in the UK. If the IOC
and international federations won't protect women's sports, there are
other ways to make sure it happens. None of those would be needed
if the transparent and balanced model my sport has opted for was
used as a template for organisations in other sports.

SWIMMING TURNS THE TIDE

The fight within sporting governance is already under way – and
women don't always lose.

It was great news from the general congress of swimming global
regulator FINA in Budapest in June 2022. Women's swimming

would be ring-fenced for females only from the very next day. Any boy who lives through male puberty is no longer eligible for the women's category. Finally, we had a big, unequivocal, game-changing decision in favour of women from a leading Olympic sport.

In my sport, too! The same policy also applies to the other three Olympic aquatics disciplines: diving, water polo and synchronised (or artistic) swimming. In water polo it was genuinely a cause for safety concerns too.

FINA, which has since rebranded as World Aquatics, had voted overwhelmingly in favour of fair play for women by excluding all biological males who experience any part of Tanner stage 2 puberty from female competition.[14] The cut-off equates to around 12 years, but is a more accurate measure than age. Inclusion was assured. All other athletes would be eligible for a men's and/or a new 'open' category, along the lines of what we'd called for back in 2019. The shape of the 'open' category is set to be announced in July 2023 after a task force was convened to work out the details.

Craig called me from Budapest for the *Sunday Times* and asked me for my response.[15] It was simple enough. I was immensely proud of our international federation, and on the reform road to a much better place. They'd not only done the right thing but embraced a professional, fully transparent process.

Just as World Rugby had done when adopting a gender-inclusion policy that protected the women's game for females only, the policy that FINA leaders recommended to the global membership of aquatics was informed by the collective opinions of female athletes, coaches, doctors, lawyers versed in sex discrimination and human rights, exercise scientists, human biologists and specialist clinicians. No one was excluded.

The recommendation of the experts citing the science was clear: transgender women who developed as males from puberty onwards should be ineligible for elite competition.

I'd been talking to coaches for a while before the vote and knew that the World Swimming Coaches Association (WSCA) and its president, Jon Rudd, the performance director in charge of Ireland's elite swimming programme, had urged World Aquatics to keep women's events for females only and to create an 'open' category to ensure inclusion for all.

The WSCA submission included the following statement: 'Competitive fairness cannot be reconciled with self-identification into the female category in a gender-affected sport such as swimming. The average differences in strength, stamina and physique between the sexes are significant. Transgender females are, on average, likely to retain physical advantages even if testosterone suppression is utilised.'[16]

That's how you stand up for fair sport for females. Swimming will always welcome everyone, no matter how they identify, but fairness is the cornerstone of sport. The World Aquatics vote followed speeches by a range of world-class experts and two female Olympic swimming champions, American Summer Sanders and Australian Cate Campbell, who spoke eloquently and with passion. All the presentations are available through the World Aquatics YouTube page.[17]

'Women, who have fought long and hard to be included and seen as equals in sport, can only do so because of the gender category distinction,' Cate said. 'To remove that distinction would be to the detriment of female athletes everywhere.'

Among the slides presented as evidence of the irreversible impact of male puberty and the strength retained even after any subsequent hormone-replacement therapy, experts noted that, by the age of 14, the best boy swimmers in the world are already racing faster than the female world-record pace. The American 13–14 age group records for boys in the 50, 100 and 200 metres freestyle are all faster than the women's world record in those events.

The World Aquatics policy states:

Because of the performance gap that emerges at puberty between biological males as a group and biological females as a group, separate sex competition is necessary for the attainment of these objectives. Without eligibility standards based on biological sex or sex-linked traits, we are very unlikely to see biological females in finals… and in sports and events involving collisions and projectiles, biological female athletes would be at greater risk of injury.[18]

A weight had been lifted and women's swimming restored to females. It had been a long, hard road. Anyone who had spoken up for women and pointed to the reality of binary sex, the differences between male and female and how those play out in sport had been bullied and harassed. Since being voted World Aquatics president in June 2021, Husain Al-Musallam had made clear that he would not compromise on fair play, while seeking to honour a commitment to inclusion.

After the vote in Budapest, he said:

We have to protect the rights of our athletes to compete, but we also have to protect competitive fairness at our events, especially the women's category. FINA will always welcome every athlete. The creation of an open category will mean that everybody has the opportunity to compete at an elite level. This has not been done before, so FINA will need to lead the way. I want all athletes to feel able to develop ideas during this process.[19]

The World Aquatics policy is obligatory for all national federations and overrides 'any domestic policies' for those seeking to race in international competition, FINA director Brent Nowicki told delegates at the regulator's congress.

Swimming had turned the tide on easy access for transwomen to female sport and that didn't go down well with everyone. Alejandra Caraballo, a transgender instructor at Harvard Law School, said the new policy would be a green light for other bodies to pass 'similarly restrictive bans and also require athletes to produce as many as ten years or more of invasive medical records and blood tests', according to a report in the *New York Times*.[20] I hope so. In fact, I hope every sport protects the women's category for females, the people it was designed for.

HOW WORLD AQUATICS BUILT
ITS GAME-CHANGING POLICY

Caraballo also made a mistake when they told the newspaper: 'This is an incredibly discriminatory policy that is attempting to fix a problem that doesn't exist. This is the result of a moral panic because of Lia Thomas.'[21] This was a reference to a popular narrative suggesting that swim bosses had been panicked into action because of the Thomas controversy in the United States. Some American outlets suggested that the whole thing was stoked up to keep Thomas out of the Olympics in 2024.

That was a total fallacy, said Brent Nowicki. He told News Corp colleagues Julian Linden and Craig: 'It's easy to say Lia Thomas was the lightning rod but that's not the case. These issues, health and safety, welfare issues, competition, fairness issues, these are issues that have been in international sport for years now.'[22]

The process of creating a new policy actually started in 2021, immediately after the IOC had issued a non-binding framework on inclusion and an instruction to international federations to form their own policies and rules based on the nature of the sports they regulate.

'We didn't start with the goalposts in front of us. We weren't trying to kick that ball through those goalposts,' Nowicki said. 'We were trying to move the ball down the field methodically, correctly, and that was the approach we had always taken.'[23]

Nowicki, who had worked for years at CAS and has a reputation for meticulous planning, found a long list of 'issues to resolve' on his desk when he took up his job at World Aquatics on 8 June 2021. Balancing fairness and inclusion was one of them. He took a deeper look into the transgender debate and soon started to assemble top international experts in various fields with no ties to the murky past of pre-reform FINA. Nowicki told News Corp:

> There was no preconceived notion. If anything, there was a desire to learn as much as we possibly could and figure out what does science say, what does it mean? I wanted an all-star team where everybody's a free agent. I wanted to know what it was. What does being transgender mean? What does it mean scientifically? What does it mean, chromosomally? What does it mean socially? What does it mean mentally? It's not just being transgender that makes you transgender. There's more to it than just the label you put on somebody. It was our duty to figure that out, educate ourselves.[24]

By November 2021, the first line-up of experts was in place. Consisting of medical and science experts, it included Dr Sandra Hunter, an Australian-born professor at the Athletic and Human Performance Research Center (AHPRC) at Marquette University in Milwaukee, Wisconsin. Nowicki got a first draft of their report in early 2022 and then began the process of completing the full version, keeping it a secret all the way to the vote in Budapest.

The scientists had stood shoulder to shoulder on the key pillars of the policy they recommended, namely:

- competition between male and female athletes is no longer fair once puberty kicks in because of the differences in testosterone values and sex-based development
- biological and physical changes can't be undone – there is no mitigating for male development to the point at which fair play might be possible.

The science was clear. Nowicki set up a second working group, with legal and human-rights experts, to look at how to frame the policy. The five members included former Federal Court of Australia judge Annabelle Bennett and James Drake, an Australian barrister and CAS Arbitrator, now based in London. Nowicki also sent out questionnaires to over 300 athletes around the world so he could hear their voices.

The response was overwhelming. More than 83 per cent said eligibility for events should be decided by birth sex. And over 63 per cent said they wanted to see an additional 'open category' created to ensure that everyone can compete. Nowicki also held one-on-one interviews with Sanders, Campbell and a number of other elite competitors whose identities remain confidential.

When the Congress voted 71 per cent in favour of adopting the new policy, it lit a fuse in world sport. Plaudits flooded in, but many are yet to take similar decisions. Several are expected to do so before the Paris Olympic Games in 2024. And that's fairly fast for the wheels of sports administration.

NO TO MAKING FEMALE SPORT A LIVE EXPERIMENT

There was also criticism of the swimming regulator from expected quarters, including LGBTQ+ campaign groups and the likes of transgender runner and scientist Dr Joanna Harper, who said that it was 'very unfortunate' because 'transwomen are not taking over women's sports and they are not going to'.[25]

That completely overlooks the potential for a small handful of transwomen competing on an unfair level to do enormous harm, as was the case in the days of the GDR. Harper said that it could take up to 20 more years of research. The mention of 20 years is particularly chilling for me. That's about the length of time that the GDR's sporting crime of the century was rolled out to catastrophic effect in women's sport. For two decades women in swimming, athletics and a variety of other sports such as rowing and cycling were subjected to the inclusion of female athletes who had been given male steroids to ensure that they could beat us. As this book has shown, the GDR's systematic cheating was highly successful because it was underpinned by cutting-edge science that made a live experiment of female sport.

Calling for 20 more years of research may well be viewed as a job-creation exercise for the trans industry. By all means let Dr Harper and others conduct their research on performance measures in trans athletes and file their academic papers accordingly, but not at the expense of females who deserve their opportunities and accolades.

Since 2019, Harper has indeed been conducting new research. She's based at Loughborough University, partly funded by an IOC grant. While universities and their sponsors are at it, perhaps they'd like to put some resources into specific studies about female sport, reflecting issues that affect women's performance specifically, such as the impact of the menstrual cycle.

SWIM BOSS NOWICKI:
'100% RIGHT BASED ON THE SCIENCE TODAY'

Some described the policy as 'aggressive', but Nowicki said in his interview with News Corp:

We went as far as we needed to go to meet the legitimate objectives we felt were necessary for competitive balance, for fairness in our sport. We had such a sound body of evidence, we had a sound body of voice, we felt comfortable in our legal skin and we were prepared to go forward. We weren't worried or concerned about what impact it would have on other federations.[26]

Among those there on the big day in Budapest were IOC president Thomas Bach and World Athletics boss Lord Coe. In Budapest, Sebastian Coe pledged a review of World Athletics transgender and DSD policies. The results were delayed until spring of 2023, but in 2022 Lord Coe told the media:

My responsibility is to protect the integrity of women's sport. We take that very seriously and, if it means that we have to make adjustments to protocols going forward, we will. And I've always made it clear: if we ever get pushed into a corner to that point where we're making a judgement about fairness or inclusion, I will always fall down on the side of fairness.[27]

He lived up to his promise! On 23 March 2023, World Athletics announced that it would follow Word Aquatics and no athlete who had experienced male puberty would be eligible for the female category. DSD athletes with access to high levels of testosterone would be eligible to compete with women if they reduced T levels below a limit of 2.5 nanomoles per litre for a minimum of 24 months.

Lord Coe's statement came as a great relief after an announcement in February 2023 of a World Athletics 'preferred option' that stuck with giving transwomen tickets to female sport if they reduced testosterone levels. The federation was clearly struggling to meet Lord Coe's pledge but a wave of opposition in the sport helped tip the balance back in favour of the president's promise.[28]

March also saw World Rowing, which could not change its rules until 2024, adopt bye-laws that effectively matched the World Athletics decision.

FIFA bosses have also indicated that they are minded to follow swimming, while the British government's Department for Culture, Media and Sport (DCMS) has recommended that 'all sports' follow the policy of World Aquatics.[29] Yet still sports bodies are dragging their feet.

They are also overlooking joint guidance from UK Sport, Sport England, Sport Wales, SportScotland and Sport Northern Ireland that concluded that

> the inclusion of transgender people into female sport cannot be balanced regarding transgender inclusion, fairness and safety in gender-affected sport... due to retained differences in strength, stamina and physique between the average woman compared with the average transgender woman or non-binary person assigned male at birth, with or without testosterone suppression.[30]

It has always been disappointing to me that this strong advice was not followed by all UK national governing bodies (NGBs) the moment it was issued in 2021. And all the more so given research that shows that strength is retained 14 years into hormone-reduction therapy.[31] It's very clear that allowing males into sport solely designed to offer females fair competition is sex discrimination – and that runs counter to the 2010 Equality Act and its sex-based provisions.

FUTURE CHALLENGES

Meanwhile, in the same June 2022 *New York Times* article reporting swimming's new policies and Caraballo's mistake on the timeline of Nowicki's plan, the paper noted that trans athletes might appeal the World Aquatics policy at CAS in Switzerland.

Any such appeal victory would also be subject to appeal to the ultimate arbiter of law in Switzerland (including CAS cases), the last-chance saloon of the Swiss Supreme Court. That particular avenue looked less hopeful for challengers on transgender issues by the close of 2022, after a 21 December decision of the Swiss government to reject the idea of introducing a 'third-gender' or 'no-gender' option for official records. Male and female remain the only two options.

'The binary gender model is still strongly anchored in Swiss society,' the Swiss Federal Council said in response to two proposals from the Swiss parliament, according to an article from the Associated Press. It added: 'The preconditions for the introduction of a third gender or for a general waiver of the gender entry in the civil registry currently are not there.'[32]

Nor is the science, according to the renowned evolutionary biologist Jerry Coyne, who tweeted in response to one such popular-science representation of sex as a spectrum. He said: '"Actual science" done by biologists shows 2 sexes, one with small mobile gametes and the other with large, immobile ones. There is no third sex. Disorders of sex development are not new sexes, and biological sex is binary. Let's not conflate sex, gender & developmental anomalies.'[33]

Indeed not. It's a message that's slowly sinking into the consciousness of Olympic bosses. In December 2022, the IOC's science team issued a new 'position statement' on their 'Framework on Fairness, Inclusion, and Non-Discrimination', issued a year earlier.[34] They appeared to have been stung by criticism of their discrimination against women, and yet they were still incapable of changing their ways.

There was a begrudging nod to female athletes but every one of the nine key points of the statement failed to acknowledge the impact on women of current policies. The science team's focus was instead almost exclusively on the rights and challenges of 'transgender and non-binary' athletes.

Thankfully, the document has no teeth. It's a series of non-binding guidelines. World Aquatics policy has already plotted a much bolder course when it comes to safeguarding women and ensuring that female athletes have a home of their own, free from unfair play in the shape of male advantage.

If you only have time to read one great paper from late 2022 on why males do not belong in female sport, then make it this one: 'When ideology trumps science: a response to the Canadian Centre for Ethics in Sport's review on transwomen athletes in the female category'.[35]

It demolishes the IOC position and the review referred to in the title. As the tide turns, female athletes owe a debt of thanks to its authors, the researchers and scientists Cathy Devine, Emma Hilton, Leslie Howe, Miroslav Imbrišević, Tommy Lundberg and Jon Pike, as well as to those colleagues whose fine work they cite, including Ross Tucker.

Lundberg joined Dr Greg Brown, professor of Exercise Science at the University of Nebraska Kearney, in an April 2023 paper that pulls together much of the science contained in the 18 peer-reviewed studies we referred to in Chapter 10. It's well worth a read.[36]

14

TRUTH AND RECONCILIATION

TRUTH

WHAT, then, are the principles that I think should shape the way forward in women's sport?

Jon Pike argues that the two most basic principles in all sports should be the safety conditional and the fairness conditional.

The first says: 'If there is an [intolerable] increased risk of injury from the inclusion of transwomen in the women's game, then it is unsafe for transwomen to compete in the women's category.'

The second states: 'If [intolerable] male advantage remains after Hormone treatment, then it is unfair for transwomen to compete in the women's category.'[1]

Allowing biological men to compete within the women's category can only be allowed if those two tests are met – and it's highly unlikely, in most cases, that they ever will be, based on the science we have to date.

Anyone trawling through the various IOC guidelines on transgender inclusion over the past two decades could be forgiven for thinking that safety and fair play are secondary concerns because inclusion of trans athletes is a priority over female athletes and their prospects. That has to stop.

How should we manage trans inclusion, given this?

Fairness and inclusion have been made opponents in a clash of rights, which must be resolved in the best interests of the vast majority in sport. We must call transwomen transwomen so they have the space to be themselves in a way that does not undermine the rights of other, much larger groups.

An 'open' category is the way forward. It's the only way to ensure that boundaries are respected and female athletes get the same level of fair play as their male counterparts. Yet everyone is included.

Federations are debating what such a category would look like. There are two basic models under consideration. The first, which I support, would mean that the category of 'men' would become 'open' and include all who are biologically male or who have chosen to have testosterone-boosting therapy on transition from female to identifying as a man. Anyone who has a chemical or biological advantage over females, including biological females taking male hormones that would lead to a woman testing positive for doping and then being banned, should have no ticket to female sport. Nor should a female who has taken testosterone at any point in their history be allowed to compete with females. Its benefits remain.

The second 'open' model would be a third category alongside men's and women's and include all trans athletes, potentially with divisions for those who identify as men, women and non-binary. I don't believe this is workable, however, because human nature says that people will identify where they think they have the best chance of success. That is the whole point of competitive sport. And for teams and races there needs to be a certain amount of depth in numbers for it to work practically.

In the back rooms of debate about what 'open' would look like, differences in the trans population have been a sticking point. Transmen and transwomen are not the same: one is still male and one still female, no matter how they choose to identify.

Most female athletes who want to be transmen choose to delay transition until their elite or college careers are over because they have almost no chance as females competing among males of ever replicating the success they enjoy as a woman competing with women. The situation is wholly different for transwomen, who bring male advantages into women's sport even during and after testosterone-reduction therapy. Where the status of transmen in sport declines significantly on transition, the status of transwomen soars.

Whether it's biological males in women's sport or biological females in men's sport – or both in an 'open' category – hormone treatment is a part of the picture, including testosterone reduction and testosterone-boosting treatment, the latter up to an allowable limit under Therapeutic Use Exemption (TUE) rules.

I question the TUE system in general. It's open to manipulation, as was shown in 2021 by the Team Sky episode in the cycling world, in which chief doctor Richard Freeman lost his medical licence.[2] In the context of trans athletes, I'm also concerned that we're straying further away from sport as a healthy pursuit for body and mind. How can it be right for the IOC to ignore the medical facts about the debilitating and even life-threatening impact of heavy hormone treatment on health, as highlighted by a study that found that people taking hormones for gender dysphoria were at greater risk of having heart attacks and strokes?[3]

As we know, swimming, having accepted expert evidence that biological males who go through puberty will always have an advantage over females, regardless of any therapy, opted for inclusion by creating a home for transgender athletes. We'll know what that looks like by the summer of 2023.

The notion of an athlete being non-binary has no place in sport. People can identify however they want, but sport is based on biological sex, a physical reality, as shown by Quinn, the Canadian international football player who identifies as non-binary.[4] Those who do not identify with one of the only two sexes available in human biology should compete in the category of their sex. Quinn still opted to compete at the Olympics with people of the same biology. I've never known anyone at Olympic level identifying as non-binary choosing to compete with the opposite sex.

There should only be one winner (individual or team) in competitive sport, in each sex category, barring ties – and there should be no medals or prize money for mediocrity.

The tendency for events to have a 'non-binary' prize should not be dragged into competitive sport. If fair play is the goal, then how would it be fair for a mediocre male athlete identifying as non-binary, as has happened, to claim a prize of thousands of dollars that much better athletes, male, female or transgender, would not be eligible for unless they also identified as non-binary? It makes a mockery of celebrating the best in a given race.

Self-declaration of a status that doesn't exist cannot be controlled. Where might it stop? The definition sport must now use is 'open'. How those whose status places them in that new category identify or choose to live their lives should not be used as a way of describing the variety of people who are either ineligible or do not wish to compete as men or women. As we established in Chapters 5 and 6, there are very sound reasons why sex, not self-declared gender, is the starting point of multiple sports categories, like age groups or Paralympic and weight divisions.

At the start of 2023, that reality was recognised in the rules of rugby and swimming, which have ring-fenced the women's category for female athletes on grounds of safety and fairness.

It's a form of inclusion trans activists don't want, but inclusion is about providing a home in sport in a category that is fair for all. There is no 'trans ban' any more than there's a ban on me being in a race for 12-year-olds. I wouldn't want to be there and I should have no right to be there. It would be a lie. There are now people who describe themselves as 'transage', and who at 30 imagine themselves to be ten.[5] Will we let a thirty-something into the ten and under race? No, of course not. Well, not yet, anyway!

It's a feeling, regardless of whether it's gender or age. But the age feeling would have no chance of becoming a part of sport, we'd like to think. Of course, we would have said that about anyone declaring themselves to be the opposite sex and entitled to a ticket to female sport only a few years ago. How would the IOC justify validation of one feeling but not another? The fact is, none of it is workable. It lacks integrity and kills participation and competition by making a mockery of sport as we've known it.

Not a single trans athlete has ever been stopped from taking part in sport in the category of their natal sex, and they can continue to do so until new open categories are in place. The process involves a degree of patience. Women fought and waited for hundreds of years for the rights we have today.

In the meantime, no one is stopping scientists and trans athletes working on research designed to show whether mitigation to the point of a level playing field is possible. But no more live experiments resulting in the destruction of women's sport, please. We've been there and suffered the consequences before.

RECONCILIATION

So, what does reconciliation look like? There is no statute of limitations on doing the right thing, no barrier but the will of men to undoing the mistakes of the past.

The IOC has made plenty of those down the decades, as we've shown. My life has been affected by two of the biggest blunders Olympic bosses have made. For the past eight years, biological males have been given a free ticket to female sport on the basis of gender self-ID and a piece of paper showing they've kept their testosterone below a level well above the average in the female range.

When the injustice being done to female athletes sank in and awoke the ghosts of the past, I had no choice but to roll up my sleeves and go into battle. The East German doping era ripped the heart and soul out of female sport for two decades. Despite the overwhelming nature and volume of evidence, the IOC did nothing, neither at the time nor since.

Back then, young female athletes were being abused by the criminals injecting them with male steroids. Today, female athletes face an even bigger threat of male advantage because sports organisations have fallen for the transgender lobby selling their science denial. They have as a result made 'inclusion' a bigger factor than the fair play and sex-based anti-discrimination rules of the Olympic Charter.

The IOC's failure to handle the crimes of the GDR included a decade in which they could have acted, followed by more than two decades of an insistence that time had run out. Time never runs out on injustice and the harm it does – from lost medals, opportunities and team places through to the implications for mental and physical health.

But there's another reason why talk of statutes of limitation does not hold water. The threat of legal action against the IOC still remains after all these years if it fails to embrace the truth, doesn't help with reconciliation and still chooses not to grant the recognition and justice for the women impacted.

Olympic bosses know they got it wrong. The biggest proof of that is their own solution to proven cheating in the past decade, a medals-reallocation scheme that sets a precedent.

TAKE THE PODIUM

The IOC now has a very welcome and much-needed 'Take the Podium' programme, in which clean athletes are finally awarded their rightful Olympic medals following the disqualification of doped athletes.[6] It's time-limited: only since 2015.

The World Anti-Doping Code provides for a ten-year window following a competition to test athletes' samples for a possible doping violation. 'Take the Podium' allowed the redistribution of medals from the Beijing Olympic Games onwards where stored samples reanalysed with updated techniques returned an adverse finding.

In the context of the GDR era, neither I nor anyone else I know is asking for medals to be taken away from East German women. Our opponents in sport were victims of abuse. In many cases, it also destroyed their health and their lives, as well as the health and lives of children born with disabilities associated with their parents' doping.

But let's be clear: they competed with an advantage, a male advantage that meant the vast majority of women had no chance of beating the best of the GDR. As we have shown, some of those responsible were caught and convicted of bodily harm against minors in the German doping trials of 1998–2000.

The IOC, on the other hand, has mishandled the whole sorry saga for decades. Remember, when the Berlin Wall fell and Manfred Höppner confessed to the systematic doping programme in an interview with *Stern* magazine in 1990, IOC president Juan Antonio Samaranch told the brave GDR girls who tried to hand in their medals so they could be given to 'those who deserve them' that they should keep the prizes because others might have doped too.

We, the generations of women impacted by poor IOC vigilance during that 20-year period, want you, Olympic leaders, to extend 'Take the Podium' to our era, because just as those denied between 2008 and today deserve to be recognised for their true achievements, so do all of us you have ignored for so terribly long.

So how can the IOC make good? Here are some ideas:

- The GDR athletes keep their medals, but athletes like myself that would be due an upgrade return them to be replaced.
- The IOC compiles a revised results sheet reflecting the truth. The doped athletes are removed from the revised list as with the 'Take the Podium' system, and a new podium is revealed as the official record of the IOC. It isn't a massive, impossible task – Craig has already done it in swimming. Computers can do it all pretty quickly these days.
- The historical results and related publications remain in the museums of sport as the contemporaneous record of sports history, but the revised list is now used in any subsequent publication of the data. Asterisks are to be placed not on us, those cheated out of medals and places, but in places that reference the GDR era.
- The IOC grants permission to NOCs to issue medals, which the IOC pays for, to any of their athletes now promoted up or onto the podium.
- The IOC provides a budget to NOCs to organise ceremonies in precisely the same fashion as takes place in the prevailing 'Take the Podium' scheme. This allows any surviving parents, coaches, family and friends to attend the celebration the athlete should have enjoyed.

That's what doing the right thing looks like. Maybe the IOC could even organise an event at Lausanne to bring surviving victims from both sides together? If the IOC is still not persuaded, all who were denied recognition and who were unable to capitalise financially on their sporting success would have nothing to lose by going down the route of class action.

The goal is simple truth and reconciliation – not retribution. Truth would replace the lies printed in the official results of Olympic history. At present there is no mention of the mass cheating or rule breaking that affected generations of females, nor is there comfort for their families, coaches and communities who missed out on celebrating excellence.

There are, sadly, tidal waves of female swimmers who ought to have been inducted into the International Swimming Hall of Fame (ISHOF) in my sport, as well as into national, regional and local halls of fame, and a number of female athletes who might have had a school, pool or track named after them.

It's both joyous and heartbreaking to watch the 'Take the Podium' film telling the story of Canadian weightlifter Christine Girard.[7] She'd finished fourth in her category at Beijing 2008 but persevered to claim bronze in her category at the London 2012 Olympics, behind athletes from China and Russia. Both those athletes were subsequently proven to have cheated when their samples were reanalysed years after the medals were handed out in London. Christine eventually got her gold.

I was suddenly back in Montreal as a 13-year-old, racing the 200 metres backstroke for Britain at my first Olympics. I'd watched Canadian Nancy Garapick take bronze medals in the 100 and 200 metres backstroke behind the same two East Germans in each final. Imagine what double gold at a home Olympics would have meant for Nancy's life. Might we have visited the 'Nancy Garapick Aquatics Centre' down the years? Would children have been inspired every time they passed the 'Wall of Fame' at the local pool where Nancy had once trained?

Nancy's Wikipedia page tells us that it took until 2008 before she was inducted into Canada's Sports Hall of Fame and it was 2018 before she was named one of the greatest 15 athletes in Nova Scotia's history.[8] Her true achievement as a 15-year-old in Montreal in 1976 would have knocked such prizes into a cocked hat, but the IOC's official athlete profile of her simply says she was 'selected to represent Canada at the 1976 Summer Olympics, where she won bronze medals in the 100 and 200 m backstroke'.[9]

GDR athletes are still celebrated in the Olympic Museum in Lausanne and at ISHOF in Florida. There is no reference to all those who finished fourth, fifth and sixth behind three doped East Germans when they should have won a medal. Or to those like Linda Blade, who sat at home and watched the 1988 Games from afar because her national authorities ratcheted up the qualification targets a few months out from the Games based on international standards set by doped athletes working in a toxic environment.

Sports leaders have failed to take responsibility for any of the people harmed by 20 years of cheating followed by more than three decades of wilful blindness. In 2023, we have witnessed the IOC's drive to have Russians back in the Olympics by 2024 despite the war in Ukraine. As it was back in my racing days, they still appear to be working for the status quo regardless of the view of athletes.

It's time for change.

THE ATHLETE VOICE

Athletes need a union, a representative body that has a seat at the top tables of sport, and that speaks the voice of the key stakeholders in sport, the folk who actually compete and provide the show for the multi-billion-dollar Olympic industry.

The trouble with the athlete commissions the IOC and international federations hold up as evidence that they're listening is that they speak the message of the machine, not the dissenting or sceptical voices of athletes calling out hypocrisy.

It shouldn't be like that. Athletes should have a paid, professional team of people representing them, chosen from former athletes with experience and knowledge backed by experts in labour relations, law, human rights and marketing.

I don't profess to have all of the answers. I just know that what we're doing at the moment is terribly wrong and we've got to give some power and a voice back to the majority. In many sports, a lot of the best were teenagers like me in swimming in years gone by. I was 11 to 18 during my first international career, but the top athletes in most sports aren't children any more. They are fully grown adults in their mid-twenties earning a very good living. Sport isn't just an all-consuming hobby: it's a high-profile, potentially high-earning career.

Their sport is effectively their job, like any other, but we're not treating Olympic athletes with the same respect professional footballers and rugby, baseball and basketball players enjoy. Olympic bosses decided long ago that they knew best and that, like children of the fifteenth century when the phrase was coined, athletes 'should be seen and not heard'.

Putting Olympic swimming finals in the morning not the evening because it suits American prime-time TV is an example of money talking. It's the kind of topic in-house athlete groups tend to steer clear of. That's not good enough.

Naive is the kindest word I can find to describe Kirsty Coventry, the US-based Olympic 200 metres backstroke swimming champion from Zimbabwe. She became an in-house 'athlete representative' and now she's an IOC member rocketing up the ranks of Olympic politicians, with big ambitions. Sadly, like others who enter the corridors of IOC power with good intentions, however, Kirsty seems to have morphed into the mindset of the status quo.

It was 2019 when Global Athlete (GA) was founded as an independent representative organisation.[10] It noted the weakness of in-house athlete groups, and from the moment Rob Koehler took up his position at the helm, Kirsty and the IOC Athletes' Commission hit back.

When Callum Skinner, Olympic cycling champion and member of GA, told CBC that the in-house group 'maybe pushes the end goals of the IOC more than the athletes', Kirsty and co. said GA 'seems to believe that none of us care about athletes and that none of us do a good job for athletes if we are part of the Olympic movement'.[11]

That missed the point. It's not about caring; it's about listening and then representing athletes with votes and actions. True leadership is what athletes need, not an IOC version of compromise.

To represent all athletes Kirsty would have to consider the following issues and raise them at the top table for starters:

- Exorcising the ghosts of a rotten past
- Upholding sex-based policies and rules
- Replacing the way Olympic hosting rights are granted with a robust alternative that recognises the importance of human rights
- Making sure rules do what they say, so that if a whole-nation ban is required, it is extended to athletes, IOC members and other officials
- Insisting that the voices of athletes are heard on Russian reinstatement.

For me, any athletes' commission should have the backs of the athletes who will lose out because of bad decisions, before the backs of the organisation enabling it.

The voice of athletes challenging the status quo began in 1981 when the current president of the IOC, Thomas Bach, Olympic fencing champion for Germany in 1976, was one of the chosen few sportsmen and women invited to speak for the first time at the IOC Congress. Just over a decade later, Bach became an IOC member on his way to the top. Four decades on, his role in appeasing Russia ahead of the Rio 2016 Olympics, then, in 2018, in the biggest doping scandal since the GDR, and more recently in the drive to reinstate Russians for the Paris Olympics in 2024 despite the war in Ukraine, have left Bach bruised by criticism from former athletes turned politicians and soldiers, like Ukrainian boxer Wladimir Klitschko.[12]

The clash of cultures between athletes who want change and those who back the status quo led to disagreement between the IOC Athletes' Commission run by Kirsty and the WADA Athlete Committee run by retired Olympic cross-country ski champion Beckie Scott, of Canada.

The full WADA report into allegations of bullying and harassment in the saga of Russia's 2018 reinstatement is revealing.[13]

When GA came along to question the IOC, Beckie welcomed the group as 'a fresh positive new platform for the voice and rights of athletes', while Kirsty questioned where the funding was coming from for the new independent group and issued a press release that stated that 'there remain many unanswered questions about universality, accountability and funding'.[14]

I'm always amused by people in Olympic governance who raise questions about the transparency and funding of others but don't ask the same questions of fellow IOC members and leadership figures at international federations who have been called out by investigative journalists unearthing wrongdoing.

THE ATHLETE CONTRACT AND
OLYMPIC CHARTER RULE 50

Kirsty says she and other athlete representatives have been democratically elected by peers from all 206 NOCs. It's not quite as simple as that, but even if she is spot on, it's a moot point if representatives sided with the IOC and not athletes. In all the years I was an athlete I was never approached by an athlete representative or an IOC official seeking my views on matters that affected me and my teammates.

When athletes call for the scrapping of Olympic Charter Rule 50.2, which limits the right to freedom of speech during an Olympics, athlete representatives have a duty to reflect those views and put them to the IOC. They should not just toe the official line.

Rule 50 provisions are written into the contracts many athletes selected to compete at the Olympic Games (and other major internationals) for their countries must sign if they want to take up their place. No signature = no selection, no Games, no status. No voice. No platform to run. No funding.

It's why a union is so desperately needed. Athletes need a common and combined voice on big issues that has no ties to the IOC or big sports federations.

Matters like Rule 50 need calm consideration beyond the fray of debate during a Games. I'm not a fan of podium virtue-signalling. But such protests would be far less likely if athletes got the independent representation and agency they ought to have in the decision-making process. Enabling the athletes to stand together and say, 'Unless you fix this, we don't compete' puts power back into the hands of those who deliver the show that drives the tills.

In a missive to Team USA athletes ahead of the Beijing Winter Olympics in 2020, USOPC said that Rule 50 is 'not intended to stifle public debate on any topic'.[15]

Except, that is, topics such as China being accused of the genocide of the Uyghurs, when freedom of expression is restricted by this (Rule 50.2):

No kind of demonstration or political, religious or racial propaganda is permitted in any Olympic sites, venues or other areas.[16]

This implies that you could protest off-site, but then the laws of China would stop you doing that, too, and the IOC sides with the host, not the athlete.

To some extent, the Olympic Movement is like the Vatican: it has its own rules and they must be observed even if they clash with

cultural norms and even the laws of member countries, such as the
First Amendment in the United States.

In January 2021, GA issued an appeal to Olympic partners and
sponsors to tell the IOC that suppression of freedom of speech was
antithetical to and out of step with their corporate values.[17]

On the way to the Covid-delayed Tokyo Olympics, the BOA
let it be known that they would 'find a way' for Team GB athletes
to protest during the Games if they had cause to do so, despite
indications of an IOC Rule-50 crackdown. The BOA stance won
the backing of athletes, with Olympic champion swimmer Adam
Peaty telling us: 'I've always had a certain belief that the Olympics
and sport in general shouldn't be political. But there are so many
issues in the world, you don't want to take away the right of those
athletes to protest.'[18]

THE ROLE OF RETIRED ATHLETES

In 2022, Adam Peaty joined the Athletes' Committee of World
Aquatics. The involvement of the likes of Adam is essential, but the
truth is that active athletes have limited time and energy to devote
to campaigns for change. They have a job to do. And it's full on.

International athletes have to be quite selfish because it's the
nature of the beast. You have to put yourself first because that's
how you get your best performance. Of course you want to influence the decision-making process and get it right. But on the
other hand, you're keeping your head down and looking after
yourself – you're not inviting criticism or controversy because
you've got work to do.

That's where retired athletes come in. They understand. They've
been there and got the T-shirt, and there's now nothing in it for
them other than just trying to do something for the sports they love.
When it comes to forming athlete unions, a trusted combination of

active and retired athletes working together is probably the ideal. But it must be present-day and athlete-centric, and not be about creating new hierarchies.

In May 2022, two athletes said to be well known and established high achievers spoke to the BBC on condition of anonymity to say that they believed sport needed to be kept in sex categories because that was the only way it would remain fair.[19] They had a lot of good things to say but the self-protection of anonymity removed power from their message.

Thank goodness more athletes are now finding their voices. Shot-putter Amelia Strickler led the way among track-and-field athletes in Britain when she said that allowing biological males into female competition would be the death of women's sport.[20] She was responding to what many regarded as a World Athletics fudge.[21]

Amelia called for many more athletes to speak out: 'I hope more of us band together to prevent this because it is going to be the end.' Two-time European indoor 800 metres track medallist Jamie Webb soon joined her when he tweeted: 'With this and other things, I've lost a lot of faith in the sport. Sad to see. Make the male category open. Male athletes won't be affected whatsoever.'[22]

It's been heartening to see many more athletes, including some men, use their voices and call on regulators to do the right thing.

LESSONS FROM A SWIM LEAGUE

Those are some of the lessons that Konstantin Grigorishin taught swimmers when the Ukrainian energy magnate was setting up the International Swimming League (ISL) in a challenge to the status quo in 2018, until the Russian invasion of his country in 2022 brought a final halt to the project.[23]

On the road to breaking a World Aquatics stranglehold in the sport, Grigorishin introduced swimmers to Rachel Aleks, assistant professor on labour relations at Cornell University in New York. She told more than 30 Olympic and World Championship medallists at a gathering in London in late 2018 that 'boycotts are not something anyone wants. You also have to understand that your power is the right to withdraw your services until you are treated to the civility of having your voice heard in a negotiation over pay and conditions.'[24]

Adam Peaty had suggested that he might boycott the Tokyo 2020 Olympics if the swimming federation threatened him for racing in League competition.[25] In the same *Sunday Times* article noting Peaty's position, Grigorishin scoffed at the treatment of swimmers in the Olympic world. They were, he said, treated 'like experimental laboratory rats, with risks to their health', and had 'no salary, social guarantees, no welfare, no medical and life insurance, no pension rights, no insurance'.[26]

His stance coincided with a ruling that backed his right to hold competitions within FINA rules but without their involvement or permission.

The EU's competition authority came down on the side of speed skaters who had wanted to race in an independent event for money but were told by their global federation that they could not without being penalised. The EU ruled that no sports federation has the right to tell athletes where they can and cannot earn their money in competition that is a part of their livelihood.[27] It also said that while it was not rolling the decision out to all sports in general, the same ruling would be applied if there were any challenges from athletes in other sports.

HUMAN RIGHTS

Thomas Bach and the IOC often cite 'human rights' as a key reason why they have prioritised inclusion of trans athletes over safety and fair play by setting conditions that allow biological males into female sport.

They didn't apply any of those very same human rights to the victims of doping down the years. Did they consider the human rights of clean athletes when Russia was reinstated to the Olympic Movement in 2018, at a time when whistleblower Grigory Rodchenkov was making headlines around the world with excruciating revelations of systematic cheating?[28] His evidence led to the adoption of the Rodchenkov Act in the United States but did not lead to a change of mindset at the IOC.[29]

Recent events have highlighted yet again how the IOC has all too often been on the wrong side of history. Through Putin's war on Ukraine, Bach has kept Russian and Belarusian officials in the IOC and wants athletes from those countries at the Paris 2024 Olympic Games, making them pawns in Putin's propaganda.[30]

The IOC would do well to remember that it shut South Africa out of the Olympic Games throughout the apartheid years. That kind of pressure contributed to global embargoes that helped bring an end to systematic discrimination.

In a telling thread on Twitter, Rob Koehler, the head of GA, urged the IOC to change tack, and pointed out that in the first year of Putin's war, 231 Ukrainian athletes were killed, 343 sports facilities were destroyed, 40,000 athletes were forced to live abroad and 140,000 young athletes were left without sports venues, according to the Ukrainian government statistics. Rob also noted that 45 of the 71 Russian medals at the Tokyo Olympic Games were won by athletes engaged in military service.[31]

A year after Putin ordered Russian troops into Ukraine, I saw a picture of a young girl holding a pair of goggles and peering into the bombed-out swimming pool in her shattered neighbourhood. How does Thomas Bach square that with his campaign to have Russians at the Paris Olympics while there are calls for Putin to be tried at the International Criminal Court (ICC) and for Russia to be forced to pay reparations for the destruction it has wrought on a sovereign land?

Bach's argument is that the IOC is non-political and neutral, just wants peace and is on the right side of history.[32] Ukraine athletes responded by saying that the IOC was on 'the wrong side of history.'[33] Russia's presence in Paris would be a 'manifestation of violence', Ukraine's president, Volodymyr Zelenskiy, told a summit of 35 sports ministers chaired by the UK government.[34]

Thirty-four of those countries, including the 2024 hosts France, told the IOC in February 2023 that the aggressor nations must be banned from the Paris Olympics, a move supported by EU lawmakers, who condemned the IOC stance, while Anne Hidalgo, the mayor of Paris, said that Russians and Belarusians would not be welcome at the 2024 Games if the war in Ukraine is not over.[35]

The IOC's version of neutrality calls on the oppressed to shake the hands of their oppressors in an illegal war that has torpedoed the world economy.

I have no issue with Olympic leaders talking about sport as a vehicle for spreading harmony and understanding between diverse nations and people. But the IOC is not a peace organisation. It's the extremely commercial organiser of the biggest multi-sports event in the world and it should be athlete-centric and a part of the real world. Olympians are its key stakeholders and the people who generate the interest and the revenue.

It's madness to think that removing the Russian flag means that the athlete is no longer under the control of Putin's Russia. No Russian official or athlete would be in Paris without Putin's say-so.

In March 2023, 40 leading Canadian Olympians signed a petition calling on the Canadian Olympic Committee (COC) to reverse its position and withdraw support for the IOC's plan to have

Russian and Belarusian athletes compete at the Paris Olympics as 'neutrals'.

Neutrality is impossible under the prevailing circumstances. Canada's Olympic bosses responded to athletes by saying that it had joined more than 30 other nations in calling 'for the continuation of the ban in the absence of clarity and concrete details on a workable neutrality model'.[36]

On that score, the IOC would be wise to turn to a champion of reconciliation for wisdom.

INJUSTICE IS NOT HISTORIC — IT'S TIMELESS

When the Reverend Desmond Tutu passed away in December 2021, the IOC was among those keen to pay plaudits to the South African Anglican Archbishop who played a key role in bringing apartheid to an end in his country.[37] In a glowing tribute to the Nobel Peace Prize recipient, the IOC failed to use the word 'neutrality' once, bypassing one of the key issues raised by Archbishop Tutu, who once said: 'If you are neutral in situations of injustice, you have chosen the side of the oppressor. If an elephant has its foot on the tail of a mouse and you say that you are neutral, the mouse will not appreciate your neutrality.'[38]

But the IOC can correct mistakes of the past when they choose to. Take Jim Thorpe, the teenage Native American who won the decathlon at the 1912 Olympic Games and then had the title stripped away a year later because it was discovered that he'd accepted a small fee for playing baseball three years earlier.[39]

It was 1982 when Jim's family was told that, even though prevailing rules had been broken, the IOC had awarded a shadow gold medal to their hero in recognition of the pettiness of the judgment made back in 1913. Honour and pride were restored three decades after Jim passed away – and right in the middle of the GDR doping era, a time when I was barred from returning to swimming because I'd been paid £40 for appearing on a TV game show unrelated to sport. Oh, the irony.

Then, in 2022, that shadow gold was upgraded to outright gold. The IOC took the decision to change the result sheet back to the way it looked after the competition 110 years earlier. If it can be done for one man surely it can be done for countless women who lost out?

In 2021, thanks to 30 years of campaigning by my co-writer Craig, World Aquatics finally stripped Dr Lothar Kipke of the honour it had given him in 1986, at a time when he was on the regulator's medical committee as a spy in the camp watching for new testing methods that might expose East Germany's doping programme.[40] As we mentioned in Chapter 3, Kipke was convicted of bodily harm to minors in the German doping trials way back in 1998–2000. Yet nothing was done at the time.

Swimming bosses acted as part of a reform process that has raised great hopes for the future of my sport. An independent Aquatics Integrity Unit opened in January 2023; time will tell if it can be as effective as the equivalent body established by World Athletics in 2017.[41]

So far, it's been heart-warming watching the change of culture at the helm of aquatics. It led to governance calling in professional experts and delivering the decision to hand the women's category in aquatics back to female athletes.

Swimming's leadership deserves plaudits and our encouragement. At last, the new management is one that clearly gets it, and has delivered on a pledge to have a 40 per cent female quota at board and committee level. Executive director Brent Nowicki now operates an open-door policy in an atmosphere of cooperation. There is dialogue between him, the president, athletes, coaches, stakeholders and media.

That may sound strange to those of you who work in places where such things are common best practice. It hasn't been like that in

Olympic sport for a very long time. It's good to see the tide turning. When Craig raised the possibility of a truth-and-reconciliation process with the president of World Aquatics, this is what Mr Al-Musallam said:

> Fina understands the concerns of athletes who have competed against others subsequently proved to have cheated. Athletes work their entire lives for a mere chance to compete for a medal, yet alone win one. So when athletes are denied the reward they worked so hard to achieve, Fina must do everything it can to right this wrong. Once established, the independent Aquatics Integrity Unit will investigate the matter to determine what recourse may be taken in support of Ms Davies and all similarly situated other aquatics athletes.[42]

It was the first time we'd ever heard any such encouragement. For it to come from an IOC member meant a lot. A process has begun to find a way. Let's get around a table and talk it through with Olympic leaders. Sadly, the transgender issue has again reminded female athletes and their supporters the world over that sometimes standing up and being counted is what you have to do.

On 9 January 2023, the day we completed the first draft of this book, the International Consortium on Female Sport (ICFS; see Appendix 2) was launched as an international lobby group to advocate for the preservation of the female sport category worldwide. I'm right with them. This comes at a time when more international governing sports bodies, including the IOC, are opening up female sport to more male competitors than ever before.

In the 2022 spring season, the world witnessed a major turning point in US female sport when biological male swimmer Lia Thomas won the 500 yards freestyle at the NCAA championships. We need to build on the impact that had in raising awareness of the injustice faced by female athletes. No sport should need a Lia Thomas before bosses wake up to the harm being done.

FINDING SOLUTIONS — A CHARTER FOR FAIR PLAY

There are lots of solutions that women around the world would like to suggest to sports leaders, through athlete representatives, as they meet and agree rules, policies and guidelines that impact culture and the environment in which sportspeople work and compete.

Here are just a few of our thoughts to bring our book to a close.

1. *Unions.* Athletes must have a genuine, professional, voice of experience to speak on their behalf. They must be able to say no en masse, and have that voice represented at the top tables of sport.
2. *Greater transparency and accountability in IOC governance.* World Aquatics are doing a great job of reform: no more huge per diems and volunteers on large daily allowances so finances can be misrepresented rather than fees paid for a professional job well done. Other sports governing bodies should follow their lead.
3. *Athlete-centric.* There needs to be greater understanding that sports organisations exist for the athletes, not as business opportunities or deluxe-travel bureaux for committee members.
4. *Fair-share distribution of revenues to athletes.* More of the massive revenues should go to those who attract the big audience and broadcast fees at the Olympic Games. In big pro sports, athletes get a share of around 50 per cent of the take, but in Olympic sport it's an estimated 4 per cent, a figure the IOC disputes, but there can be no doubt that it's nothing remotely close to 50 per cent.
5. *Legal representation for athletes.* Contracts with national governing bodies (NGBs) or the IOC and federations tend to be all about 'you will sign this or not be allowed to compete'. Change it!

Individuals' rights to a profession have to include personal earning power at major events. It's their job and they have a right to earn a living from it.

6. *Categories based on the realities of human biology.* Eligibility for sports categories cannot be based on feelings, whims or personal choices. Sport is based on sex, age, weight or type of ability in Paralympic sport. If there's a reason why that needs changing, don't discriminate to accommodate, create new categories. Unfair inclusion ruins long-established models of fairness.

7. *Respect for privacy, safe spaces and safeguarding.* There has to be an understanding written into rules that all athletes have a right to safety and privacy. If someone identifies as a woman but their genitalia is male, they either have to change with males or in extra facilities so that all can be comfortable, with an acceptable degree of dignity and privacy. You can't say it's indecent exposure when a man strips off in the women's locker room but think it's perfectly all right for the same man to self-identify as a woman and do exactly the same thing. That's hypocrisy – and ridiculous. It's a safeguarding issue that needs to be addressed and resolved through respectful conversations and provision of changing facilities that accommodate reasonable need. If we need male, female and mixed or unisex changing, then sports facilities will have to factor that in.

8. *Female-specific promotion of sport.* NGBs need to understand that they have a responsibility to grow female participation in sport. Consistent media coverage is poor for the women's market and more needs to be done to promote female role models and encourage young girls into sport. It's vital for society as a whole, for physical and mental health. Kids cannot dream of being what they don't see. Inclusion is a part of that, but no one group should ever trump another.

9. *Transparency in drug testing and the system of penalties.* Some athletes get the standard punishment that WADA sets to fit the crime, but

we all know far too many cases of big names in sport who commit the same offence as lesser-known athletes but get reduced penalties, timed to make sure they make it back for the next major event. It's no coincidence – and shouldn't happen.

10. *Independent and random testosterone testing for trans athletes.* This should be linked to the availability system in the same way as all other athletes must be. NGBs and the IOC need to fund this if their controls for trans athletes are based on levels of testosterone, which is on the list of banned substances. Any violation of T levels should attract the same penalty applicable to all other athletes. A trans athlete's violation cannot be a 'mistake', as some rules suggest, when the same test outcome would result in another athlete being handed a penalty for cheating. There should be no special treatment in anti-doping for any demographic.

11. *A ban should mean a ban and not only for athletes.* Lifetime bans should be elevated to a bigger threat for the top tier of offences in sport. There have been too many cases of two-time offenders making it back into sport and even the Olympic Games. All top-level offences, if there are no mitigating circumstances, as judged by an independent panel subject to oversight, should result in a minimum of four years out to cover the next Olympics. And the likes of the officials who threatened anti-doping testers in the Sun Yang scandal in swimming should be banned for life. The swimmer, rightly, was banned, but none of the adults paid a price for their offending behaviour. If we really wish to stop cheating we have to get to those that supply, administer or encourage.

12. *All time limits for doping infractions should be lifted.* If there is evidence of cheating, it should be taken seriously, investigated and, if proven, ought to lead to sanction, regardless of how long ago the offence took place. It follows that there should be no time limit on the removal and reallocation of honours, including medals and prize money.

13. *Swifter inquiry processes.* At present the system takes way too long to bring investigations and sanctions and allows athletes awaiting hearings at CAS to continue to compete and win medals and money prizes that then do not get handed over to rivals, even if the court rules against the athlete.

14. *Forfeiting medals.* In the spirit of the IOC's retrospective 'Take the Podium' scheme, athletes who get to compete at major international events while awaiting judicial processes should hand back any medals and prizes won at those competitions if the subsequent hearing results in suspension. The risk of having offending athletes win and then keep medals simply because of long delays in appeal processes should be removed.

15. *Biological sex specified in rules and charters.* Not many years ago, sex was the only specification in sports regulations, but now that gender has been added and wilfully misinterpreted, it is time to enshrine the significance of biology in sport in the rule book to make it crystal clear that the women's category will always be ring-fenced for female athletes.

ACKNOWLEDGEMENTS

W HEN the men's and women's categories were conceived in sport, the meaning of gender was biological sex. It has been eroded by self-identification ideology. With a feeling being allowed to trump a fact.

International and domestic sports authorities around the world, many of them taking their steer from the IOC, have opted for a divisive inclusion model that has promoted the rights of trans-gender athletes above those of female athletes and created inequality between males and females.

Female athletes have long had to fight injustice, enduring massive challenges for decades without sports leaders lifting a finger to right past wrongs. Sex discrimination and second-class status in sport have been a woman's lot for far too long.

Just when we thought we'd won some of those battles along comes yet another hurdle to fight our way over.

I would like to acknowledge the sterling work of women's rights groups, scientists and investigative journalists, some of whom are named in this book. I'm immensely grateful for their dedication to the pursuit of truth at a time when veracity, language, the intended meaning of words, and the freedoms of expression and speech are under constant assault.

My thanks also goes to the people and organisations who have shown the courage to speak up in the face of threats to life and livelihood. Women's campaign groups, their supporters, including influential figures and leading female athletes and some of our male peers, continue to turn the tide, helped by organisations and companies that have refused to yield to the cancel culture that serves no one.

I'm particularly proud of my sport, swimming, which has led the way in redressing the balance and ring-fencing the women's category for biological females. There is still much more work to be done, but the suffragette spirit is alive and kicking. Who'd have thought that in the twenty-first century we'd have to be fighting for equality all over again!

I want to say a huge special thank you to Craig, my co-writer. It has been an emotional roller coaster – we've both put in some serious hours to deliver this book. He's been endlessly patient and I know we're both very proud of what we've produced.

Finally, thank you to every single person who has written to me or taken the time to stop me in the street and thank me for sticking with it on behalf of their daughters, sisters and friends. It keeps me going.

APPENDIX I

The Key Studies and Papers on Retained Male Advantage after Transition and the Meaning of Fair Play

After 2019, several studies assessed muscle changes such as changes in fibre size and fast-twitch proportion, and measured performance outcomes such as strength and aerobic capacity in athletes. Several scientific papers and other documents showing that transwomen retain significant levels of male strength even after years of testosterone-reduction therapy were published in 2020 and 2021.

Here's a brief summary of their findings:

Cathy Devine, 'Written evidence submitted by Cathy Devine [GRA1160]', committees.parliament.uk/writtenevidence/17227/pdf/

Cathy Devine sets out her research and explanations on 'the impact of transgender inclusion policies on the fair inclusion of girls and women in single sex sport categories both nationally and internationally' in written evidence submitted to the UK Parliament for its debates on the 2010 Equality Act and 2004 Gender Recognition Act.

Joanna Harper, Emma O'Donnell et al., 'How does hormone transition in transgender women change body composition, muscle strength and

haemoglobin? Systematic review with a focus on the implications for sport participation', *British Journal of Sports Medicine* 55 (2021), pp. 865–72, bjsm.bmj.com/content/55/15/865

Key point:
- Hormone therapy decreases strength, lean body mass (LBM) and muscle area in transwomen, yet values remain above that observed in women, even after 36 months. These findings suggest that strength may be well preserved in transwomen during the first three years of hormone therapy.

Emma N. Hilton and Tommy R. Lundberg, 'Transgender women in the female category of sport: perspectives on testosterone suppression and performance advantage', *Sports Medicine* 51 (2020), pp. 199–214, link. springer.com/article/10.1007/s40279-020-01389-3

Key points:
- Muscle mass and strength conferred by male puberty, and thus enjoyed by most transgender women, is only minimally reduced when testosterone is suppressed.
- Twelve months of hormone-replacement therapy (HRT) results show minimal reduction in male strength advantage and that there is no meaningful mitigation of the 10–50 per cent male performance advantage transwomen have at transition.
- There are 'major performance and safety implications' in relevant sports.
- The delivery of fairness and safety presumed by the criteria set out in transgender-inclusion policies is undermined.
- Targeting a certain testosterone level to be eligible to compete as a biological male in female sport will not achieve its objective of fair sport once any male has gone through any part of puberty.

- Proper risk assessment should be conducted by sports that continue to include transgender women in the female category.
- Each sports federation should evaluate its own conditions for inclusivity, fairness and safety.

Miroslav Imbrišević, 'The transgender reader: language, law, sport and reality. A collection of essays, new edition (extended)' [PDF published by Brighteye Publishing, Worthing, Sussex, 2023], https://www.researchgate.net/publication/361209724_THE_TRANSGENDER_READER_Language_Law_Sport_Reality_A_Collection_of_Essays_new_edition_extended_2023

Jon Pike, 'Safety, fairness, and inclusion: transgender athletes and the essence of rugby', *Journal of the Philosophy of Sport* 48/2 (2021), pp. 155–68, https://oro.open.ac.uk/74562/

Key points:
- The inclusion of transwomen in the women's game leads to increased risk.
- Male advantage remains after HRT.
- Where a typical player with male characteristics tackles a typical player with female characteristics, there's a greater risk for the female players of at least 20–30 per cent.

Jon Pike, 'Why "meaningful competition" is not fair competition', *Journal of the Philosophy of Sport* 50 (2023), pp. 1–17, tandfonline.com/doi/full/10.1080/00948705.2023.2167720

A new concept has arrived with the advent of transwomen gaining access to women's sport: 'meaningful competition'. In this paper, Pike argues that the concept is in itself unfair, an attempt to substitute for the perfectly serviceable concept of fair competition. Meaningful competition, he writes, is 'a snare and a delusion'.

Jon Pike, Emma Hilton and Leslie A. Howe, 'Fair game – biology, fairness and transgender athletes in women's sport' [document published by the Canadian think tank the Macdonald-Laurier Institute, 2021], macdonaldlaurier.ca/files/pdf/Dec2021_Fair_game_Pike_Hilton_Howe_ PAPER_FWeb.pdf

Highly critical of the Canadian Centre for Ethics in Sports (CCES), this paper provides an overview of much of the best evidence and research in support of protecting women's sport for females only.

As the authors noted elsewhere:

> The science is clear: athletes who were born male but who identify as women and seek participation in women's events have significant competitive advantages. Additionally, a thorough ethical examination finds that while inclusion is an important objective, safety and fairness should be higher priorities when it comes to sport.[1]

I wholeheartedly endorse that as pure common sense. Jon adds:

> In any event, gender identity (a subjective concept) is a poor basis for sports categories. It is biological sex (an objective fact) which drives the inherent differences in athletic advantage, and which makes sex-based categories in sport necessary to begin with. Numerous models for inclusion fail when examined in this light.[2]

Timothy A. Roberts, Joshua Smalley and Dale Ahrendt, 'Effect of gender-affirming hormones on athletic performance in transwomen and transmen: implications for sporting organisations and legislators', *British Journal of Sports Medicine* 55/11 (2021), pp. 577–83, https://bjsm. bmj.com/content/55/11/577.info

Key points:

- The study, based on the fitness test results and medical records of 29 transmen and 46 transwomen on gender-affirming hormones while in the United States Air Force, challenges the IOC's scientific position.
- The 15–31 per cent athletic advantage over female athletes that transwomen had before transition declined with hormone-reduction therapy, but transwomen still retained certain clear advantages.
- They had a 9 per cent faster mean run speed after the one-year period of testosterone suppression recommended by World Athletics for inclusion in women's events.
- They retained a 12 per cent advantage in running tests even after taking hormones for two years to suppress their testosterone.
- The results, researchers suggest, indicate that the current IOC guidelines may give transwomen an 'unfair competitive advantage' over biological women.
- After suppressing their testosterone for two years – a year longer than IOC guidelines – they were still 12 per cent faster in a 1.5-mile run on average than females and retained a 10 per cent advantage in push-ups and a 6 per cent advantage in sit-ups for the first two years after taking hormones.

Anna Wiik, Tommy R. Lundberg et al., 'Muscle strength, size, and composition following 12 months of gender-affirming treatment in transgender individuals', *Journal of Clinical Endocrinology and Metabolism* 105/3 (March 2020), pp. e805–e813, academic.oup.com/jcem/article/105/3/e805/5651219

Key point:

- One year of gender-affirming treatment resulted in robust increases in muscle mass and strength in transmen (who have taken testosterone) but modest changes in transwomen (who have reduced testosterone and/or taken oestrogen).

APPENDIX 2

Resources

- Champion Women (advocacy by Nancy Hogshead-Makar and team): championwomen.org/
- Equality Act 2010 (UK): gov.uk/guidance/equality-act-2010-guidance
- Fair Play for Women (including resources on UK law, science, sex vs gender and consultation submissions): fairplayforwomen.com
- Independent Council on Women's Sports (ICONS): iconswomen.com
- International Bill of Human Rights: https://www.ohchr.org/en/what-are-human-rights/international-bill-human-rights
- International Consortium on Female Sport (ICFS): icfsport.org
- Protection of Women and Girls in Sports Act of 2023: congress.gov/bill/118th-congress/house-bill/734/text
- *The Real Science of Sport Podcast* (with Professor Ross Tucker and Mike Finch): podcasts.apple.com/gb/podcast/the-real-science-of-sport-podcast/id1461719225
- Save Women's Sports: facebook.com/savewomenssports/
- Save Women's Sport Australasia: savewomenssport.com
- Sex Matters (including resources for parents): sex-matters.org
- Sporting Integrity (founded by Michele Verroken): sportingintegrity.com/index.html
- United Nations Convention on the Elimination of All Forms of Discrimination Against Women (CEDAW; see Article 10 (g),

which states that 'states parties' should ensure for women 'the same opportunities to participate actively in sports and physical education'): www.ohchr.org/en/instruments-mechanisms/instruments/convention-elimination-all-forms-discrimination-against-women

- Women's Declaration International (WDI): https://www.womens declaration.com/en/declaration-womens-sex-based-rights-full-text/

APPENDIX 3

Fair Play for Women's Guide to UK Equality Law and a Woman's Right to Single-Sex Spaces and Services

Fair Play for Women has comprehensive guides and explanatory documents and articles on its website. For further information on a woman's right to single-sex spaces and services, see fairplayforwomen.com/equality-act-2010_womens-rights/.

The Equality Act 2010 provides legal protection from discrimination, harassment and victimisation based on the protected characteristics of age, disability, marriage/civil partnership, pregnancy/maternity, race, religion/belief, sexual orientation, sex and gender reassignment.

Sex discrimination is being treated unfairly because of what sex you are. It's about being treated unfairly just because you are a woman (or a man).

Gender reassignment discrimination is being treated unfairly because you have proposed, started or completed a process to change attributes of your sex. It's about being treated unfairly just because you are transgender or transsexual.

The Gender Recognition Act 2004 sets out the legal requirements a transgender person must meet to get a gender recognition certificate (GRC) and to change their legal sex to the opposite of their biological sex.

This requires a medical diagnosis of gender dysphoria and two years living in the role of the preferred sex. By March 2018 only 4,910 people had a GRC in the UK according to government figures.

For the vast majority of transgender people their birth sex remains the legal sex.

Sometimes sex and gender reassignment discrimination can be lawful in situations when it is a proportionate means to provide a legitimate aim. Equality decisions should be evidence-based and must fairly balance the needs of all groups affected. This does not mean treating everyone the same. Sometimes treating people differently is the least discriminatory outcome.

There are six such legal exemptions in the Equality Act 2010 for organisations to use to support women's rights to access single-sex spaces and services:

WOMEN-ONLY SERVICES
Schedule 3, Part 7, Sections 26–8

In some cases it is lawful to discriminate on the grounds of sex and gender. It is also lawful to exclude someone because they are transgender even if they have changed their legal sex to female via a GRC. Single-sex services are lawful when provided in a hospital or other place where users need special care, supervision or attention. It is also lawful if the service involves physical contact between people and a woman might reasonably object to the presence of a male person.

ALL-WOMEN SHORTLISTS
Part 7, Section 104 (7)

It is lawful for political parties to restrict the selection of election candidates to only those who share the protected characteristic of

the female. It is lawful to exclude legal males, including those who
self-identify as transgender women, from all-women shortlists
(AWS) because they are not legally female. AWS is not designed
to address the under-representation of any of the other protected
characteristics. This must be addressed only using reserved places
on non-AWS lists.

WOMEN-ONLY CLUBS
Schedule 16, Part 1

It is lawful for a club or association to restrict its membership
to only those who share the protected characteristic of sex. It is
lawful to exclude legal males, including those who self-identify
as transgender women, from clubs dedicated to people who are
legally female.

COMPETITIVE SPORTS
Part 14, Section 195

It is lawful to exclude people born male from women-only sporting
competitions when physical strength, stamina or physique are major
factors in determining success or failure. This includes people who
are born male even if they self-identify as transwomen and/or have
changed their legal sex status to female.

This is necessary to uphold fair or safe competition.

OCCUPATIONAL REQUIREMENTS
Schedule 9, Part 1

It is lawful to make it a requirement for a worker not to be of the
male sex and/or not to be a transgender person if this is a crucial
requirement for the work.

Considerations can include privacy and decency, cultural and religious sensitivities, psychological vulnerabilities and other reasons that are deemed crucial for the provision of services for women.

COMMUNAL ACCOMMODATION
Schedule 23, Part 3

In some cases it is lawful to discriminate on the grounds of both sex and gender reassignment. It is lawful to exclude legal males, including those who self-identify as transgender women, from communal accommodation for women which has either shared sleeping arrangements or shared sanitary facilities. It is also lawful to exclude someone because they are transgender even if they have changed their legal sex to female (using a GRC).

APPENDIX 4

Letter from Fair Play for Women to the IOC Executive Board

For the attention of Thomas Bach, IOC
5 September 2019

Dear members of the IOC Executive Board,

This is a private letter signed by over sixty British Olympic medallists, world-class sports men and women, and leading scientists. We have come together because we share a single purpose: to help ensure the integrity and fairness of the Olympic games

We believe the IOC's revised (2015) transgender guidelines do not guarantee safe and fair competition for female athletes.

These recommendations are based on flawed science.

IOC guidelines recommend that male-born transgender athletes demonstrate their testosterone level has been below 10 nmol/L for at least one year before their first female competition. However, there is currently no scientifically robust, independent research showing that all male-like performance advantage is eliminated under these conditions.

There is no list of reference works or papers that were consulted that can be made available to other researchers. It appears the only published research underpinning the guidelines is the unscientific, small retrospective study performed by two of the twenty members of the consensus meeting. The study size is tiny but the impact it may have on both women's sport and the Olympics is enormous.

Put simply, there's more to male performance advantage than testosterone.

The legacy effect of exposure to high levels of testosterone in early life and puberty is well known. Growing up male will give transgender athletes a lifelong edge that simply cannot be fully negated by a period of testosterone suppression.

Higher testosterone levels after birth mean males have larger hearts and lungs, on average. Females have a wider pelvis, altering hip rotation and making them inherently slower. Males have longer and stronger bones from puberty. Longer bones allow for increased reach and a wider articular surface, allowing them to put down more skeletal muscle. Muscle memory resulting from a male physiology prior to transition provides the permanent ability to regain or maintain muscle. Only females face the problems of managing a menstrual cycle and the effect on performance and training.

Let's not change the rules without proper evidence.

Such an important subject demands proper research of a significantly large population and using robust scientific measurements. Only then will we be able to have a true understanding of whether a transwoman has an unfair sporting advantage over her fellow competitors. Properly designed intervention studies are urgently required to investigate the effect of transition on trainability and performance.

We ask the IOC to listen to other, well-informed voices and consider commissioning studies that look at muscle physiology and strength adaptations pre- and post-transition.

These guidelines were never meant to be mandatory.

We note that the guidelines were designed as recommendations – not rules or regulations – for sporting bodies to take into account. They were published after a consensus meeting of Olympic officials and medical experts in November 2015 in Lausanne, Switzerland, but they were not approved by the IOC Executive Board. However, they have now been widely used as the justification for opening the female category to athletes who were born male by most national and international sport governing bodies throughout the world.

Therefore, we ask the International Olympic Committee to suspend its transgender guidelines regarding the eligibility of male-born transgender athletes into female competition pending further scientific study and analysis.

If based on the IOC guidelines, the sporting world changes its rules prematurely and transwomen are found to unfairly dominate, it will be to the detriment of sport, women and the Olympics.

Signatories:

Sharron Davies MBE

[other names redacted]

APPENDIX 5

The State of Inclusion Policies – Global Federations, March 2023

SPORTS WHERE THE WOMEN'S CATEGORY
IS LARGELY RING-FENCED FOR FEMALES ONLY

SPORT	POLICY AS AT MARCH 2023
Aquatics/ swimming	**World Aquatics**, June 2022: no biological male who has experienced Tanner stage 2 male puberty (around 12 years of age) is eligible for women's competition. Open category due July 2023. See fina.orq/fina/document/2022/06/19/525de003-51f4-47d3-8d5a-716dac5f77c7/FINA-INCLUSION-POLICY-AND-APPENDICES-FINAL-.pdf.
Athletics/ track and field	**World Athletics**, March 2023: no biological male who has experienced Tanner stage 2 male puberty is eligible for women's competition; DSD cases restricted by event and testosterone monitoring; working group to look at further sports-related trans research. See worldathletics.org/news/press-releases/council-meeting-march-2023-russia-belarus-female-eligibility.
Boxing	**The World Boxing Council**, January 2023: 'WBC completely rejects any boxing activity between people born male against born female, regardless of their current sexuality; so the creation of a Committee to create a competition manual was approved, with the possibility of having a transgender league welcoming those who wish to participate in our sport. This decision is about safety and inclusion.' See wbcboxing.com/en/round-12-a-promising-2023/.
Rowing	**World Rowing**, March 2023: a change to bye-laws states that only those born or assigned female at birth are eligible for the women's category. DSD cases restricted by event and testosterone monitoring and subject to executive discretion. See worldrowing.com/2023/03/15/ world-rowing-adopts-tighter-rules-for-transgender-women-athletes/.
Rugby	**World Rugby**, October 2020: Transgender women many not play women's rugby, on grounds of safety and fairness. world.rugby/news/591776

SPORTS THAT CONTINUE TO
DISCRIMINATE AGAINST FEMALE ATHLETES

SPORT	POLICY AS AT MARCH 2023
Basketball	**FIBA** follows IOC guidelines but those now require international federations to formulate new rules appropriate to the sport(s) they govern. FIBA is yet to announce any new measures beyond its 2020 position of allowing biological males into female games if testosterone levels are reduced below a limit well outside the female range. See fiba.basketball/her-world-her-rules-global.
Cycling	**UCI** updated its policy in June 2022 but continues to allow biological males into female sport: the maximum permitted plasma testosterone level was reduced from 5 nmol/L to 2.5 nmol/L and the period that level has to be maintained was extended from 12 to 24 months. See bicycling.com/news/a40320907/uci-transgender-policy-2022/.
Football	**FIFA** stated in June 2022 that it would review its inclusion policy and was minded to match the World Aquatics decision. Until then, 'any such case will be dealt with on a case-by-case basis.' See reuters.com/lifestyle/sports/fifa-world-athletics-review-transgender-rules-after-swimmings-change-2022-06-20/.
Triathlon	**World Triathlon**: males can race females if the concentration of testosterone in the athlete's serum is less than 2.5 nmol/L continuously for at least 24 months and then only four years after last racing as a male. See triathlon.org/news/article/world_triathlon_executive_board_approves_transgender_policy.
Weightlifting	The **IF** supports 'gender equity', but has no published guidelines on inclusion. It says it follows 'IOC guidelines', but those include permission for each regulator to set its own rules.

NOTES

INTRODUCTION

1. 'Olympic Charter', olympics.com/ioc/olympic-charter.
2. United Nations, 'Women's rights are human rights' [PDF] (2014), ohchr.org/sites/default/files/Documents/Events/WHRD/WomenRightsAreHR.pdf; UN Women, 'The facts about gender equality and the Sustainable Development Goals' [video], YouTube [website] (14 February 2018), www.youtube.com/watch?v=K-oc4GOoWOI.
3. Nicholas D. Kristof, *Half the Sky: Turning Oppression into Opportunity for Women Worldwide* (New York: Alfred A. Knopf, 2009).
4. UN Women, 'Poverty deepens for women and girls, according to latest projections' (February 2022), data.unwomen.org/features/poverty-deepens-women-and-girls-according-latest-projections.
5. Rob Goldberg, 'Martina Navratilova: transgender athletes in women's sport is insane, cheating', Bleacher Report [website] (18 February 2019), bleacherreport.com/articles/2821380-martina-navratilova-transgender-athletes-in-womens-sport-is-insane-cheating.
6. 'Transgender cyclist defends her right to compete in women's sport', News24 [website] (18 October 2019), news24.com/sport/transgender-cyclist-defends-her-right-to-compete-in-womens-sport-20191018.
7. Margaret Heffernan, *Willful Blindness: Why We Ignore the Obvious at Our Peril* (New York: Bloomsbury, 2012).

CHAPTER 1

1. 'IOC sends extremely strong message that gender balance is a reality at the Olympic Games' [media statement], International Olympic Committee [website] (4 March 2020), olympics.com/ioc/news/ioc-sends-extremely-strong-message-that-gender-balance-is-a-reality-at-the-olympic-games.
2. 'Gender equality through time at the Olympic Games', International Olympic Committee [website], olympics.com/ioc/gender-equality/gender-equality-through-time.
3. Ibid.
4. Quoted in Laura Chase, 'A policy analysis of gender inequality within the Olympic Movement', in Robert K. Barney and Klaus V. Meier, eds, *Proceedings: First International Symposium for Olympic Research* (London, ON: Centre for Olympic Studies, 1992),

academia.edu/490645/A_Policy_Analysis_of_Gender_Inequality_within_the_Olympic_Movement.

5. Quoted in Tina Hynes, '"An Olympiad with females would be impractical, uninteresting, unaesthetic and improper" – Baron Pierre de Coubertin', *Irish Times* (7 August 2008), irishtimes.com/news/an-olympiad-with-females-would-be-impractical-uninteresting-unaesthetic-and-improper-baron-pierre-de-coubertin-1.1222948.

6. 'International Women's Sports Federation', Wikipedia [website], en.wikipedia.org/wiki/International_Women%27s_Sports_Federation.

7. Stefan Nestler, '100 years ago: Women's Olympic Games in Monte Carlo', Deutsche Welle [website] (23 March 2021), dw.com/en/100-years-ago-womens-olympic-games-in-monte-carlo/a-56962107.

8. 'Fanny Durack', Wikipedia [website], en.wikipedia.org/wiki/Fanny_Durack.

9. 'Fanny Durack', She's Game, Women Making Australian Sporting History [website], womenaustralia.info/exhib/sg/durack.html.

10. 'The victorious English 400 m. women's relay swimming team' [archive photo, 1912], commons.wikimedia.org/wiki/File:The_victorious_English_400_m._women%27s_relay_swimming_team_at_Wellcome_V0048555.jpg.

11. Craig Lord, 'Stockholm 1912', in Craig Lord, ed., *Aquatics 1908–2008: 100 Years of Excellence in Sport* (Lausanne: FINA, 2008), p. 65. Available at the Olympic Library, Lausanne, Switzerland.

12. 'Stamata Revithi', Wikipedia [website], en.wikipedia.org/wiki/Stamata_Revithi.

13. Ailsa Ross, 'The woman who crashed the Boston Marathon', JSTOR Daily [website] (18 March 2018), daily.jstor.org/the-woman-who-crashed-the-boston-marathon/.

14. Kathrine Switzer, 'The real story of Kathrine Switzer's 1967 Boston Marathon', Kathrine Switzer Marathon Woman [website], kathrineswitzer.com/1967-boston-marathon-the-real-story/.

15. Quoted in Tejas Kotecha, 'Kathrine Switzer: first woman to officially run Boston Marathon on the iconic moment she was attacked by the race organiser', Sky Sports [website] (15 December 2021), https://www.skysports.com/more-sports/athletics/news/29175/12475824/kathrine-switzer-first-woman-to-officially-run-boston-marathon-on-the-iconic-moment-she-was-attacked-by-the-race-organiser.

16. Linda J. Borish, 'Charlotte Epstein', Jewish Women's Archive [website], jwa.org/encyclopedia/article/epstein-charlotte.

17. Craig Lord, 'Epstein's vision', in Craig Lord, ed., *Aquatics 1908–2008: 100 Years of Excellence in Sport* (Lausanne: FINA, 2008), p. 37. Available at the Olympic Library, Lausanne, Switzerland.

18. 'Joseph Goebbels on women 1933', Alpha History [website], alphahistory.com/nazigermany/joseph-goebbels-on-women/.

19. John Hoberman, 'Think again: the Olympics', *Foreign Policy* 167 (2008), pp. 22–28, http://www.jstor.org/stable/25462313.

20. 'Carl von Ossietzky', Wikipedia [website], en.wikipedia.org/wiki/Carl_von_Ossietzky.

21. 'All Nobel Peace Prizes', The Nobel Prize [website], nobelprize.org/prizes/lists/all-nobel-peace-prizes/.

22. Phillip Barker, 'Drut calls for modern Olympics founder Coubertin to enter Paris

Panthéon in time for 2024 Olympics', Inside the Games [website] (6 February 2022), insidethegames.biz/articles/1118829/drut-coubertin-pantheon.

23. 'French Olympic Committee unveiled the sculpture of Alice Milliat', International Committee of the Mediterranean Games [website] (17 March 2021), cijm.org.gr/french-olympic-committee-unveiled-the-sculpture-of-alice-milliat/.

24. Murad Ahmed and David Keohane, 'Élysée lunch with Sarkozy at heart of Platini corruption probe', *Financial Times* (19 June 2019), ft.com/content/d45b1e6e-91df-11e9-b7ea-60e35ef678d2.

25. 'Global gender gap report 2022: insight report' [PDF], World Economic Forum [website] (July 2022), https://www3.weforum.org/docs/WEF_GGGR_2022.pdf.

26. 'Qatar: male guardianship severely curtails women's rights', Human Rights Watch [website] (29 March 2021), hrw.org/news/2021/03/29/qatar-male-guardianship-severely-curtails-womens-rights.

27. Cathrin Schaer, 'Did LGBTQ rights campaigns in Qatar help or hinder?', Deutsche Welle [website] (30 December 2022), dw.com/en/did-lgbtq-rights-campaigns-in-qatar-help-or-hinder/a-64239795.

28. Guardian Football, '"I feel Qatari, I feel gay": Infatino defends Fifa decision to host World Cup in Qatar' [video], YouTube [website] (19 November 2022), youtube.com/watch?v=KwBoSuMuK4Y.

29. Quoted in Sean Ingle, '"I feel gay, disabled… like a woman too!": Infantino makes bizarre attack on critics', *Observer* (18 November 2022), theguardian.com/football/2022/nov/19/fifa-gianni-infantino-world-cup-qatar.

30. 'Members', International Olympic Committee [website], olympics.com/ioc/members.

31. 'Countries', Amnesty International [website], amnesty.org/en/countries/; Human Rights Watch [website], hrw.org.

32. 'Nearly 2.4 billion women globally don't have same economic rights as men', World Bank (1 March 2022), worldbank.org/en/news/press-release/2022/03/01/nearly-2-4-billion-women-globally-don-t-have-same-economic-rights-as-men.

33. Craig Lord, 'FINA sinks to bottom of league on Olympic governance with weightlifting & judo feds', SOS [website] (17 June 2020), stateofswimming.com/fina-sinks-to-bottom-of-league-on-olympic-governance-with-weightlifting-judo-feds/.

34. Craig Lord, 'A 40% female quota, new name & hoisting honoraries overboard highlight the good news on a FINA reform voyage in its infancy', SOS [website] (9 December 2022), stateofswimming.com/a-40-female-quota-new-name-hoisting-honoraries-overboard-highlight-the-good-news-on-a-fina-reform-voyage-in-its-infancy/.

35. Chris Jewers, 'Norway condemns "ridiculous" €1,500 fine for their women's beach handball team after punishment for wearing shorts instead of bikini bottoms is confirmed', *Daily Mail* (20 July 2021), dailymail.co.uk/news/article-9806507/Norways-womens-handball-team-fined-1-500-wearing-shorts-instead-bikini-bottoms.html.

36. C. Cooky, L. D. Council, M. A. Mears and M. A. Messner, 'One and done: the long eclipse of women's televised sports, 1989–2019', *Communication & Sport* 9/3 (2021), pp. 347–71. For the 2010 report, see M. A. Messner and C. Cooky, 'Gender in televised sports: news and highlight shows, 1989–2009' [PDF], USC Dornsife College of Letters, Arts and Sciences [website] (June 2010), https://dornsife.usc.edu/assets/sites/80/docs/tvsports.pdf.

37. 'World of Sport unusual moments with Dickie Davies (1981)' [video], YouTube [website] (7 March 2019), youtube.com/watch?v=tPe8IoXV3ZE.

38. Dominic King, 'England's women take EasyJet flight for Portugal clash as travel plans come under more scrutiny just months after men's under 21 squad used private jet while they flew to the World Cup on British Airways', Daily Mail (7 October 2019), https://www.dailymail.co.uk/sport/football/article-7546381/Englands-women-EASYJET-flight-Portugal-clash-travel-plans-come-scrutiny.html.

39. Alicia Turner, 'England women's football team to fly in premium economy for SheBelieves Cup as men get private jet', World of Women's Sport [website] (27 February 2020), https://www.worldofwomenssport.com/football/england-womens-football-team-to-fly-in-premium-economy-for-shebelieves-cup-as-men-get-private-jet-4497.

40. Sarah Harvey, 'Lionesses' win watched by record-breaking 17.4million', Evening Standard (1 August 2022), standard.co.uk/news/uk/lionesses-england-win-germany-tv-audience-numbers-euros-2022-b1015901.html.

41. ESPN, 'NCAA called out for women's basketball weight room for March madness' [video], YouTube [website], youtube.com/watch?v=oSrGB_P3iGU.

CHAPTER 2

1. Werner W. Franke and Brigitte Berendonk, 'Hormonal doping and androgenization of athletes: a secret program of the German Democratic Republic government', Clinical Chemistry 43/7 (July 1997), pp. 1262–79. The details of Berendonk's book are as follows: Brigitte Berendonk, Doping: von der Forschung zum Betrug (Reinbek bei Hamburg: Rowohlt, 1992).

2. USADA, 'Andreas Krieger: Heidi's farthest throw' [video], YouTube [website] (19 November 2015), youtube.com/watch?v=KQhUjaiveAg.

3. Carolin Emcke and Udo Ludwig, 'Blaue Bohnen von Dr. Mabuse', Der Spiegel (27 February 2000), spiegel.de/politik/blaue-bohnen-von-dr-mabuse-a-6b93a ff8-0002-0001-0000-000015807565.

4. Oliver Fritsch, 'Poisoned by East Germany', Die Zeit (26 March 2018), https://www.zeit.de/sport/2018-03/doping-ddr-sport-dopingopfer-kinder-folgen-hilfe-english?utm_referrer=https%3A%2F%2Fwww.google.com%2F.

5. Ibid.

6. Franke and Berendonk, 'Hormonal doping and androgenization of athletes'.

7. Ibid.

8. Susanne Kranz, 'Women's role in the German Democratic Republic and the state's policy toward women', Journal of International Women's Studies 7/1 (November 2005), vc.bridgew.edu/cgi/viewcontent.cgi?article=1423&context=jiws.

9. Lucas Aykroyd, 'Fall of Berlin Wall brought curtain down on GDR's doping program', Global Sport Matters [website] (6 November 2019), globalsportmatters.com/culture/2019/11/06/fall-of-berlin-wall-brought-curtain-down-on-gdrs-doping-program/.

10. Craig Lord, 'GDR 30 years on: the day in 1989 the Berlin Wall came tumbling down on doping regime', SOS [website] (9 November 2019), stateofswimming.com/gdr-30-years-on-the-day-in-1989-the-berlin-wall-came-tumbling-down-on-doping-regime/.

11. Craig Lord, 'Ignorance is bliss: Kornelia Ender speaks for the first time since the fall of the Berlin Wall and revelations that her coaches gave her performance-enhancing drugs', *Times* (7 December 1991).

12. Quoted in Alan McDougall, 'Sport under communism: behind the East German "miracle"', *Sport in Society* 16/6 (2013), pp. 841–3.

13. Franke and Berendonk, 'Hormonal doping and androgenization of athletes'.

14. 'African nations boycott Montreal Olympics', *Guardian* (19 July 1976), theguardian.com/sport/2021/jul/19/african-nations-boycott-montreal-olympics-1976.

15. 'Top 10 notable drug scandals: East Germany's Olympic miracle', CBCSports [website] (27 July 2006), web.archive.org/web/20121103091941/http://www.cbc.ca/sports/photoessay/top10-doping/index2.html.

16. For information about this film, directed by Brian T. Brown and written by Casey Barrett and Brian T. Brown, see imdb.com/title/tt5958174/.

17. 'National Living Treasure (Australia)', Wikipedia [website], https://en.wikipedia.org/wiki/National_Living_Treasure_(Australia).

18. Shirley Babashoff and Chris Epting, *Making Waves: My Journey to Winning Olympic Gold and Defeating the East German Doping Program* (Solana Beach, CA: Santa Monica Press, 2016).

19. *Stern* 49 (November 1990), altezeitschriften.de/stern-magazin/6412-stern-heft-nr49-29-november-1990-helft-russland.html.

20. Jim Bronskill, 'E. Germans tossed drugs in St Lawrence at '76 Games', Canadian Press [news agency] (9 November 2009), thestar.com/sports/olympics/2009/11/09/e_germans_tossed_drugs_in_st_lawrence_at_76_games.html.

21. Ibid.

CHAPTER 3

1. *Stern* 49 (November 1990), altezeitschriften.de/stern-magazin/6412-stern-heft-nr49-29-november-1990-helft-russland.html.

2. 'Doping-Prozess: ex-DDR-Sportchef Ewald ist verhandlungsfähig', *Der Spiegel* (16 May 2000), spiegel.de/sport/sonst/doping-prozess-ex-ddr-sportchef-ewald-ist-verhandlungsfaehig-a-76619.html.

3. 'Olympic Order', Wikipedia [website], en.wikipedia.org/wiki/Olympic_Order.

4. The study is referred to in Werner W. Franke and Brigitte Berendonk, 'Hormonal doping and androgenization of athletes: a secret program of the German Democratic Republic government', *Clinical Chemistry* 43/7 (July 1997), pp. 1262–79.

5. See www.icarus.film.

6. 'Germany: ex chief doctor of swimming team convicted' [video], AP NewsRoom Archive [website] (12 January 2000), newsroom.ap.org/editorial-photos-videos/detail?itemid=d412374a317193c6181ef34b15b167e5&mediatype=video&source=youtube.

7. Quoted in Hans-Joachim Seppelt and Holger Schück, *Anklage: Kinderdoping. Das Erbe des DDR-Sports* (Berlin: Tenea Verlag, 1999).

8. John Borneman, *Settling Accounts: Violence, Justice, and Accountability in Postsocialist Europe* (Princeton: Princeton University Press, 1998).

9. Werner Franke, 'Funktion und Instrumentalisierung des Sports in der DDR:

Pharmakologische Manipulationen (Doping) und die Rolle der Wissenschaft', in Deutscher Bundestag, ed., *Bericht der Enquete-Kommission 'Aufarbeitung von Geschichte und Folgen der SED-Diktatur in Deutschland'*, iii/2 (Frankfurt am Main: Suhrkamp Verlag, 1995), pp. 904–1143. Available online at the website enquete-online.de, document wp12b3_2_150-389.pdf.

10. The website of Heidi's Heroes can be found at heidisheroes.co.uk.

11. Franke, 'Funktion und Instrumentalisierung des Sports in der DDR'.

12. Verena Kemna, 'Sportler auf der Flucht', Deutschlandfunk [website] (posted online 24 July 2011), deutschlandfunk.de/sportler-auf-der-flucht-100.html.

13. 'Renate Vogel', Olympics [website], olympics.com/de/athleten/renate-vogel.

14. Fritz Neumann, 'Christiane Sommer: Sie haben uns süchtig gemacht', *Der Standard* (18 September 2017), derstandard.de/story/2000064142264/christiane-sommersie-haben-uns-suechtig-gemacht.

15. Craig Lord, 'East German doping: "My father was heartbroken back then and the drug injustice still tortures him at 85"', *Times* (13 October 2021), thetimes.co.uk/article/east-german-doping-my-father-was-heartbroken-back-then-and-the-drug-injustice-still-tortures-him-at-85-j75bhcr9p.

16. Giselher Spitzer, *Doping in der DDR: Ein historischer Überblick zu einer konspirativen Praxis* (Cologne: Sportverlag Strauß, 2018).

CHAPTER 4

1. 'Schneider: I was doped', Eurosport [website] (22 December 2005), eurosport.com/swimming/schneider-i-was-doped_sto806055/story.shtml.

2. Jens Weinreich, 'The IOC, the Olympic family and the absolutely impeccable reputation of KGB/FSB agents', Sport & Politics [website] (23 July 2016), jensweinreich.de/2016/07/23/the-ioc-the-olympic-family-and-the-absolutely-unimpeachable-reputation-of-kgbfsb-agents/.

3. 'USA: President Carter suggests moving the Olympic Games from Moscow to Greece unless Soviet troops leave Afghanistan' [archive video from 21 January 1980], British Pathé [website], https://www.britishpathe.com/asset/179207/.

4. 'Moscow 1980 Olympic Games', *Britannica* [website], www.britannica.com/event/Moscow-1980-Olympic-Games.

5. 'Great Britain at the 1980 Summer Olympics', Wikipedia [website], en.wikipedia.org/wiki/Great_Britain_at_the_1980_Summer_Olympics.

6. Kevin Klose, 'Moscow prepares purge before Summer Olympics', *Washington Post* (17 December 1979, washingtonpost.com/archive/politics/1979/12/17/moscow-prepares-purge-before-summer-olympics/3ebe7938-2283-4660-9d45-aef5e5e2d8f8/.

7. David Jones, 'Sportsperson 137', *Daily Mail* (10 January 1998).

8. Craig Lord, 'GDR 30 years on: the day in 1989 the Berlin Wall came tumbling down on doping regime', SOS [website] (9 November 2019), stateofswimming.com/gdr-30-years-on-the-day-in-1989-the-berlin-wall-came-tumbling-down-on-doping-regime/.

9. 'The Order of Merit of the Federal Republic of Germany', Der Bundespräsident [website], https://www.bundespraesident.de/EN/Role-and-Functions/HonoursAndDecorations/TheOrderOfMerit/theorderofmerit-node.html.

10. Alan Maimon, 'One tale of doping and birth defects', *New York Times* (6 February 2000), archive.nytimes.com/www.nytimes.com/library/sports/other/020600swim-germany.html.

11. The documentary was made by Joe Layburn and titled *Joe Public – Miscarriages of Justice: East German Doping*, and aired on Channel 4 on 19 November 1998.

12. See the website of the Stasi Records Archive, www.stasi-unterlagen-archiv.de/en/.

13. Jones, 'Sportsperson 137'.

14. Aud Krubert, 'Lasting bodily harm and injustice – the story of Birgit Böse', *Welt Am Sonntag* (3 October 2004), welt.de/print-wams/article116126/Beharrlich-schmerzen-der-Koerper-und-die-Ungerechtigkeit.html.

15. 'Jenapharm zahlt, Opfer sind ruhig', *Der Spiegel* (21 December 2006), www.spiegel.de/sport/sonst/doping-in-der-ddr-jenapharm-zahlt-opfer-sind-ruhig-a-455929.html.

16. See the website of Doping-Opfer-Hilfe, no-doping.org.

17. 'Entschädigung für 240 DDR-Dopingopfer', *Die Zeit* (16 August 2017), zeit.de/sport/2017-08/doping-ddr-opfer-entschaedigung-bundesrepublik?utm_referrer=https%3A%2F%2F.

18. Cyrus Engineer, 'Why was Max Clifford in prison and what were his offences?', *Sun* (1 March 2021), thesun.co.uk/news/5107296/max-clifford-inquest-jail-net-worth-offences-family-overturn-convictions/.

19. Karin Helmstaedt, 'German trials: the conspiracy of lies has been cracked beyond a doubt', *SwimNews Magazine* (August 1998), swimnews.com/Magazine/1998/augmag98/drugtrials.shtml.

20. Jere Longman, 'East Germany's doping chief, Manfred Ewald, is dead at 76', *New York Times* (23 October 2002), nytimes.com/2002/10/23/sports/east-germany-s-doping-chief-manfred-ewald-is-dead-at-76.html.

21. Harry Peart, 'Endless battle to outsmart the dopes', BBC News [website] (15 January 1998), news.bbc.co.uk/2/hi/special_report/1998/drugs_in_sport/47692.stm.

22. Cecil M. Colwin, 'Swimming fights for its life', *SwimNews Magazine* (February 1998), swimnews.com/Magazine/1998/febmag98/swimfight.shtml.

23. 'The politics of doping and anti-doping in Chinese sport', *International Journal of the History of Sport* 29/1 (2012), pp. 132–44.

24. Justine McCarthy, 'Who are these Guys?', *Irish Independent* (15 August 1998), independent.ie/irish-news/who-are-these-guys-26177435.html.

25. Craig Lord, 'Drug test threat to Michelle Smith's future', *Times* (29 April 1998).

26. 'Court hears de Bruin appeal', *Irish Echo* [n.d.], group.irishecho.com/2011/02/court-hears-de-bruin-appeal-3/.

27. Rick Morrisey, 'The tarnished golden girl', *Chicago Tribune* (14 August 2000), archive.seattletimes.com/archive/?date=20000814&slug=4036702.

28. Steve Wilstein, 'Drug OK in baseball, not Olympics', Associated Press [website] (22 August 1998), apnews.com/article/87e8d2a7928c8de874fdc3f43b53a33a.

29. 'The CAS statement', *Irish Times* (6 August 1998), www.irishtimes.com/sport/the-cas-statement-1.193588.

30. 'Positive test ended promising discus career of Erik de Bruin', *Irish Times* (7 August 1998), irishtimes.com/news/positive-test-ended-promising-discus-career-of-erik-de-bruin-1.180605.

31. Christopher Clarey, 'East Germans will keep medals', *New York Times* (13 December

1998), nytimes.com/1998/12/13/sports/olympics-east-germans-will-keep-medals-from-76-olympics.html.

32. Christopher Clarey, 'Despite doping, Olympic medals stand', *New York Times* (16 December 1998), https://www.nytimes.com/1998/12/16/sports/IHT-despite-doping-olympic-medals-stand.html.

33. Werner W. Franke and Brigitte Berendonk, 'Hormonal doping and androgenization of athletes: a secret program of the German Democratic Republic government', *Clinical Chemistry* 43/7 (July 1997), pp. 1262–79.

34. 'Petra Schneider (GDR)', International Swimming Hall of Fame [website], ishof.org/honoree/honoree-petra-schneider/.

35. Jones, 'Sportsperson 137'.

36. This quotation is taken from the author's original notes for an interview that was published as 'Craig Lord catches up with Petra Schneider' in *SwimNews Magazine* in June 2005.

37. 'Eberhard Mothes' [article available on the 'Doping in the DDR' archive of newspaper cuttings and references], cycling4fans [website], cycling4fans.de/index.php?id=5674.

38. 'DSV Erklärungen zur Anstellung Doping belasteter ehemaliger DDR-Trainer' [article available on the 'Doping in the DDR' archive of newspaper cuttings and references], cycling4fans [website], cycling4fans.de/index.php?id=5674.

39. 'Eberhard Mothes' [article available on the 'Doping in the DDR' archive of newspaper cuttings and references], cycling4fans [website], cycling4fans.de/index.php?id=5674.

40. 'Drugs stance stirs outrage', BBC News [website] (27 July 1998), news.bbc.co.uk/2/hi/sport/140315.stm.

41. Quoted in Barrie Houlihan, *Dying to Win: Doping in Sport and the Development of Anti-Doping Policy* (Strasbourg: Council of Europe Publishing, 1999), p. 54.

42. Clarey, 'Despite doping, Olympic medals stand'.

43. Michael Mielke, 'Geldstrafen im Doping-Prozeß', *Die Welt* (21 August 1998), welt.de/print-welt/article6252250/Geldstrafen-im-Doping-Prozess.html.

44. Vyv Simson and Andrew Jennings, *The Lords of the Rings: Power, Money and Drugs in the Modern Olympics* (London: Simon & Schuster, 1992).

45. Craig Lord, 'Sharron Davies in line for gold medal 41 years later as swimming chief Husain al-Musallam vows to confront Olympic doping', *Times* (13 October 2021), thetimes.co.uk/article/sharron-davies-in-line-for-gold-medal-41-years-later-as-swimming-chief-husain-al-musallam-vows-to-confront-olympic-doping-9otkctpjw. For the BSCA Historic Achievement Awards, see 'BSCA Recognition Awards for swim coaches', Somerset ASA [website], somersetasa.org/sasa/en/News/News-Items?newsid=6342&smallscreen=0&printview=1.

46. Ibid.

47. 'BSCA Recognition Awards for swim coaches', Somerset ASA [website], https://www.somersetasa.org/sasa/en/News/News-Items?newsid=6342&smallscreen=0&printview=1.

CHAPTER 5

1. 'The evolution of the sex chromosomes: step by step', UChicagoMedicine [website] (27 October 1999), uchicagomedicine.org/forefront/news/the-evolution-of-the-sex-

chromosomes-step-by-step. For 'two million years', see 'How did humans evolve?', History.com [website] (1 April 2021), history.com/news/humans-evolution-neanderthals-denisovans.

2. 'How many chromosomes do people have?', MedlinePlus [website], https://medlineplus.gov/genetics/understanding/basics/howmanychromosomes/.

3. 'Trisomy', Wikipedia [website], en.wikipedia.org/wiki/Trisomy.

4. 'Turner syndrome 74', Wikipedia [website], en.wikipedia.org/wiki/Turner_syndrome 74.

5. The new technique is known as Electron Spin Resonance (ESR). See 'New technique dates fossil teeth', European Commission [website] (19 June 2017), cordis.europa.eu/article/id/198922-new-technique-dates-fossil-teeth.

6. A copy of the speech was supplied to Craig by David Gerrard. The website of the IWG is available at https://iwgwomenandsport.org/.

7. Carole Hooven, *Testosterone: The Story of the Hormone that Dominates and Divides Us* (London: Cassell, 2021).

8. Emma N. Hilton and Tommy R. Lundberg, 'Transgender women in the female category of sport: perspectives on testosterone suppression and performance advantage', *Sports Medicine* 51 (2020), pp. 199–214, link.springer.com/article/10.1007/s40279-020-01389-3.

9. For Hilton's presentation, see 'A woman's place is on the podium: Emma Hilton' [video], YouTube [website] (18 July 2019), youtube.com/watch?v=pzg9QtQelR8.

10. Jon Pike, 'Why "meaningful competition" is not fair competition', *Journal of the Philosophy of Sport* 50 (2023), pp. 1–17, tandfonline.com/doi/full/10.1080/00948705.2023.2167720.

11. Ibid.

12. Maya Yamauchi, 'To make sure everyone is aware, here is Veronica Ivy, of multiple name changes, saying women should die in a grease fire […]' [Twitter post] (9 April 2022), twitter.com/mara_yamauchi/status/1512732324861038593.

13. Hannah Witton with Veronica Ivy, 'Trans People in Elite Sport and Testosterone Myths with Dr. Veronica Ivy' [episode of Doing It! podcast, 9 November 2022], doingitpodcast.co.uk/transcripts/dr-veronica-ivy-transcript.

14. Quoted in Hooven, *Testosterone*.

15. Valérie Thibault et al., 'Women and men in sport performance: the gender gap has not evolved since 1983', *Journal of Sports Science and Medicine* 9/2 (June 2010), pp. 214–23. For Title IX, see 'Title IX', Wikipedia [website], en.wikipedia.org/wiki/Title_IX.

16. Linda Blade and Barbara Kay, *Unsporting: How Trans Activism and Science Denial Are Destroying Sport* ([n.p.]: Rebel News, 2020), p. 48.

17. Naomi Cunningham, 'Sex, gender and fair competition in sport', Legal Feminist [website] (7 July 2020), legalfeminist.org.uk/2020/07/07/sex-gender-and-fair-competition-in-sport/.

CHAPTER 6

1. Nick Thierry, Craig Lord and Gido Weidlich, 'Swim rankings database 1896–2023' [private resource].

2. Jason Herbert, 'The transition of athletes and the impact it has on women's sports', Sports Room (28 June 2021), thesportsroom.org/transition-of-athletes-impact-womens-sports/.

3. Katie Barnes, 'Amid protests, Penn swimmer Lia Thomas becomes first known transgender athlete to win Division I national championship', ESPN [website] (17 March 2022), espn.com/college-sports/story/_/id/33529775/amid-protests-pennsylvania-swimmer-lia-thomas-becomes-first-known-transgender-athlete-win-division-national-championship.

4. The quality of images 10 and 11 reflects the unpaid, unresourced efforts made by women's groups around the world. For the full presentation, see https://womensclearinghouse.org/wp-content/uploads/CWI-Transgender-Inclusion-LAW-Hogshead-Makar-5-2022.pdf.

5. 'World record progression 200 metres backstroke', Wikipedia [website], en.wikipedia.org/wiki/World_record_progression_200_metres_backstroke.

6. Craig Lord, 'Great Britain mixed medley 3:37.58 world record victory makes pioneers of Dawson, Peaty, Guy, Hopkin & Anderson', SOS [website] (31 July 2021), stateofswimming.com/great-britain-mixed-medley-337-58-world-record-victory-makes-pioneers-of-dawson-peaty-guy-hopkin-anderson/.

7. Kishan Vaghela, 'Arsenal Women suffer an embarrassing 5–0 defeat by their boys' U15 side in behind closed doors friendly', Daily Mail (31 August 2022), dailymail.co.uk/sport/football/article-11160861/Arsenal-Women-suffer-5-o-defeat-boys-U15-closed-doors-friendly-London-Colney.html.

8. Boys vs Women, boysvswomen.com.

9. Doriane Lambelet Coleman and Wickliffe Shreve, 'Comparing athletic performances: the best elite women to boys and men', Duke Law [website], law.duke.edu/sports/sex-sport/comparative-athletic-performance/.

CHAPTER 7

1. Craig Lord, 'Tucker & the fallacy of "T"', SOS [website] (22 February 2022), stateofswimming.com/tucker-the-fallacy-of-t-when-it-comes-to-reasons-why-transgender-athletes-dont-belong-in-womens-sport/.

2. For the decision by World Rugby, see Sean Ingle, 'World Rugby bans trans women from elite women's game due to injury risks', Guardian (9 October 2020), theguardian.com/sport/2020/oct/09/world-rugby-bans-trans-women-from-elite-womens-game-due-to-injury-risks.

3. 'Hannah Mouncey', Wikipedia [website], en.wikipedia.org/wiki/Hannah_Mouncey.

4. Jens Krepela (with SID/DPA), 'Doping, made easy', Deutsche Welle [website] (5 May 2015), dw.com/en/doping-made-easy/a-18431887.

5. Werner W. Franke and Brigitte Berendonk, 'Hormonal doping and androgenization of athletes: a secret program of the German Democratic Republic government', Clinical Chemistry 43/7 (July 1997), pp. 1262–79.

6. Emma N. Hilton and Tommy R. Lundberg, 'Transgender women in the female category of sport: perspectives on testosterone suppression and performance advantage', Sports Medicine 51 (2020), pp. 199–214, link.springer.com/article/10.1007/s40279-020-01389-3.

7. Alex Hutchinson, 'Why sprinters don't have the fastest finishing sprint', Outside [website] (4 November 2021), outsideonline.com/health/training-performance/sprint-speed-anaerobic-capacity-research/.

8. Chris Hatler, 'Jake Caswell wins nonbinary division at the 2022 New York City Marathon', Runner's World [website] (7 November 2022), runnersworld.com/news/a41879395/new-york-city-marathon-nonbinary-results-2022/.

9. Mara Yamauchi and Robert Johnson, 'Gender identity has no place in sport', LetsRun [website] (8 November 2022), letsrun.com/news/2022/11/gender-identity-has-no-place-in-sport/.

10. Mara Yamauchi, 'The NYC Marathon NB winner won $5000 for 2:45:12, slower than 146 men and 25 women, most of whom won nothing. More easy NB money in this race. And NB Q time half-way btw M & W times – so NB males get luxury of running slower & NB females must run faster than their peers' [Twitter post] (22 April 2023), twitter.com/mara_yamauchi/status/1649680814496526336.

11. S. F. Witchel, 'Disorders of sex development', *Best Practice and Research Clinical Obstetrics and Gynaecology* 48 (April 2018), pp. 90–102, ncbi.nlm.nih.gov/pmc/articles/PMC5866176/.

12. I. A. Hughes, C. Houk, S. F. Ahmed, P. A. Lee and LWPES1/ESPE2 Consensus Group, 'Consensus statement on management of intersex disorders', *Archives of Disease in Childhood* 91/7 (July 2006), pp. 554–63, https://www.ncbi.nlm.nih.gov/pmc/articles/PMC2082839.

13. E. Vilain et al., 'We used to call them hermaphrodites', *Genetics in Medicine* 9 (2007), pp. 65–66, doi.org/10.1097/GIM.0b013e31802cffcf.

14. 'F1000 commentary: changes over time in sex assignment for disorders of sex development / what is 5-alpha-reductase deficiency (5-ARD)?', Accord Alliance [website], accordalliance.org/faqs/what-is-5-alpha-reductase-deficiency-5-ard/.

15. Niamh Shackleton, 'Caster Semenya can't defend Olympic title due to new testosterone rules', Unilad [website] (3 July 2021), unilad.com/sport/caster-semenya-cant-defend-olympic-title-due-to-new-testosterone-rules.

16. Quoted in 'Caster Semenya accuses IAAF of using her as a "guinea pig experiment"', *Guardian* (18 June 2019), https://www.theguardian.com/sport/2019/jun/18/caster-semenya-iaaf-athletics-guinea-pig.

17. Megha Mohan, 'What Caster Semenya IAAF discrimination case means for women and sport', BBC News [website] (1 May 2019), https://www.bbc.co.uk/news/world-africa-48120228. For the UN document, see United Nations for LGBT Equality, 'Fact sheet, intersex' [PDF], UN Free & Equal [website], unfe.org/wp-content/uploads/2017/05/UNFE-Intersex.pdf.

18. Fausto-Sterling's book is *Sexing the Body: Gender Politics and the Construction of Sexuality* (New York: Basic Books, 2000).

19. For books by Leonard Sax, see amazon.com/stores/Leonard-Sax/author/B001JSEHTW.

20. Leonard Sax, 'How common is intersex? A response to Anne Fausto-Sterling', *Journal of Sex Research* 39/3 (August 2002), pp. 174–8, https://www.tandfonline.com/doi/abs/10.1080/00224490209552139.

21. Ross Tucker, 'The Caster Semenya debate', The Science of Sport [website] (16 July 2016), sportsscientists.com/2016/07/caster-semenya-debate/.

22. 'IOC releases Framework on Fairness, Inclusion and Non-discrimination on the basis of gender identity and sex variations', International Olympic Committee [website] (16 November 2021), olympics.com/ioc/news/ioc-releases-framework-on-fairness-inclusion-and-non-discrimination-on-the-basis-of-gender-identity-and-sex-variations.

23. M. Martowicz, et al., 'Position statement: IOC framework on fairness, inclusion and non-discrimination on the basis of gender identity and sex variations', *British Journal of Sports Medicine* 57 (2023), pp. 26–32, https://bjsm.bmj.com/content/57/1/26.

24. Louis J. Elsas et al., 'Gender verification of female athletes', *Genetics in Medicine* 2/4 (July–August 2000), pp. 249–54, https://doi.org/10.1097/00125817-200007000-00008.

25. Ibid.

26. IOC, 'Statement of the Stockholm consensus on sex reassignment in sports' [PDF] (18 October 2003), stillmed.olympic.org/Documents/Reports/EN/en_report_905.pdf.

27. Cathy Devine, Emma Hilton, Leslie Howe, Miroslav Imbrišević, Tommy Lundberg and Jon Pike, 'When ideology trumps science: a response to the Canadian Centre for Ethics in Sport's review on transwomen athletes in the female category', idrottsforum.org [website] (29 November 2022), idrottsforum.org/devineetal221129/.

28. Save Women's Sports, 'Fallon Fox on Twitter' [Facebook post] (17 June 2020), facebook.com/savewomenssports/posts/fallon-fox-on-twitter-for-the-record-i-knocked-two-out-one-womans-skull-was-frac/1614713022011984/.

CHAPTER 8

1. John Hoberman, 'The myth of sport as a peace-promoting political force', SAIS Review of International Affairs 31/1 (2011), pp. 17–29, https://www.researchgate.net/publication/236768613_The_Myth_of_Sport_as_a_Peace-Promoting_Political_Force.

2. Associated Press, 'IOC rules transgender athletes can take part in Olympics without surgery', *Guardian* (26 January 2016), theguardian.com/sport/2016/jan/25/ioc-rules-transgender-athletes-can-take-part-in-olympics-without-surgery.

3. I. T. Nolan, C. J. Kuhner and G. W. Dy, 'Demographic and temporal trends in transgender identities and gender confirming surgery', *Translational Andrology and Urology* 8/3 (June 2019), pp. 184–90, https://pubmed.ncbi.nlm.nih.gov/31380225/.

4. 'Access to sex reassignment surgery', EU Agency for Fundamental Rights [website], fra.europa.eu/en/publication/2017/mapping-minimum-age-requirements-concerning-rights-child-eu/access-sex-reassignment-surgery.

5. Helen Davidson, 'Transgender weightlifter Laurel Hubbard's eligibility under scrutiny', *Guardian* (9 April 2018), theguardian.com/sport/2018/apr/09/transgender-weightlifter-laurel-hubbards-eligibility-under-scrutiny.

6. Sina Filifilia Seva'aetasi, 'Woman lifter beaten by transgender speaks up', *Samoa Observer* (23 March 2017), samoaobserver.ws/category/samoa/8993.

7. 'Tokyo Olympics: Laurel Hubbard out of weightlifting after failing to register successful lift', BBC Sport [website] (2 August 2021), bbc.com/sport/olympics/58054891.

8. Sean Ingle, 'Sports stars weigh in on row over transgender athletes', *Guardian* (3 March 2019), theguardian.com/society/2019/mar/03/sports-stars-weigh-in-on-row-over-transgender-athletes.

9. Veronica Ivy, 'I won a World Championship. Some people aren't happy', *New York*

Times (5 December 2019), https://www.nytimes.com/2019/12/05/opinion/i-won-a-world-championship-some-people-arent-happy.html.

10. 'Heinrich Ratjen' [Dora Ratjen], Wikipedia [website], en.wikipedia.org/wiki/Heinrich_Ratjen.

11. 'Erik Schinegger' [Erika Schinegger], Wikipedia [website], en.wikipedia.org/wiki/Erik_Schinegger.

12. David Gerrard was speaking at the eighth International Working Group (IWG) World Conference on Women and Sport in New Zealand in November 2022. A copy of the speech was supplied to Craig by Gerrard. The website of the IWG is available at https://iwgwomenandsport.org/.

13. International Olympic Committee, 'IOC consensus meeting on sex reassignment and hyperandrogenism November 2015' [PDF], https://stillmed.olympic.org/Documents/Commissions_PDFfiles/Medical_commission/2015-11_ioc_consensus_meeting_on_sex_reassignment_and_hyperandrogenism-en.pdf. The remainder of the quotations in this section are also from this document.

14. Joanna Harper, 'Race times for transgender athletes', *Journal of Sporting Cultures and Identities* 6/1 (2015), pp. 1–9, https://cgscholar.com/bookstore/works/race-times-for-transgender-athletes?category_id=common-ground-publishing.

15. Alex Hutchinson, 'What's the ideal age for marathoning?', Runner's World [website] (6 November 2014), runnersworld.com/advanced/a20833515/whats-the-ideal-age-for-marathoning/.

16. Linda Blade and Barbara Kay, *Unsporting: How Trans Activism and Science Denial Are Destroying Sport* ([n.p.]: Rebel News, 2020), p. 73.

17. Emma N. Hilton and Tommy R. Lundberg, 'Transgender women in the female category of sport: perspectives on testosterone suppression and performance advantage', *Sports Medicine* 51 (2020), pp. 199–214, link.springer.com/article/10.1007/s40279-020-01389-3.

18. Martyn Ziegler and Craig Lord, 'Three of four transwomen athletes drop out of IOC study', *Times* (1 February 2023), www.thetimes.co.uk/article/three-of-four-transwomen-athletes-drop-out-of-ioc-study-nrh2hpx8m.

19. James Witts, 'Technological doping: the science of why Nike Alphaflys were banned from the Tokyo Olympics', BBC Science Focus [website], (4 September 2021), sciencefocus.com/the-human-body/nike-alphafly-banned-technological-doping/.

20. Craig Lord, 'FINA announce ban on bodysuits from 2010', *Times* (31 July 2009), thetimes.co.uk/article/fina-announce-ban-on-bodysuits-from-2010-tdsdb9twp9f.

21. 'A woman's place is on the podium: Emma Hilton' [video], YouTube [website] (18 July 2019), youtube.com/watch?v=pzg9QtQelR8. For a transcript, see 'Emma Hilton reviews the science supporting the IOC decision to let male-born transgender athletes into female competition', Fair Play for Women [website] (14 July 2019), fairplayforwomen.com/emma_hilton/. For details of the conference, see womansplaceuk.org/2019/09/26/a-womans-place-is-at-conference/.

22. L. J. Gooren and M. C. Bunck, 'Transsexuals and competitive sports', *European Journal of Endocrinology* 151/4 (October 2004), pp. 425–9, https://pubmed.ncbi.nlm.nih.gov/15476439/.

23. Timothy A. Roberts, Joshua Smalley and Dale Ahrendt, 'Effect of gender-affirming hormones on athletic performance in transwomen and transmen: implications for

sporting organisations and legislators', *British Journal of Sports Medicine* 55/11 (2021), pp. 577–83, https://bjsm.bmj.com/content/55/11/577.info.

24. Brent Schrotenboer, 'Lance Armstrong and the apology that never happened', *USA Today* (17 March 2016), eu.usatoday.com/story/sports/cycling/2016/03/17/lance-armstrong-movie-the-program-david-walsh/81933880/.

25. Sophie Law, 'BBC in "no platform" row after axing a guest from discussion on transgender athletes', *Daily Mail* (3 March 2019), dailymail.co.uk/news/article-6718921/BBC-no-platform-row-axing-guest-discussion-transgender-athletes.html.

26. Quoted in Andres Ybarra and Associated Press, 'Beckie Scott's heartfelt going-away speech marks end of era at WADA', CBC [website] (9 November 2019), cbc.ca/sports/olympics/beckie-scott-wada-speech-1.5352817.

27. Yoo Jee-ho, 'British swimmer Peaty hoping athletes will have more "voice"', Yonhap News Agency [website] (25 July 2019), en.yna.co.kr/view/AEN20190725009600315. For the controversy over Chinese cheat Sun Yang, see Craig Lord, 'Olympic champion Sun Yang abuses drug testers', *Sunday Times* (27 January 2019), thetimes.co.uk/article/olympic-champion-sun-yang-abuses-drugtesters-flgppztl3.

28. Linda Blade and Barbara Kay, *Unsporting: How Trans Activism and Science Denial Are Destroying Sport* ([n.p.]: Rebel News, 2020), pp. 154–5.

29. 'Convention on the Elimination of All Forms of Discrimination against Women New York, 18 December 1979', United Nations [website], https://www.ohchr.org/en/instruments-mechanisms/instruments/convention-elimination-all-forms-discrimination-against-women.

30. Thomas Airey, 'Feagaiaga Stowers – I used to be afraid of the outside world', *Samoa Observer* (30 December 2018), www.samoaobserver.ws/category/samoa/29367.

31. Mata'afa Keni Lesa, 'Hubbard moment the biggest and most blatant injustice in Samoa XVI Pacific Games', *Samoa Observer* (15 July 2019), samoaobserver.ws/category/samoa/45741.

32. For books by Andrew Jennings exposing corruption at the IOC and FIFA, see thriftbooks.com/a/andrew-jennings/343962/.

33. Andrew Jennings, 'Some thoughts on our simple craft', *Sport and Politics* ['The Andrew Jennings Edition'] (January 2022), jensweinreich.de/produkt/sap-3-2020/.

34. 'Yoshiaki Tsutsumi', Wikipedia [website], https://en.wikipedia.org/wiki/Yoshiaki_Tsutsumi#1998_Winter_Olympics.

35. Kyodo, AFP–Jiji, 'Former Tokyo Olympics operations exec and three others arrested over bid-rigging', *Japan Times* (8 February 2023), japantimes.co.jp/news/2023/02/08/national/crime-legal/olympics-bid-rigging-arrest/.

36. Stephen Wilson and Associated Press, 'IOC releases compensation figures for Bach and members', *USA Today* (2 April 2015), https://eu.usatoday.com/story/sports/olympics/2015/04/02/ioc-releases-compensation-figures-for-bach-and-members/70816678/.

37. Reuters, 'IOC releases compensation figures for President Thomas Bach, members', *Sports Business Journal* (3 April 2015), https://www.sportsbusinessjournal.com/Global/Issues/2015/04/03/Olympics/IOC-compensation.aspx.

38. 'Victims share what Larry Nassar did to them under the guise of medical treatment', *Indianapolis Star* (25 January 2018), eu.indystar.com/story/news/2018/01/25/heres-what-larry-nassar-actually-did-his-patients/1065165001/.

39. See athleteafilm.com.

40. Christine Hauser and Maggie Astor, 'The Larry Nassar case: what happened and how the fallout is spreading', *New York Times* (25 January 2018), nytimes.com/2018/01/25/ sports/larry-nassar-gymnastics-abuse.html.

41. Rachel Axon and Nancy Armour, 'Entire USA Gymnastics board resigns in wake of Larry Nassar scandal', *USA Today* (31 January 2018), eu.usatoday.com/story/ sports/olympics/2018/01/31/entire-usa-gymnastics-board-resigns-usoc-larry-nassar-scandal/1082855001/.

42. AFP, 'Outrage as disgraced former US Olympic chief Scott Blackmun gets US$2.4-million payoff', *Straits Times* (4 July 2019), straitstimes.com/sport/outrage-as-disgraced-former-us-olympic-chief-scott-blackmun-gets-us24-million-payoff.

43. Ram Gopal, 'Sports ethics beyond the rules', *International Journal of Research in Engineering* 5/11 (November 2015), indusedu.org/pdfs/IJREISS/IJREISS_338_17659. pdf.

44. 'Open Letter: 500+ Canadian gymnasts' concerns about a toxic and abusive sport culture continue to be ignored', Global Athlete [website] (26 October 2022), globalathlete.org/our-word/500-canadian-gymnasts-concerns-about-a-toxic-abusive-sport-culture-continue-to-be-ignored.

45. 'List of individuals permanently suspended or ineligible for membership', USA Swimming [website], usaswimming.org/safe-sport/individuals-suspended-or-ineligible.

46. Craig Lord, 'USA swimming handed safe sport manifesto by special "abuses" committee 27 years ago', SOS [website] (9 March 2018), stateofswimming.com/usa-swimming-handed-safe-sport-manifesto-by-special-abuses-committee-27-years-ago/.

47. Associated Press, 'Deena Deardurff Schmidt, a 1972 Olympic gold medalist, says the governing body of the U.S. swim team' [video], YouTube [website] (19 March 2010), https://www.youtube.com/watch?v=zj8AJdjphgU.

48. Safe Sport, 'USA Swimming' [website], sftest.usaswimming.org/safe-sport.

49. 'Paul Bergen (USA/CAN)', International Swimming Hall of Fame [website], ishof. org/honoree/honoree-paul-bergen/.

50. Craig Lord, 'Great day for athlete safety as U.S. House matches Senate to pass Empowering Olympic, Paralympic, and Amateur Athlete Act (S2330)', SOS [website] (1 October 2020), stateofswimming.com/great-day-for-athlete-safety-as-u-s-house-matches-senate-to-pass-empowering-olympic-paralympic-and-amateur-athlete-act-s2330/. For the USA Gymnastics sex-abuse scandal, see 'Larry Nassar', Wikipedia [website], en.wikipedia.org/wiki/Larry_Nassar.

51. Jerry Moran and Richard Blumenthal, 'Senate Olympics Investigation – Empowering Olympic, Paralympic, and Amateur Athletes Act' [PDF], moran.senate.gov/public/_ cache/files/1/e/1e4e590c-5d02-4629-8347-4ae1a2f3f058/1588EC5DF1475803 1013 F503E3505F23.2020.7.22-olympics-bill-one-pager.pdf.

52. 'NBCUniversal's acquisition of media rights through 2032', NBCPress Box [website] (7 May 2014), nbcsportsgrouppressbox.com/2022/02/01/nbcuniversals-acquisition-of-media-rights-through-2032-3/.

53. Quoted in Lord, 'Great day for athlete safety'.

CHAPTER 9

1. Ron Dicker, 'Transgender swimmer Lia Thomas is destroying records at Penn and aiming to make history', HuffPost [website] (7 December 2021), uk.sports.yahoo.com/news/transgender-swimmer-lia-thomas-destroying-121513000.html.

2. "'That sounds like a guy to me…" – Bill Maher and Mike Tyson on Lia Thomas and transgender athletes' [video], YouTube [website] (11 July 2022), youtube.com/watch?v=8nS0VhkszvU90.

3. Quoted in Ryan Glasspiegel, 'Michael Phelps: NCAA's Lia Thomas issue shows need for level playing field', *New York Post* (17 January 2022), https://nypost.com/2022/01/17/michael-phelps-ncaas-lia-thomas-controversy-very-complicated/.

4. Joshua Rhett Miller, 'USA Swimming official quits over transgender swimmer Lia Thomas: "I can't support this"', *New York Post* (24 December 2021), nypost.com/2021/12/24/usa-swimming-official-quits-over-transgender-swimmer/.

5. Patrick Reilly, 'Teammates say they are uncomfortable changing in locker room with trans UPenn swimmer Lia Thomas', *New York Post* (27 January 2022), https://nypost.com/2022/01/27/teammates-are-uneasy-changing-in-locker-room-with-trans-upenn-swimmer-lia-thomas/.

6. Craig Lord, 'Indecent exposure laws cited in letter to U.S. legal authorities highlights litigation threat to sports & college bosses blind to women's rights in transgender debate', SOS [website] (4 March 2022), stateofswimming.com/indecent-exposure-laws-cited-in-letter-to-u-s-legal-authorities-highlights-litigation-threat-to-sports-college-bosses-blind-to-womens-rights-in-transgender-debate/.

7. Reilly, 'Teammates say they are uncomfortable'.

8. Quoted in Lord, 'Indecent exposure laws cited in letter'.

9. Quoted ibid.

10. Craig Lord, 'The 200 free time trial that became a yardstick of how much poison is being poured in the women's swimming pool', SOS [website] (19 February 2022), stateofswimming.com/the-200-free-time-trial-that-became-a-yardstick-of-how-much-poison-is-being-poured-in-the-womens-swimming-pool/.

11. ESPN, 'Swimmer Lia Thomas breaks silence about backlash, future plans' [video], YouTube [website] (31 May 2022), youtube.com/watch?v=wMrZ2T46ZXs.

12. Matt Bonesteel, 'USA Swimming issues new policy for transgender athletes in elite competition', *Washington Post* (1 February 2022), washingtonpost.com/sports/2022/02/01/usa-swimming-transgender-policy/.

13. Robert Sanchez, "'I am Lia": the trans swimmer dividing America tells her story', *Sports Illustrated* (3 March 2022), si.com/college/2022/03/03/lia-thomas-penn-swimmer-transgender-woman-daily-cover.

14. Champion Women and the Women's Sports Policy Working Group, '7605 people, including almost 400 Olympians and Paralympians, petition Congress and sport governing organizations to prioritise competitive fairness and safety for biological women' [PDF], Champion Women [website] (15 April 2022), championwomen.org/wp-content/uploads/2022/06/Press-Release-Champion-Women-and-WSPWG-Petitions-updated-2022.pdf.

15. 'Sex Matters – the statement on the petitions from the Women's Sports Policy

Working Group and Champion Women', quoted in Craig Lord, 'Sex matters in sport: 3,000 athletes among more than 5k who signed petitions calling on fair play for women in transgender inclusion debate', SOS [website] (15 March 2022), https://www.stateofswimming.com/sex-matters-in-sport-3000-athletes-among-more-than-5k-who-signed-petitions-calling-on-fair-play-for-women-in-transgender-inclusion-debate/.

16. Amanda McMaster, Henderson Hewes and Douglas Lantz, 'Penn transgender swimmer Lia Thomas speaks out about backlash, future plans to compete', ABC/ESPN [website] (31 May 2022), abc7ny.com/lia-thomas-transgender-woman-university-of-pennsylvania-swimmer-good-morning-america/11911743/.

17. Senator Tommy Tuberville, 'Senator Tuberville delivers a floor speech on the real March Madness' [video], YouTube [website] (17 March 2022), www.youtube.com/watch?v=AVnWlXJg6RY.

18. Mara Yamauchi, 'At what point do all these male-inclusion rules just boil down to allowing what wd otherwise be crimes? Collisions in sports – assaults. Naked males in women's changing rooms – indecent exposure & voyeurism. CPS legalising rape. So men can freely commit crimes w no consequences' [Twitter post] (14 December 2022), twitter.com/mara_yamauchi/status/1602934340635312129.

19. Anonymous, 'TTT / Transphobe/TERF Tracker – tracking transphobes in sports', ttt.lgbt.

20. 'Gun violence: how does public health tackle gun violence?', American Public Health Association [website], apha.org/topics-and-issues/gun-violence.

21. Quoted in Alex Azzi, 'Women's Tour de France revival is reminder that "the fight for equality is far from over"', NBC Sports [website] (4 August 2021), onherturf.nbcsports.com/2022/08/04/womens-tour-de-france-revival-is-reminder-that-the-fight-for-equality-is-far-from-over/.

22. Quoted ibid. For Kathyrn Bertine's film, see halftheroad.com.

23. Quoted in Azzi, 'Women's Tour de France revival is reminder'.

24. Nate Llerandi, Orion Coaching, 'The "trans movement" – for want of a better way to describe it; if there is one, let me know – is akin to the Salem witch trials, with those who support fair sport for biological women being branded as witches. By screeching "transphobe!," the power of the accusers is absolute' [Twitter thread] (9 December 2022), twitter.com/ORION_coaching/status/1601025321415094272.

25. US Center for SafeSport, uscenterforsafesport.org.

26. Char Adams, 'USA Gymnastics worked with Larry Nassar to concoct "false excuses" to hide abuse claims', *People* (24 May 2018), people.com/sports/larry-nassar-excuses-usa-gymnastics/.

27. Dan Boyce, 'U.S. Olympic report: 93 percent of athletes surveyed who experienced sexual harassment or unwanted contact say they didn't report it', CPR News [website] (15 July 2021), cpr.org/2021/07/15/u-s-olympic-report-93-percent-of-athletes-surveyed-say-they-didnt-report-sexual-harassment-or-unwanted-contact-they-experienced-as-children/.

28. For the First Amendment, see constitution.congress.gov/constitution/amendment-1/.

29. Tom Pearman, 'Forget the fact that AK is a biological male. He/she should have been DQ for this move which was only one of at least 3 attempts to put Arnesman into the tape. I was standing right there when one of the others happened. You

can do better' [Twitter post] (12 December 2022), twitter.com/TomHPearman/status/1602134082976096256.

30. Dawn Ennis, 'USA Cycling investigating trans cyclist in championship', Los Angeles Blade [website] (16 December 2022), losangelesblade.com/2022/12/16/exclusive-usa-cycling-investigating-trans-cyclist-in-championship/; Ryan Gaydos, 'US cyclocross champion reveals she retired from sport over emergence of transgender athletes in women's sports', Fox News [website] (23 March 2023), foxnews.com/sports/us-cyclocross-champion-reveals-she-retired-sport-emergence-transgender-athletes-womens-sports.

31. 'Convention on the Elimination of All Forms of Discrimination against Women New York, 18 December 1979', United Nations [website], https://www.ohchr.org/en/instruments-mechanisms/instruments/convention-elimination-all-forms-discrimination-against-women.

32. Inga Thompson, 'Adam brought in the Militia to intimidate any and All that don't agree' [Twitter post] (12 December 2022), twitter.com/ithompsonfdn/status/1602402271593058305; Inga Thompson, 'Looks like Adam coordinated with the Gun Club to intimidate the women' [Twitter post] (12 December 2022), twitter.com/ithompsonfdn/status/1602380794462625792.

33. 'Transgender and non-binary participation policy', British Cycling [website] (October 2020), britishcycling.org.uk/about/article/20201009-British-Cycling-publishes-Transgender-and-Non-Binary-Participation-policy-0.

34. 'Millar, R., positive 14/05/1992, positive test ID 811', Dopeology [website], dopeology.org/incidents/Millar%2C-R-positive/.

35. 'Philippa York', Wikipedia [website], en.wikipedia.org/wiki/Philippa_York.

36. LW, 'Transgender cyclist disqualified prior to competing in women's race', Marca (30 March 2022), marca.com/en/more-sports/2022/03/31/624604d0268e3ebc1b8b4651.html.

37. John Westerby and Craig Lord, 'Trans cyclist Emily Bridges blocked from Laura Kenny race', Times (31 March 2022), thetimes.co.uk/article/trans-cyclist-emily-bridges-barred-from-competition-by-uci-h2nvo6f6w.

38. Dame Laura Kenny, 'I couldn't agree more – well said, well written, thank you' [Twitter post] (22 April 2022), twitter.com/LauraKenny31/status/1517416605520699393.

39. Megan Hinton, 'Olympic cycling chief calls for sport to ban trans athletes from competing against women', LBC [website] (6 April 2022), lbc.co.uk/news/olympic-cycling-chief-ban-trans-athletes-competing/.

40. 'UCI halves testosterone threshold, doubles transition period for transgender women', Cycling News [website] (17 June 2022), cyclingnews.com/news/uci-halves-testosterone-threshold-doubles-transition-period-for-transgender-women/.

41. 'Emily Bridges: why I've made a documentary about my transgender journey', ITV News [website] (29 November 2022), itv.com/news/wales/2022-11-29/emily-bridges-why-ive-made-a-documentary-about-my-transgender-journey.

42. Quoted in Patrick Burke, 'British Rowing chair claims World Rowing transgender policy "less protective of women's sport"', Inside the Games [website] (8 October 2022), https://www.insidethegames.biz/articles/1128964/british-rowing-transgender-world-rowing.

43. 'Opinion: rowing denies fairness for female athletes', Newsweek (2 February 2023), newsweek.com/usrowing-denies-fairness-female-athletes-opinion-1777151.

44. USA Rowing, 'NOTE: While we encourage open dialogue and discussion, our top priority is creating a safe, welcoming community for all. Comments constituting hate speech, bullying or transphobia will be reported, and corresponding accounts blocked', [Twitter post] (2 December 2022), twitter.com/usrowing/status/1598784648137826305.

45. ViaSport British Colombia, 'Creating inclusive environments' [PDF], viasport.ca/sites/default/files/LGBTQI2S_Creating_Inclusive_Environments.pdf.

46. Linda Blade and Barbara Kay, *Unsporting: How Trans Activism and Science Denial Are Destroying Sport* ([n.p.]: Rebel News, 2020), p. 92.

47. CCES, 'Creating inclusive environments for trans participants in Canadian sport' [PDF], cces.ca/sites/default/files/content/docs/pdf/cces-transinclusionpolicyguidance-e.pdf.

48. Jon Pike, 'Transgender women athletes and elite sport: misleading at best, intellectually dishonest at worst', Macdonald Laurier Institute [website] (8 December 2022), macdonaldlaurier.ca/transgender-women-athletes-and-elite-sport-misleading-at-best-intellectually-dishonest-at-worst/.

49. Ibid.

CHAPTER 10

1. 'Kim Jones, aka "Mother of Swimmer" and her fight for women and girls in sport', Fair Play for Women [website] (7 December 2022), fairplayforwomen.com/kim-jones-aka-swim-mom-and-her-fight-for-women-and-girls-in-sport/.

2. 'One-child policy', *Britannica* [website], www.britannica.com/topic/one-child-policy.

3. 'The lesbians who feel pressured to have sex and relationships with trans women', BBC News [website] (26 October 2021), https://www.bbc.co.uk/news/uk-england-57853385.

4. Stephanie Hegarty, 'Are women getting angrier?', BBC News [website] (7 December 2022), bbc.com/news/world-63874001.

5. Nicola Davis, 'Self-harm among girls aged 13 to 16 rose by 68% in three years, UK study finds', *Guardian* (18 October 2017), theguardian.com/society/2017/oct/18/self-harm-girls-aged-13-to-16-rose-68pc-three-years.

6. May Bulman, 'Nearly one in four girls aged 14 self-harmed in past year, study shows', *Independent* (29 August 2018), www.independent.co.uk/news/uk/home-news/teenage-girls-self-harm-report-childrens-society-a8511686.html.

7. 'IOC releases Framework on Fairness, Inclusion and Non-discrimination on the basis of gender identity and sex variations', International Olympic Committee [website] (16 November 2021), olympics.com/ioc/news/ioc-releases-framework-on-fairness-inclusion-and-non-discrimination-on-the-basis-of-gender-identity-and-sex-variations.

8. Madeleine Pape [website], madeleinepape.com.

9. 'Macintosh Lecture 2022' [video of Madeleine Pape's lecture 'Biofeminism: the epistemic politics of inclusion in women's sport', delivered 27 January 2022], YouTube [website] (2 February 2022), youtube.com/watch?v=dEunnSVlh2U&t=2347s.

10. 'Our supporters', Fair Play for Women [website], https://fairplayforwomen.com/about-us/our-supporters/.

11. Gregory A. Brown and Tommy Lundberg, 'Should transwomen be allowed to compete in women's sports? A view from an exercise physiologist', Center on Sport

Policy and Conduct [website] (17 April 2023), sportpolicycenter.com/news/2023/4/17/
should-transwomen-be-allowed-to-compete-in-womens-sports.

12. 'Macintosh Lecture 2022'.

13. 'Cathy Devine', Sex Matters [website], sex-matters.org/people/advisory-group/cathy-
devine/; Miroslav Imbrišević, 'The transgender reader: language, law, sport and reality. A
collection of essays, new edition (extended)' [PDF published by Brighteye Publishing,
Worthing, Sussex, 2023], https://www.researchgate.net/publication/361209724_THE_
TRANSGENDER_READER_Language_Law_Sport_Reality_A_Collection_of_
Essays_new_edition_extended_2023.

14. 'Landmark World Rugby transgender workshop important step towards appropriate
rugby-specific policy', World Rugby [website] (27 February 27 2020), world.rugby/
news/563437/landmark-world-rugby-transgender-workshop-important-step-towards-
appropriate-rugby-specific-policy.

15. Joanna Hoffman, '200+ scholars and athletes condemn Sport Canada's funding
of anti-trans research', Athlete Ally [website] (9 May 2022), athleteally.org/scholars-
athletes-condemn-sport-canadas-funding-of-anti-trans-research/.

16. James Brinsford, 'World Athletics tightens rules on trans athletes: why this matters',
Newsweek (15 April 2023), newsweek.com/world-athletics-tightens-rules-trans-athletes-
why-this-matters-1792467.

17. James Brinsford, 'World Athletics hits back at claims over transgender competitors',
Newsweek (19 April 2023), newsweek.com/world-athletics-responds-transgender-
athletes-claims-1795338.

18. Save Women's Sports, 'Fallon Fox on Twitter' [Facebook post] (17 June 2020),
facebook.com/savewomenssports/posts/fallon-fox-on-twitter-for-the-record-i-knocked-
two-out-one-womans-skull-was-frac/1614713022011984/.

19. Quoted in Bhavesh Purohit, 'When transgender fighter Fallon Fox broke her
opponent's skull in MMA fight', SportsSkeeda [website] (30 September 2021),
sportskeeda.com/mma/news-when-transgender-fighter-fallon-fox-broke-opponent-
s-skull-mma-fight.

20. Mark Tighe, 'LGFA "developing policy" on transgender players after ladies' shield
final incident', Irish Independent (7 August 2022), independent.ie/sport/gaelic-games/
ladies-football/lgfa-developing-policy-on-transgender-players-after-ladies-shield-final-
incident-41894821.html.

21. Reduxx Team, 'Irish 'LGBTQ+ inclusive' football team with transgender player
wins women's junior final', Reduxx [website] (5 August 2022), reduxx.info/irish-lgbtq-
inclusive-football-team-with-transgender-player-wins-womens-junior-final/.

22. Women's Sports Foundation, womenssportsfoundation.org.

23. The quotations from Nancy in this section are taken from Craig's notes from the
interview that was published as Craig Lord, 'IWD: Nancy Hogshead-Makar, rape
survivor & fighter for an end to abuse in sport', SOS [website] (8 March 2021),
stateofswimming.com/iwd-nancy-hogshead-makar-rape-survivor-fighter-for-an-end-
to-abuse-in-sport/.

24. See Richard Lapchick, 'Violence against women needs action', ESPN [website]
(30 November 2011), espn.com/espn/commentary/story/_/page/lapchick-111130/
the-public-underwhelming-reaction-athletes-assault-women.

25. Nancy Hogshead, JD, 'Dr Mike Joyner on sex differences and human physiology' [video], YouTube [website] (8 June 2022), www.youtube.com/watch?v=5aJg7eDzmAc.

26. For the US Equality Act, see PBS NewsHour, 'Senate Judiciary committee holds hearing on Equality Act for LGBTQ rights' [video], YouTube [website] (17 March 2021), www.youtube.com/watch?v=iK7eOudkkZg.

27. Scott M. Reid, 'Did Women's Sports Foundation try to silence a leading voice fighting sexual abuse in sports?', *Orange County Register* (12 October 2021), ocregister. com/2021/10/12/did-womens-sports-foundation-try-to-silence-leading-advocate-for-athlete-protections-against-sexual-abuse/. For Nancy's tweet, see 'After 30y w the @WomensSportsFdn , my renewal contract had a paragraph forbidding me from advocating for athlete sexual safety on @TeamUSA [...]' [Twitter poat] (13 October 2021), https://twitter.com/Hogshead3Au/status/1448100015528890373.

28. Nancy's statement appeared on the 'Champion Women' Facebook page on 13 October 2021. See facebook.com/iChampionWomen/photos/a.632950943505631/2432463623 554345/?type=3&paipv=0&eav=AfZMiwxkvrxhZtNvQxeg2-ODTFYvXcYv4qo-pM WjAvb6yqPpJKvVg8eNuo5qlwSw6Uo&_rdr.

29. Reid, 'Did Women's Sports Foundation try to silence a leading voice fighting sexual abuse in sports?'.

30. Katie Herzog, 'Med Schools are now denying biological sex', The Free Press [website] (27 July 2021), thefp.com/p/med-schools-are-now-denying-biological.

31. Quoted in Meimei Xu, 'Biology lecturer's comments on biological sex draw backlash', Harvard Crimson [website] (11 August 2021), https://www.thecrimson. com/article/2021/8/11/biology-lecturer-gender-comments-backlash/. Hooven appeared on *Fox and Friends* on 28 July 2021.

32. Harvard University, Faculty of Arts and Sciences, 'Free speech guidelines' [PDF] (1990), https://www.thefire.org/sites/default/files/2015/08/17163021/freespeech_guidelines_19903.pdf.

33. Carole Hooven, 'Academic freedom is social justice: sex, gender, and cancel culture on campus', *Archives of Sexual Behavior* 52 (2023), pp. 35–41, https://link.springer.com/article/10.1007/s10508-022-02467-5.

34. Quoted in Oliver Brown, 'I raced Lia Thomas – and I still feel the burning injustice', *Daily Telegraph* (8 November 2022), telegraph.co.uk/swimming/2022/11/08/raced-lia-thomas-still-feel-burning-injustice/.

35. Independent Women's Forum, 'Our Bodies, Our Sports – speech' [TikTok video] (3 November 2022), www.tiktok.com/@independentwomensforum/video/7161892861598797098.

36. Quoted in Asra Q. Nomani, 'Dream Team rallies for America's daughters in sports', Asra Investigates [Substack] (14 June 2022), https://asrainvestigates.substack.com/p/dream-team-rallies-for-americas-daughters.

37. Quoted ibid. See also Lee Brown and Joshua Rhett Mille, 'Skateboarder Taylor Silverman rips trans competitors who win: "unfair"', *New York Post* (20 May 2022), https://nypost.com/2022/05/20/skateboarder-taylor-silverman-rips-trans-competitors-who-win/.

CHAPTER 11

1. Peter Verry, 'Nike is facing backlash over its partnership with transgender activist Dylan Mulvaney', Yahoo Life [website] (7 April 2023), yahoo.com/lifestyle/nike-facing-backlash-over-partnership-163607593.html.

2. Allyson Felix, 'My own Nike pregnancy story – I've been one of Nike's most widely marketed athletes. If I can't secure maternity protections, who can?', New York Times (22 May 2019), nytimes.com/2019/05/22/opinion/allyson-felix-pregnancy-nike.html.

3. Sean Gregory, 'Exclusive: Allyson Felix launches her own shoe company two years after breaking up with Nike', Time (23 June 2021), https://time.com/6073949/allyson-felix-launching-saysh-shoes/.

4. Jordan Valinsky, 'Nike further expands protections for pregnant athletes after fierce backlash', CNN Business [website] (19 August 2019), edition.cnn.com/2019/08/19/business/nike-pregnant-policy/index.html.

5. Alex Hammer, 'Bud Light's parent company Anheuser-Busch InBev has lost more than $6 BILLION in market cap in just six days after Dylan Mulvaney partnership sparked backlash', Daily Mail [website] (13 April 2023), dailymail.co.uk/news/article-11967335/Bud-Lights-parent-company-Anheuser-Busch-InBev-lost-6-BILLION-market-cap.html.

6. Rena Afami, 'Gender inequality in sports sponsorship', Sports Financial Literacy Academy [website] (31 March 2021), moneysmartathlete.com/women-athletes/gender-inequality-in-sports-sponsorships/.

7. Diversity Champions Programme, Stonewall, stonewall.org.uk/global-diversity-champions-programme.

8. 'ACLU announces Jon L. Stryker and Slobodan Randjelović LGBTQ & HIV project', ACLU [website] (4 March 2021), aclu.org/press-releases/aclu-announces-jon-l-stryker-and-slobodan-randjelovic-lgbtq-hiv-project.

9. The Gender Mapping Project, gendermapper.org.

10. 'The sex reassignment surgery market size', Global Market Insights [website] (January 2023), gminsights.com/industry-analysis/sex-reassignment-surgery-market.

11. Associated Press, 'China caught offering gene doping to athletes', NBC News [website] (23 July 2008), nbcnews.com/id/wbna25816605.

12. 'Bostock v. Clayton County', Wikipedia [website], en.wikipedia.org/wiki/Bostock_v._Clayton_County.

13. Ankita Rao, 'Biden health pick Rachel Levine set to become first trans Senate confirmee', Guardian (19 January 2021), theguardian.com/us-news/2021/jan/19/joe-biden-rachel-levine-transgender-assistant-health-secretary.

14. See 'Title IX', Wikipedia [website], en.wikipedia.org/wiki/Title_IX.

15. Joseph Clark, 'Biden reminds transgender females that they still must register for the draft', Washington Times (11 October 2022), www.washingtontimes.com/news/2022/oct/11/biden-reminds-trans-females-they-still-must-regist/.

16. Quoted in Chris Dickerson, 'Federal judge denies stay in case involving transgender athletes in school sports', West Virginia Record (7 February 2023), https://wvrecord.com/stories/639343191-federal-judge-denies-stay-in-case-involving-transgender-athletes-in-school-sports.

17. Quoted ibid.

18. Dave Collins, 'Court to reconsider Connecticut's transgender athlete policy', NBC New York [website] (15 February 2023), nbcnewyork.com/connecticut/court-to-reconsider-connecticuts-transgender-athlete-policy/4105936/.

19. Anne Branigin, 'A battle over Title IX: can it be used to exclude trans athletes?', *Washington Post* (29 September 2022), https://www.washingtonpost.com/nation/2022/09/29/connecticut-trans-athlete-lawsuit/.

20. Quoted in 'Female athletes urge 2nd Circuit to protect women's sports in rehearing of CT case', Alliance Defending Freedom [website] (23 March 2023), https://adflegal.org/press-release/female-athletes-urge-2nd-circuit-protect-womens-sports-rehearing-ct-case.

21. 'Bans on transgender youth participation in sport', Movement Advancement Project [website], lgbtmap.org/equality-maps/sports_participation_bans.

22. Helena Kelly, 'Kansas becomes first to pass Women's Bill of Rights that defines "woman" as someone who is "biologically born a female"', *Daily Mail* (24 February 2023), dailymail.co.uk/news/article-11789269/Kansas-state-define-woman-biologically-born-female.html.

23. Jon Brown, 'Bill to ban biological males from girls' sports teams fails in Ohio General Assembly', Fox News [website] (18 December 2022), foxnews.com/us/bill-ban-biological-males-from-girls-sports-teams-fails-ohio-general-assembly.

24. Quoted in Craig Lord, 'Trans inclusion part 2: will women have all lanes that life & rights promise them by the time regulators are done deciding?', SOS [website] (19 March 2020), https://www.stateofswimming.com/trans-inclusion-part-2-will-women-have-all-lanes-that-life-rights-promise-them-by-the-time-regulators-are-done-deciding/.

25. Quoted ibid.

26. 'Ramsey county judge orders USA Powerlifting to cease operations in Minnesota', USA Powerlifting [website] (15 April 2023), usapowerlifting.com/ramsey-county-judge-patrick-diamond-orders-usa-powerlifting-to-cease-operations-in-minnesota/.

27. Ari Blaff, 'USA Powerlifting must allow male athletes to compete against females, Minnesota court rules', *National Review* (6 March 2023), nationalreview.com/news/usa-powerlifting-must-allow-male-athletes-to-compete-against-females-minnesota-court-rules/.

28. 'H.R.734 – Protection of Women and Girls in Sports Act of 2023', Congress.gov [website] (2 January 2023), https://www.congress.gov/bill/118th-congress/house-bill/734/text?s=2&r=7.

29. Josh Christenson, 'House Republicans vote to bar transgender athletes from women's sports', *New York Post* (20 April 2023), nypost.com/2023/04/20/house-gop-votes-to-ban-transgender-athletes-from-womens-sports/.

30. Kishwer Falkner, 'Kishwer Falkner: a biological definition of sex is needed', *Times* (4 April 2023), https://www.thetimes.co.uk/article/kishwer-falkner-a-biological-definition-of-sex-is-needed-qrt7vdzw2.

31. See 'Suffragette city/the Pankhursts', New Manchester Walks [website], newmanchesterwalks.com/walks-tours/political-manchester/suffragette-city-dying-for-the-vote/.

32. Quoted in Henry Zeffman, 'Trans women are women, says Keir Starmer in call for

legal reform', *Times* (12 March 2022), thetimes.co.uk/article/trans-women-are-women-says-keir-starmer-in-call-for-legal-reform-6rk9tpxsl.

33. "'So a woman can have a penis?" Nick Ferrari puts Sir Keir Starmer on the spot amid a row over trans athletes' [Twitter post including video of Nick Ferrari's interview with Sir Keir Starmer] (1 January 2023), twitter.com/LBC/status/1609459724147200001.

34. Ibid.

35. Channel 4 News, 'Germaine Greer on women's liberation, the trans community and her rape' [video], YouTube [website] (23 May 2018), youtube.com/watch?v=aU_csXGfdVM.

36. Cecilia Dhejne et al., 'Long-term follow-up of transsexual persons undergoing sex reassignment surgery: cohort study in Sweden', *PLoS ONE* 6/2 (22 February 2011), doi.org/10.1371/journal.pone.0016885. For the evidence submitted to the Women and Equalities Committee, see 'Written evidence submitted by Professor Rosa Freedman, Professor Kathleen Stock and Professor Alice Sullivan [GRA2021] / Evidence and data on trans women's offending rates' [PDF], Parliament.uk [website], committees.parliament.uk/writtenevidence/18973/pdf/.

37. Ibid.

38. Quoted ibid.

39. Martin Beckford, 'Labour at war over plan to banish trans women from female-only spaces', *Daily Mail* (5 April 2023), dailymail.co.uk/news/article-11943519/Labour-war-plan-banish-trans-women-female-spaces.html.

40. Danielle DeWolfe, 'Shocking figures reveal 6,500 sex attacks in UK hospitals in just three years as only four percent end in prosecution', LBC [website] (17 April 2023), lbc.co.uk/news/shocking-figures-reveal-6-500-attacks-in-hospitals-in-just-three-years-as-only-f/.

41. Sophie Perry, 'No, the Labour Party has not dropped its plan to reform gender recognition laws', Pink News [website] (14 April 2023), thepinknews.com/2023/04/14/labour-keir-starmer-self-id-trans-gender-law-reform/. On the Scottish legislation, see 'Gender Recognition Reform Bill (Scotland)', Scottish Parliament [website] parliament.scot/bills-and-laws/bills/gender-recognition-reform-scotland-bill.

42. Andrew MacDonald, 'Scotland passes controversial gender-recognition reforms', Politico [website] (22 December 2022), politico.eu/article/scotland-gender-recognition-reform-bill-change-gender-reform-passed/.

43. Pippa Crerar and Libby Brooks, 'Rishi Sunak blocks Scotland's gender recognition legislation', *Guardian* (16 January 2023), theguardian.com/world/2023/jan/16/rishi-sunak-blocks-scotlands-gender-recognition-legislation.

44. Debbie Jackson, 'Why did Nicola Sturgeon resign as first minister?', BBC News [website] (16 February 2023), bbc.com/news/uk-scotland-scotland-politics-64661974.

45. Beira's Place, beirasplace.org.uk.

46. Megan Phelps-Roper, 'The Witch Trials of J. K. Rowling' [podcast from the Free Press, from February 2023], thefp.com/witchtrials.

47. See '16 days of activism against gender-based violence', UN Women [website], https://www.unwomen.org/en/what-we-do/ending-violence-against-women/unite/16-days-of-activism.

48. Cathy Devine, 'This is policy capture pure and simple. All the core human rights

instruments explicitly protect the human rights of girls and women on the basis of sex. Not gender identity. Yet here is the UN High Commissioner for Human Rights advocating for gender identity to overwrite sex' [Twitter post] (5 December 2022), https://twitter.com/cathydevine56/status/1599909825198292992?lang=en-GB.

CHAPTER 12

1. Nicky Swire, 'Research confirms being active helps pupils in school' [report on study by Sport England, Activity Alliance, the Association for Physical Education and the Youth Sport Trust], Sheffield Hallam University [website] (8 October 2020), shu.ac.uk/news/all-articles/latest-news/research-confirms-being-active-helps-pupils-in-school.

2. Jo Swinson and Government Equalities Office, 'New research shows seven is heaven for girls and sports', Gov.uk [website] (27 March 2015), www.gov.uk/government/news/new-research-shows-seven-is-heaven-for-girls-and-sports.

3. 'Girls put off exercise for life by PE lessons', *Irish Independent* (8 May 2012), www.independent.ie/life/family/learning/girls-put-off-exercise-for-life-by-pe-lessons-26851106.html.

4. Abigail Shrier, *Irreversible Damage: The Transgender Craze Seducing Our Daughters* (London: Swift, 2020).

5. Brendan McFadden, 'Primary school scraps boys and girls-only races from its sports day because they exclude transgender children', *Daily Mail* (1 June 1 2018), dailymail.co.uk/news/article-5794361/Primary-school-Inverness-scraps-boys-girls-races.html.

6. John Glover, 'Primary school that made sports day non-binary is now asking kids as young as five if they are gay or transgender', *Scottish Daily Express* (4 January 2023), scottishdailyexpress.co.uk/news/scottish-news/primary-school-made-sports-day-28873390.

7. 'Outing', ACLU [website], aclu.org/issues/lgbtq-rights/lgbtq-youth/outing.

8. Grace Holden, 'Gender equality in school sports', Not Only Pink and Blue [website] (2 September 2021), notonlypinkandblue.com/gender-equality-in-school-sports/.

9. B. Masanovic et al., 'Trends in physical fitness among school-aged children and adolescents: a systematic review', *Frontiers in Pediatrics* 11/8 (December 2020), https://www.frontiersin.org/articles/10.3389/fped.2020.627529/full.

10. Eileen Bailey, 'Why childhood obesity rates are rising and what we can do?', Healthline [website] (4 July 2022), healthline.com/health-news/why-childhood-obesity-rates-are-rising-and-what-we-can-do.

11. Quoted in Craig Lord, 'Kathleen Dawson perseverance pays off: back-to-back 100m bests end on 58.65 as first Brit inside 59 in textile', SOS [website] (13 March 2021), stateofswimming.com/kathleen-dawson-perseverance-pays-off-back-to-back-100m-bests-end-on-58-65-as-first-brit-inside-59-in-textile/.

12. Leo Benedictus, 'Are "non-competitive sports days" really better for school kids?', *Guardian* (9 July 2017), theguardian.com/education/shortcuts/2017/jul/09/are-non-competitive-sports-days-really-better-for-school-kids.

13. Craig Lord, 'Precocious Popovici fit to make a porpoise blush at school of Rădulescu thinking', SOS [website] (14 August 2022), https://www.stateofswimming.com/precocious-popovici-fit-to-make-a-porpoise-blush-at-school-of-radulescu-thinking/.

For David Popovici, see Dan D'Addona et al., '2022 Swimmers of the year', *Swimming World* 63/12 (December 2022), https://www.swimmingworldmagazine.com/news/product/swimming-world-magazine-december-2022-issue-pdf-only/; Yanyan Li, '2022 Swammy awards: male swimmer of the year, David Popovici', SwimSwam [website] (31 December 2022), https://swimswam.com/2022-swammy-awards-male-swimmer-of-the-year-david-popovici/.

14. For the conference, see 'Meet our speakers', World Aquatic Development Conference [website], wadc.sweaquatics.com/#speakers.

15. 'USATF National Junior Olympic Track & Field Championships records', USATF [website], usatf.org/resources/statistics/records/championship-meet-records/usatf-national-junior-olympic-track-field-champion.

16. 'The Voice of Women Working in Sport' [Women's Sport Collective and Sporting Insights], Fearless Women [website] (15 February 2023), fearlesswomen.co.uk/news/the-voice-of-women-working-in-sport.

17. Quoted in Georgie Heath, 'Olympic legend Daley Thompson says transgender athletes have no place in women's sport', News Chain [website] (21 September 2019), newschainonline.com/news/olympic-legend-daley-thompson-says-transgender-athletes-have-no-place-in-womens-sport-1700.

18. 'Jimmy Savile', Wikipedia [website], en.wikipedia.org/wiki/Jimmy_Savile.

19. 'Online grooming crimes have risen by more than 80% in four years', NSPCC [website] (12 July 2022), nspcc.org.uk/about-us/news-opinion/2022/online-grooming-crimes-rise/; Nicola Davis, 'Number of children with anorexia on the rise, study suggests', *Guardian* (20 October 2019), theguardian.com/society/2019/oct/23/anorexia-rate-children-on-the-rise-study-suggests.

20. Sally Weale, 'One in 10 children "have watched pornography by time they are nine"', *Guardian* (31 January 2023), theguardian.com/society/2023/jan/31/one-in-10-children-have-watched-pornography-by-time-they-are-nine.

21. Quoted in Sanchez Manning, 'Amateur women and girls across Britain are "quitting sport" after facing male-bodied opponents, claim campaigners', *Daily Mail* (2 April 2022), dailymail.co.uk/news/article-10680003/Amateur-women-girls-Britain-quitting-sport-facing-male-bodied-opponents.html.

22. Quoted ibid.

23. Quoted ibid.

24. Quoted in Ryan Glasspiegel, 'Caitlyn Jenner fumes over transgender swimmer storm', Fox Sports Australia [website] (21 January 2022), https://www.foxsports.com.au/more-sports/caitlyn-jenner-fumes-over-transgender-swimmer-storm/news-story/a32bd40df22aa0745d8a06110b55f4c2.

25. Quoted ibid.

26. 'World surf league announces new transgender policy' [Instagram video posted by Bethany Hamilton] (5 February 2023),instagram.com/p/CoQ7ECFo-Pa/?hl=en.

27. Paula Dedaj, 'US Olympic rower Patricia Spratlen Etem calls Biden administration's proposed Title IX changes "awful threat"', Fox News [website] (24 February 2023), foxnews.com/sports/us-olympic-rower-patricia-spratlen-etem-calls-biden-administrations-proposed-title-ix-changes-awful-threat.

28. Martina Navratilova, 'Not enough fabulous biological women athletes, NCAA?!?

What is wrong with you?!!!!!!!?' [Twitter post] (16 July 2022), twitter.com/Martina/status/1548320784715616257.

29. Quoted in Amanda McMaster, Henderson Hewes and Douglas Lantz, 'Penn transgender swimmer Lia Thomas speaks out about backlash, future plans to compete', ABC7 Eyewitness News [website] (31 May 2022), abc7ny.com/lia-thomas-transgender-woman-university-of-pennsylvania-swimmer-good-morning-america/11911743/.

30. Quoted in Luke Gentile, '"Don't need anybody's permission to be myself": trans swimmer Lia Thomas eyes Olympics', *Washington Examiner* (31 May 2022), https://www.washingtonexaminer.com/news/dont-need-anybodys-permission-to-be-myself-trans-swimmer-lia-thomas-eyes-olympics.

CHAPTER 13

1. 'Landmark World Rugby transgender workshop important step towards appropriate rugby-specific policy', World Rugby [website] (27 February 2020), world.rugby/news/563437/landmark-world-rugby-transgender-workshop-important-step-towards-appropriate-rugby-specific-policy.

2. The words 'like a deckchair' come from the captain of Porth Harlequins Ladies, Jessica Minty-Madley, quoted in Ceri Coleman-Phillips, 'Transgender rugby player playing with "a smile on my face"', BBC Sport [website] (22 August 2019), bbc.com/sport/rugby-union/49298550.

3. Rupert Kisser and Robert Bauer, 'The burden of sport injuries in the European Union' [PDF], Stiftung Sicherheit im Sport [website] European Network for Sports Injury Prevention (February 2012), https://www.sicherheit.sport/app/uploads/2014/12/burden_report.pdf.

4. P. Prieto-González et al., 'Epidemiology of sports-related injuries and associated risk factors in adolescent athletes: an injury surveillance', *International Journal of Environmental Research and Public Health* 18/9 (2 May 2021), https://pubmed.ncbi.nlm.nih.gov/34063226/.

5. Nicholas Hellen, 'Too strong trans players in women's rugby are driving referees away', *Sunday Times* (28 September 2019), thetimes.co.uk/article/injury-fears-over-rugbys-trans-women-drive-referees-off-pitch-877hjsfzo.

6. Quoted ibid.

7. 'Transgender women guidelines', World Rugby [website], world.rugby/the-game/player-welfare/guidelines/transgender/women.

8. 'World Rugby approves updated transgender participation guidelines', World Rugby [website] (9 October 2020), https://www.world.rugby/news/591776/world-rugby-approves-updated-transgender-participation-guidelines.

9. Virginia Allen and Lauren Evans, 'One female powerlifter's fight to defend women's sports', Daily Signal [website] (18 March 2021), dailysignal.com/2021/03/18/one-female-powerlifters-fight-to-defend-womens-sports/.

10. For Our Bodies, Our Sports, see 'Tell the NCAA: stop discriminating against female athletes – petition', Our Bodies, Our Sports [website], ourbodiesoursports.com.

11. USA Powerlifting, 'USA Powerlifting 2019 NGB transgender policy change discussion' [video], YouTube [website] (11 May 2019), youtube.com/watch?v=370OHWNTsqs.

12. Ibid.

13. 'IOC releases Framework on Fairness, Inclusion and Non-discrimination on the basis of gender identity and sex variations', International Olympic Committee [website] (16 November 2021), olympics.com/ioc/news/ioc-releases-framework-on-fairness-inclusion-and-non-discrimination-on-the-basis-of-gender-identity-and-sex-variations.

14. For the Tanner scale, see en.wikipedia.org/wiki/Tanner_scale.

15. Craig Lord, 'Fina bans transgender swimmers from women's elite races', *Sunday Times* (19 June 2022), thetimes.co.uk/article/fina-bans-transgender-swimmers-from-women-s-elite-races-q8q7ktm2f.

16. Quoted in Craig Lord, 'World coaches urge FINA to back model of trans inclusion that protects women through birth-sex catgorisation', SOS [website] (13 May 2022), www.stateofswimming.com/world-coaches-wsca-urge-fina-to-back-model-of-trans-inclusion-that-protects-women-through-birth-sex-catgorisation/.

17. FINA, 'FINA Extraordinary General Congress | 19th FINA World Championships | Budapest' [video], YouTube [website] (19 June 2022), World Aquatics YouTube, youtube.com/watch?v=tiujU5nUq6A.

18. 'Policy on eligibility for the men's and women's competiton [*sic*] categories' [PDF], World Aquatics [website], resources.fina.org/fina/document/2022/06/19/525de003-51f4-47d3-8d5a-716dac5f77c7/FINA-INCLUSION-POLICY-AND-APPENDICES-FINAL-.pdf.

19. Quoted in Craig Lord, 'Male puberty rules out access to female racing as FINA "gold-standard" policy safeguards fair play for women & creates open category for transgender athletes', SOS [website] (19 June 2022), https://www.stateofswimming.com/women-swimmers-transgender/.

20. Alejandra Caraballo, 'FINA restricts transgender women from competing at elite level', *New York Times* (19 June 2022), nytimes.com/2022/06/19/sports/fina-transgender-women-elite-swimming.html.

21. Ibid.

22. Quoted in Julian Linden, 'The uneasy truth about swimming's transgender ban', *Daily Telegraph* [Australia] (27 June 2022), dailytelegraph.com.au/subscribe/news/1/?sourceCode=DTWEB_WRE170_a_GGL&dest=https%3A%2F%2Fwww.dailytelegraph.com.au%2Fsport%2Folympics%2Fswimming%2Finside-story-the-truth-about-finas-transgender-vote-and-what-the-critics-got-so-wrong%2Fnews-story%2F36405a933-6065f655aoe8abf5a397bbb&memtype=anonymous&mode=premium&BT=sport.

23. Quoted ibid.

24. Quoted ibid.

25. Matthew Futterman, 'FINA restricts transgender women from competing at elite level', *San Juan Star* (21 June 2022), https://www.sanjuandailystar.com/post/fina-restricts-transgender-women-from-competing-at-elite-level.

26. Quoted in Linden, 'The uneasy truth about swimming's transgender ban'.

27. Quoted in Sean Ingle, 'Coe hints athletics may bar transgender women from female competition', *Guardian* (20 June 2022), theguardian.com/sport/2022/jun/20/sebastian-coe-hints-athletics-may-bar-transgender-women-from-female-competition.

28. Sean Ingle, 'World Athletics proposals to preserve path for trans women in female category', *Guardian* (21 January 2023), https://www.theguardian.com/sport/2023/jan/21/world-athletics-proposals-preserve-path-trans-women-female-category.

29. Reuters, 'Swimming – minister wants UK sports bodies to follow FINA's lead in transgender policy', Euronews [website] (20 June 2022), euronews.com/2022/06/20/uk-swimming-world-transgender.

30. Quoted in Craig Lord, 'Tucker & the fallacy of "T"', SOS [website] (22 February 2022), stateofswimming.com/tucker-the-fallacy-of-t-when-it-comes-to-reasons-why-transgender-athletes-dont-belong-in-womens-sport/.

31. L. A. M. Alvares et al., 'Cardiopulmonary capacity and muscle strength in transgender women on long-term gender-affirming hormone therapy: a cross-sectional study', *British Journal of Sports Medicine* 56 (2022), pp. 1292–9, bjsm.bmj.com/content/56/22/1292.

32. 'Swiss government rejects 3rd gender option, at least for now', Associated Press [website] (21 December 2022), apnews.com/article/switzerland-gender-a48e05b6e5 doc307b3ead2bdd686f9a5.

33. Jerry Coyne, '"Actual science" done by biologists shows 2 sexes, one with small mobile gametes and the other with large, immobile ones. There is no third sex. Disorders of sex development are not new sexes, and biological sex is binary. Let's not conflate sex, gender & developmental anomalies' [Twitter post] (14 November 2022), https://twitter.com/Evolutionistrue/status/1592224185832837121?lang=en.

34. M. Martowicz et al., 'Position statement: IOC framework on fairness, inclusion and non-discrimination on the basis of gender identity and sex variations', *British Journal of Sports Medicine* 57 (2023), pp. 26–32, https://bjsm.bmj.com/content/57/1/26. For the 2021 framework, see 'IOC releases Framework on Fairness, Inclusion and Non-discrimination on the basis of gender identity and sex variations', International Olympic Committee [website] (16 November 2021), olympics.com/ioc/news/ioc-releases-framework-on-fairness-inclusion-and-non-discrimination-on-the-basis-of-gender-identity-and-sex-variations.

35. Cathy Devine, Emma Hilton, Leslie Howe, Miroslav Imbrišević, Tommy Lundberg and Jon Pike, 'When ideology trumps science: a response to the Canadian Centre for Ethics in Sport's review on transwomen athletes in the female category', idrottsforum.org [website] (29 November 2022), idrottsforum.org/devineetal221129/.

36. Gregory A. Brown and Tommy Lundberg, 'Should transwomen be allowed to compete in women's sports? A view from an exercise physiologist', Center on Sport Policy and Conduct [website] (17 April 2023), sportpolicycenter.com/news/2023/4/17/should-transwomen-be-allowed-to-compete-in-womens-sports.

CHAPTER 14

1. Jon Pike, 'Safety, fairness, and inclusion: transgender athletes and the essence of rugby', *Journal of the Philosophy of Sport* 48/2 (2021), pp. 155–68, https://oro.open.ac.uk/74562/.

2. Sean Ingle, 'Team Sky and British Cycling in dock after Freeman guilty verdict', *Guardian* (12 March 2021), https://www.theguardian.com/sport/2021/mar/12/dr-richard-freeman-found-guilty-of-ordering-banned-testosterone-for-unnamed-rider.

3. Kat Lay, 'Trans people taking hormones at higher risk of stroke and heart attack', *Times* (23 February 2023), https://www.thetimes.co.uk/article/transgender-hormone-drugs-therapy-risk-heart-attack-stroke-seven-times-cr9mqbn3q.

4. 'Quinn', Wikipedia [website], en.wikipedia.org/wiki/Quinn_(soccer).

5. Gina Florio, 'Transage activists now claim "age is a social construct," just like we predicted would happen', Evie [website] (4 January 2023), eviemagazine.com/post/transage-activists-now-claim-age-is-a-social-construct-just-predicted-happen.

6. 'Take the Podium', IOC [website], olympics.com/en/original-series/take-the-podium/.

7. 'How Christine Girard was finally awarded the gold medal she deserved' [video], IOC [website], olympics.com/en/original-series/episode/how-christine-girard-was-finally-awarded-the-gold-medal-she-deserved.

8. 'Nancy Garapick', Wikipedia [website], https://en.wikipedia.org/wiki/Nancy_Garapick.

9. 'Nancy Ellen Garapick', IOC [website], olympics.com/en/athletes/nancy-ellen-garapick.

10. Global Athlete, globalathlete.org.

11. Skinner is quoted in Doug Harrison, 'New athlete-led movement aims to drive change across the sporting world', CBC Sports [website] (13 February 2019), cbc.ca/sports/olympics/global-athlete-movement-koehler-skinner-1.5016446. The IOC Athletes' Commission is quoted in Liam Morgan, 'Global Athlete criticised by IOC Athletes' Commission as Koehler insists organisation is not a threat to existing bodies', Inside the Games [website] (14 February 2019), https://www.insidethegames.biz/articles/1075526/global-athlete-criticised-by-ioc-athletes-commission-as-koehler-insists-organisation-is-not-a-threat-to-existing-bodies.

12. Wladimir Klitschko, 'Today russians have the gold medal in war crimes, deportation of children and rape of women. You can't put your @Olympics emblem on these crimes dear Thomas Bach' [Twitter post] (30 January 2023), twitter.com/Klitschko/status/1620086215121965057.

13. 'Report to the World Anti-Doping Agency concerning allegations of bullying and harassment' [PDF], WADA [website] (15 May 2019), wada-ama.org/sites/default/files/resources/files/report.pdf.

14. Beckie Scott and the IOC Athletes' Commission press release are quoted in 'Global Athlete criticised by IOC Athletes' Commission as Koehler insists organisation is not a threat to existing bodies', Team TTO [website] (15 February 2019), teamtto.org/index.php/international-games/olympic-games/7261-global-athlete-criticised-by-ioc-athletes-commission-as-koehler-insists-organisation-is-not-a-threat-to-existing-bodies.

15. 'Rule 50 of the Olympic Charter: what you need to know as an athlete' [PDF], Team USA [website], https://www.teamusa.org/team-usa-athlete-services/athlete-marketing/-/media/1710DC792CE84AAAAB50D6F5D2FA6A65.ashx.

16. 'Olympic Charter', olympics.com/ioc/olympic-charter. For the Uyghurs, see 'Who are the Uyghurs and why is China being accused of genocide?', BBC News [website] (24 May 2022), https://www.bbc.com/news/world-asia-china-22278037.

17. 'Olympic and Paralympic sponsors must protect athletes' rights to freedom of expression: media release', Global Athlete [website] (29 January 2021), globalathlete.org/our-word/olympic-and-paralympic-sponsors-must-protect-athletes-rights-to-freedom-of-expression.

18. Quoted in Craig Lord, 'Adam Peaty & Duncan Scott back TeamGB stance on Rule 50: we will find a way for athletes to protest at Tokyo Olympics if they wish to', SOS [website] (27 April 2021), https://www.stateofswimming.com/adam-peaty-duncan-scott-back-

teamgb-stance-on-rule-50-we-will-find-a-way-for-athletes-to-protest-at-tokyo-olympics-if-they-wish-to/. See also 'Tokyo 2020: British athletes free to take a knee at rescheduled Olympics', BBC Sport [website] (22 July 2020), bbc.com/sport/olympics/53505737.

19. Jane Dougall and Katie Falkingham, 'Transgender athletes: "Protect women's sport," say two British elite athletes', BBC Sport [website] (9 May 2022), bbc.com/sport/athletics/61332123.

20. 'World Athletics: new transgender rules "would leave women at serious disadvantage", says Amelia Strickler', BBC Sport [website] (25 January 2023), bbc.com/sport/athletics/64396740.

21. Sean Ingle, 'World Athletics' transgender regulations see scientific rigour give way to a fudge', *Guardian* Sportblog [website] (23 January 2023), theguardian.com/sport/blog/2023/jan/23/world-athletics-transgender-regulations-see-scientific-rigour-give-way-to-a-fudge.

22. Amelia Strickler and Jamie Webb are quoted ibid.

23. Craig Lord, 'Proposed new swimming competition is making waves', *Sunday Times* (18 November 2018), thetimes.co.uk/article/proposed-new-swimming-competition-is-making-waves-s86fcxfhz.

24. Quoted in Craig Lord, 'Solidarity swim camp: "graduate class in professional mindsets for ISL pioneers"', SOS [website] (9 September 2020), stateofswimming.com/solidarity-swim-camp-graduate-class-in-professional-mindsets-for-isl-pioneers/.

25. Craig Lord, 'Adam Peaty threatens boycott of Tokyo 2020 Olympics', *Times* (20 December 2018), thetimes.co.uk/article/adam-peaty-threatens-boycott-of-tokyo-2020-olympics-jh76s32wz.

26. Quoted in Lord, 'Proposed new swimming competition is making waves'.

27. 'Antitrust: International Skating Union's restrictive penalties on athletes breach EU competition rules', European Commission [website] (8 December 2017), ec.europa.eu/commission/presscorner/detail/en/IP_17_5184.

28. 'Grigory Rodchenkov', Wikipedia [website], en.wikipedia.org/wiki/Grigory_Rodchenkov.

29. 'H.R.835 – Rodchenkov Anti-Doping Act of 2019', Congress.gov [website] (29 January 2019), www.congress.gov/bill/116th-congress/house-bill/835/text.

30. Louise Radnofsky and Rachel Bachman, 'Olympics president signals he wants russian athletes at Paris 2024', *Wall Street Journal* (7 December 2022), wsj.com/articles/olympics-russia-paris-2024-ioc-thomas-bach-11670438528.

31. Rob Koehler, 'Where do I start with this one from @DShoemaker_COC @TeamCanada? 1. It's a crime in Russia to denounce the war. 2. You cannot compare the NHL to @Olympics. For Russia Olympians, there is no distinction between the athlete and the state' [Twitter thread] (25 February 2023), twitter.com/RobKoehler2/status/1629500036903239680.

32. Andrew Dampf and Graham Dunbar, 'Olympics not on wrong side of history over Russia, insists defiant IOC president Thomas Bach', *Independent* (14 February 2023), independent.co.uk/news/thomas-bach-ap-russia-ioc-ukraine-b2280657.html.

33. Sean Ingle, '"Wrong side of history": Ukraine athletes accuse IOC of "kowtowing" to Russia', *Guardian* (9 February 2023), theguardian.com/sport/2023/feb/09/ukraine-athletes-ioc-of-kowtowing-to-russia-paris-olympics-2024.

34. Agence France-Presse, 'Zelensky says Russian athletes at Olympics a "manifestation of violence"', France24 [website] (10 February 2023), france24.com/en/live-news/20230210-zelensky-says-russian-athletes-at-olympics-a-manifestation-of-violence.

35. For the 34 countries' position, see Ali Walker, 'IOC should consider banning Russia from Paris 2024 Olympics, 34 countries urge', Politico [website] (20 February 2023), politico.eu/article/boot-russia-from-paris-2024-olympics-more-than-30-countries-urge-ioc-neutral-flags-vladimir-putin-zelenskyy/. For the support of EU lawmakers, see 'Lawmakers ask EU countries to pressure IOC for Russia's ban', Associated Press [website] (17 February 2023), apnews.com/article/politics-sports-european-union-europe-cea558059dfdf0e9a544c6b6886d6f2a. For Anne Hidalgo's position, see 'Mayor Anne Hidalgo wants Russia banned from Games', BBC Sport [website] (8 February 2023), bbc.com/sport/olympics/64567709.

36. Quoted in 'Canadian Olympians demand COC withdraw support of "neutral" Russian athletes at Paris Games', CBC [website] (8 March 2023), https://www.cbc.ca/news/canada/olympians-coc-letter-olympics-paris-russia-belarus-1.6771468.

37. 'Desmond Tutu biographical', The Nobel Prize [website], nobelprize.org/prizes/peace/1984/tutu/biographical/.

38. Quoted in 'Archbishop Desmond Tutu', Justice Innovation Lab [website] (January 2022), justiceinnovationlab.org/movingtheneedle/desmond-tutu. For the IOC's tribute, see 'Olympic Movement mourns the death of Archbishop Desmond Tutu', IOC [website] (26 December 2021), olympics.com/ioc/news/olympic-movement-mourns-the-death-of-archbishop-desmond-tutu.

39. 'Jim Thorpe', Wikipedia [website], en.wikipedia.org/wiki/Jim_Thorpe.

40. Craig Lord, 'FINA finally sends strong message in reform process by stripping "disgraced" GDR Dr. Lothar Kipke of 1980s honour 20 years after criminal conviction', SOS [website] (16 November 2021), stateofswimming.com/fina-sends-strong-message-in-reform-process-by-stripping-disgraced-gdr-dr-lothar-kipke-of-1980s-honour-20-years-after-criminal-conviction/.

41. See Aquatics Integrity Unit, athletics integrity unitquaticsintegrity.com and World Athletics Integrity Unit, athleticsintegrity.org.

42. Quoted in Craig Lord, 'Hail the day when the criminal Kipke is a member of the FINA family no more at the dawn of hope on healing & reconciliation', SOS [website] (14 October 2021), stateofswimming.com/hail-the-day-when-the-criminal-kipke-is-a-member-of-the-fina-family-no-more-at-the-dawn-of-hope-on-healing-reconciliation/.

APPENDIX 1

1. Jon Pike, Emma Hilton and Leslie A. Howe, 'Body check: reconciling biology and fairness for female athletes while supporting trans inclusion in sport', Macdonald-Laurier Institute [website] (7 December 2021), https://macdonaldlaurier.ca/biology-fairness-trans-inclusion-sport-paper/.

2. Ibid.